SALKELDS
through
Seven Centuries

Lilian Salkeld, 1904.

SALKELDS
through
Seven Centuries

J. Grange Moore

Phillimore

1988

Published by
PHILLIMORE & CO. LTD.
Shopwyke Hall, Chichester, Sussex

ISBN 0 85033 644 9

Printed and bound by
Richard Clay Ltd.
Chichester, Sussex

Contents

List of Illustrations

Frontispiece: Lilian Salkeld, 1904

List of Salkeld Wills and Inventories

The 32 wills and inventories presented below have been selected from some 150 of which I have copies. The year shewn against each is the date of signature or compilation (if an inventory), or of probate. Copyright is held by the county record offices, the most helpful being those at Carlisle, Kendal, Preston, Ipswich, York and Chester.

Acknowledgements

During the summer months of the years 1977 to 1985 my sister Joan and I visited the homes and sites of many of the Salkelds discussed in this book, and the County Records Offices and Libraries likely to have Salkeld wills or other information. The purpose of this note is to place on record our sincere thanks for the kindness we met and the permission we received to use the information we so collected.

As the Bibliography shows, our largest single source of Salkeld material was the *Transactions of the Cumberland and Westmorland Antiquarian and Archaeological Society*, to the Council of which we are most grateful.

Without the help of the County Archivists and their staff, and in particular Mr. Bruce Jones at Carlisle, Miss Sheila Macpherson, then at Kendal, and the Archivists at Preston, Chester, Shrewsbury and Ipswich, and the County Librarians alongside them, this book could certainly not have been written.

We thank the Dean of Carlisle for verbal permission to publish a small drawing of a section of the Salkeld Screen, by the Lakeland artist Mr. Harley Rycroft; and Canon T. E. H. Baily for his introduction to Shap and to Mr. and Mrs. Weightman who in turn permitted Mr. Rycroft to draw the Salkeld stained glass windows in their home at Rosgill Hall, which drawings provide the coloured cover of this book. Nearby, the Vicar of Bampton gave details of Salkelds there from 1654 to 1717, and the Rev. F. B. Swift sent papers on early schools. Mrs. Evelyn Pawley of Thrimby Grange entertained us with Canon Markham of Morland church, and Mrs. Irving of nearby Thrimby Hall, all buildings with Salkeld connections.

We were especially grateful to be shown round some of the famous Cumbrian buildings in which Salkelds in past years had lived or had drawn their brides. Mrs. Mary Dent did this for Catterlen Hall – the Vaux family – Mrs. Sharp for Little Salkeld Hall, Mr. and Mrs. John Philip Howard for Corby Castle, and the Earl and Countess of Carlisle showed us Naworth and spoke of the records there. Mrs. Parkin Moore kindly arranged for us to wander round what is now left of Whitehall (near Cockermouth), once one of the most prosperous Salkeld homes.

The late Mr. Cave Brown Cave was most helpful in unravelling for us the Salkeld Tenement of Winster and Miss Margaret Coutts, who lives there, added background. Miss Jane Peat who farms nearby Broadgate was most kind and interested as was Mr. Walling of nearby Mislet, and Mr. Robert of the Mockerkin Salkelds introduced us to Mrs. Jane Rooney who was largely rebuilding the old Pardshaw Hall.

Our exploration of Dent was much helped by the Rev. Malcolm Robinson and his wife Joyce who gave us a guided tour of Dentdale farms; in particular we met Mrs. Pigott of Broadfield, Mrs. Timpson of Clint, and Mrs. Mason of

Birchentree, all intimately connected with past Salkelds. Thomas Salkeld the joiner lived of course at Blandsgill, and in the absence of the now owner Mrs. Howell, we were shown the outside by her agent Mr. J. T. Sedgwick of Craglea, Dent. Mr. David Butler of the Society of Friends, Kendal, kindly let us study their Salkeld minutes of this area.

In Whitby we were helped by Mrs. Olive Sewell, a very active widow whose husband had had a deep knowledge of local Quaker history. In Suffolk the County Archivist supplied copies of Salkeld documents, and Mr. George Arnett, a Woodbridge writer, showed us tithe maps. Mrs. M. B. Cambridge of Grange Farm showed us her house at Hasketon, once a Salkeld home, with the private burial ground opposite. Near the centre of Woodbridge, Mrs. Uloth showed us her Red Maltings home, overlooking the rear of the Salkeld town house in Kingston Road.

In Cheshire the Vicar of Rainow near Macclesfield told us of the Salkeld-related graves of the Morris family, which we visited. Miss Elsie Guest my cousin in Prestatyn was most helpful in providing documents and diaries and a painting in colour of Elizabeth Morris and information on the Salkeld step-children in Runcorn.

We were much encouraged through all this work by that past President of the CWAA Society Mr. Roy Hudleston, who very generously lent his Salkeld papers to study, and whose joint papers with Mr. R. S. Boumphrey have become standard text books on Cumberland and Westmorland families. He also put me in touch with Mr. Robert E. Salkeld of Sherborne, Dorset, a keen researcher of Salkeld history.

In all the above any errors are mine, not theirs.

Other sources of help must be recorded. The first was the translation, by Mr. C. Richardson, Head of Classics at Cranleigh School, of the Corby papers quoted in this book. The second was the transcription by Mr. Robert Pickavance of a number of wills in Middle English, often with very interesting inventories. And the third, the excellent typing of drafts of this book, by Mrs. Jeanne Wood of Nailsea, and the patient proof reading by my daughter Mrs. Gillian Dunsterville.

J.G.M. 1987

It is with great regret that the death on Friday 4th December 1987 of J. Grange Moore is announced. Sadly, he did not live to see his book in print. Publication has gone ahead, as he would have wished, and this book will serve as a lasting memorial to its author.

Summary

In the first pages of this summary I have indicated the main roads we must take, and the side roads we must avoid, if we wish to arrive at a fair view across some twenty-two or so generations which ended in the person of my maternal ancestor MARY ELIZABETH LILIAN SALKELD. The whole, contained in 15 chapters of varying lengths, may later be supplemented by glimpses down a few side roads – but that will be a bonus, confined to interesting Salkeld characters who are not *direct* ancestors and so have been relegated to the appendices at the end of the book.

The name 'Salkeld', applied to a *person* rather than to a place, first occurs in the Pipe Roll of 10 John 1208[1] (a Treasury account), and is repeated some three years later. But as a *place*, there is mention of a 'Salehild' in 10 Henry II[2] – (that is in 1164) in connection with rents to be paid to the King for land and a tan mill. The village of Little Salkeld is near the lovely River Eden and some six miles north-east of Penrith; the first mention, even of Carlisle, in these Pipe Rolls was in 1130.

The second chapter examines what little is known about the earliest Salkelds – where they lived and worked – and I conclude that most of them held tenancies in such Cumbrian villages as Old Salkeld, Hunsonby, Maughanby, the now disappeared original Addingham (swept at some unknown dates into the River Eden) and Huddlesceugh, all within a few miles of each other. These I shall call 'the Salkelds of Addingham', to include also those nearby in Gamblesby, Glassonby, and from Lazonby to Addingham's adjacent parish of Kirkoswald. One of the best documented of these Salkeld families is that of John (son of Nicholas) who married Joan in 1242. I have tried to fit many of these early Salkelds, who lived in or near the parish of Addingham, into the top reaches of a three-page family tree (pp. 7-9), and rather than repeat them would suggest that the reader consults that 'tree' for details. We are specially fortunate in that the will (dated 1358) of John's son John of Maughanby, who married Margaret of nearby Croglin, has survived, for though John was not a *direct* ancestor of Lilian Salkeld, his brother Richard – later to become Sir Richard – certainly was; this will throw much light on the current scene in Richard's days. To pinpoint which John – or Richard – is referred to I have added Roman numerals as they occur, and these are repeated in the text; John of the will of 1358 becomes John (II) – his father being John (I). The other most interesting will is that of John (II's) nephew Roger, proved in 1378, which I also give.

'Put not thy trust in Princes' might well have been muttered by Andrew Harcla, first earl of Carlisle, as he was treacherously seized when writing letters in the hall of his castle of Carlisle, on the orders of King Edward II – to be hanged, drawn and quartered at nearby Harraby on 3 March 1323. The arresting party, under the command of Sir Anthony de Lucy, included other knights and 'four men at arms of good mettle', one of whom was named Richard Salkeld. For this, and later good services to the Crown, Richard was granted the escheated vill of Great Corkeby and, on 14 October 1335, by the new king, Edward III, the manor of Corby for service of half a knight's fee. His family was to occupy Corby Castle for more than three hundred years. Richard died in 1368 leaving a large family, the most important of whom proved to be his second son Hugh (I). Although John (III) was the *eldest* son, Hugh had the foresight to marry Christiana the daughter and heiress of Sir John Rosgill, thus increasing the Salkeld landowning of Corby by the addition of areas of Shap fells. There is some uncertainty regarding the date of this important marriage, and indeed about when father Richard Salkeld and son Hugh occupied on the one hand the manor of Little Salkeld, the Castle of Corby, and the manor of Rosgill. I present the various possibilities, with estimates of dates.

Hugh (I) was the father of Hugh (II), known as 'The Wise', whose wife was Margaret of Tymparon; their family included Hugh (III) who in 1433 married Isabel Broughton and had a son Thomas. His son, another Thomas (III), by marrying 'Domina' Katherine the co-heiress of Sir Richard Salkeld of Corby (who had six daughters by Jane Vaux but no sons) kept the Salkeld surname alive. This Sir Richard (III) died in 1501 and was a direct descendant, through several generations, of John (III), elder brother of the Hugh who had married Christiana of Rosgill.

Space does not permit much detail in this summary, but we may note that in 1436 a list was compiled of those men living in Westmorland who had lands worth a hundred shillings or more. It gave 52 names in all; fifth, with tenements worth £46, was Hugh Salkeld marked 'senior', and lower down a Hugh Salkeld 'junior' – obviously Hugh (II) and Hugh (III).

Parallel with the Hughs come the Thomases, directly descended from Hugh I's elder *brother* John (III). My book, directly quoting Lord William Howard of Naworth in 1625, shows how, by marriage to the Blenkinsops, was lost a moiety of Corby to the Howards in 1605, and how the Thomases' estates at Rosgill, for lack of male heir, were sold to the Lowthers. These are matters well known to readers of papers in the *Transactions of the Cumberland & Westmorland Antiquarian & Archaeological Society* (CWAA), but they contain practically nothing of the next step in our story, of how the descendants of Hugh Salkeld (II) encouraged Henry Salkeld to bring up his family in Pardshaw Hall, and of Henry's will of November 1584 containing thanks to Richard Salkeld (IV) 'his uncle', and his 'uncle' John the Younger, for their kindness. In short, Henry's will provides a direct link back to Thomas Salkeld (IV) the Younger, who was the son of Thomas (III) of Rosgill. But whereas the Rosgill Salkelds were for many years wealthy landowners, those Salkelds of whom we read in Henry's Pardshaw will were for the most part only able to survive illness, plague, and famine perhaps, by the kindness of their immediate ancestors.

We now come to a difficult hiatus in the records which, for the parish of Dean (in which lies Pardshaw Hall), are often missing. We know from these records that Henry Salkeld of Pardshaw Hall had an eldest son John, a second son Thomas, and a third son Richard, the latter baptised at Dean on 13 February

1578; we know of the children of the elder brothers John and Thomas. But of Richard's family all is silence except for recording the birth of a daughter Clara. It is this Richard's absence, apparently, from the scene, which forms the weakest link in the saga of my mother's ancestors. My reasons for supposing that this Richard, son of Henry, was in fact the Richard found later working in the village of Winster, and dying there in 1616, are set out as fully as possible in this book, in the studies for which I came across a tiny group of houses at Winster labelled – in stone – 'the Salkeld Tenement'. There is information about this Richard of Winster from an inventory made in July 1615, but sadly, no will. His eldest son was Thomae, who left a will dated 23 August 1667; mostly it would seem to ensure that his various 'breetches' were made use of! I have been able to construct some interesting charts of this Salkeld Tenement and of its inhabitants before it disappeared.

The other son of Richard (VI) was Francis, born in 1614 at Winster. Francis left Winster and settled at nearby Broadgate, got himself an unnamed wife, and had his first child baptised at Windermere in April 1646, named Thomas (VII). Tragedy almost at once 'o'ertook' Francis – he died and was buried in Windermere within a month, leaving his widow and infant son to the mercies of their friends in the area of Broadgate and, 300 yards away, the Quaker vill of Mislet. I have come to the conclusion – and present the evidence for it in this book – that the unknown wife, now widow, was until her marriage Isabell Braithwaite, born at Broadgate, baptised on 29 June 1619 in Windermere Church, and daughter of William Braithwaite. Quaker records show that an Isabell SALKELD, widow, of Broadgate, died there a Quaker on 4 September 1688, having, as I shall show later, been visited by her son Thomas from their later farmhouse in the village of Dent in Yorkshire.

In the last few paragraphs of this summary the discerning reader will have detected a change from the Salkelds of Corby and of Rosgill, with their military background and vast acres and tenements, to a quite impoverished yeoman as personified by old Thomae and his nephew Thomas (VII) of Broadgate. But these *are* our ancestors, as I shall in the next few pages, hope to show.

So far, I have scarcely done justice to the *military* achievements of the various Salkelds – Richards and Hughs and Thomases – not even mentioned the alabaster tomb of Sir Richard (III) and his wife Jane in Wetheral church, nor have I pointed out the importance of the Salkelds of Whitehall, descended from the loins of Hugh (I) and at one time living in splendour in the Hall of that name near Cockermouth. But there is so much to tell.

With Thomas Salkeld (VII) we take a great step, geographically, out of Cumbria proper into the vale of Dent in Yorkshire. Our hero is now no longer a fighting man but a peace-loving hill farmer, whose worst wars are not those of the Border raiders but of the weather in his isolated valley, and the fear of ill-health.

His mentors at Broadgate had the young Thomas (VII) apprenticed to a joiner in one of the back yards for which *Kendal* was famous. In this period he was exposed, probably through his mother at Broadgate, to the very new influences of George Fox and his Quakers, and in later years we find Thomas (VII) taking a militant part (as did his mother) in their meetings and preachings. Soon after completing his indentures,

Thomas met Ann, daughter of a well-off farmer from the nearby village of Dent; she was not a Quaker, but Thomas did not have too much difficulty in arranging their wedding in the Quaker centre of Brigflatts, a mile south-west of Sedbergh. Ann Haygarth married Thomas Salkeld (VII) at Brigflatts on 25 June 1672 and they set up house at Blandsgill, next door to her father's farm named Broadfield, where Ann had spent her childhood; Blandsgill had been kept for just such a purpose, and on her marriage she conveyed the title to Thomas (VII) her husband. He I suspect put aside his joiner's bag and set about learning farming from his father-in-law next door.

The wealth of detail in the Quaker records, and in the various wills and non-Quaker registers, makes it possible to build up a picture of their home, surroundings, friends and possessions, and to analyse the town of Dent into its salient parts. The church register is especially helpful in listing not only births, marriages and deaths, but also the places of residence and occupation of those born and died.

Ann was 29 years old when she married Thomas (VII); and their first child was born at Blandsgill 15 months later. She recovered from a difficult birth and made her will; but the birth of their second child John, killed her, and she was buried at Brigflatts, a Quaker, though her son survived. With these very young children and a farm to look after, it is not surprising that, aged 31, Thomas soon decided to remarry; she was Grace Capstack, living at Clint Farm just over the valley from Blandsgill. The first child of this second marriage was baptised Ann, but the excellent Quaker records show that Thomas had taken Grace across the hills to his own mother at Broadgate, for this birth, and duly registered it as at Broadgate not at Dent. (Without this detail of birth, there would have been no indication of the critical connection between Thomas and the joiner/farmer of Blandsgill, and his earlier Salkeld ancestors from Mislet, Pardshaw, Rosgill, Corby and Addingham.) Their later children were born back at Blandsgill including William, our direct ancestor, on 8 December 1683.

Thomas (VII), their father, made his will in 1694, and there is a fully copy of it in this book; he died in 1700 and his wife Grace died in 1702; although his will specified that on her death the property was to be sold and the proceeds shared amongst the six children, it was not in fact sold until 1712. Francis married and moved to Whitby where he was to live, with a small family, for 50 years a local Quaker executive. Ann his sister married Joseph Linskill of Whitby. Our own ancestor young William turned up in Suffolk as a schoolmaster in the little boat-building town of Woodbridge, and found himself a Suffolk wife, one Elizabeth Riggs, whom he married in April 1707.

Our story moves to the little town of Woodbridge in Suffolk, in the person of William Salkeld who had been born in the valley of Dent on 8 December 1683 and who died in May 1760 in Woodbridge. It is said that William prospered, and even became mayor of Woodbridge, but I can find no details about him at Woodbridge school; Elizabeth his wife died in 1758, being interred in the Quaker burial ground at Woodbridge on 29 October of that year. They had only two children, both boys, the elder Thomas born July 1710 who married Elizabeth Routh in London, and the younger William (II), born 20 February 1713 who married Hannah Gooding at Clopton on 22 September 1737.

William and Hannah had six children, of whom two died young, two went to London, and, of the remaining two, Thomas stayed on at Woodbridge and inherited considerable wealth and property for his 12 children, and the other, our ancestor William, born

1742, emigrated to Shrewsbury for no known reason and died there in 1782, many years before his mother, and so had practically nothing from the various Woodbridge estates. Detail of his mother's family is scarcely warranted as the only one who matters was this William who went to Shrewsbury in time to marry another Hannah – this time a Hannah Cross (in St Chad's church) on 30 August 1770. This move from Woodbridge to Shrewsbury seems to have killed the tendency of our Salkeld ancestors to be Quakers. Had William not abandoned Woodbridge and his relatives there, but stayed on for his share of their estates, he would have had a standard of living little short of that attained amongst his Cumbrian ancestors in the grand days of Rosgill, Corby and, particularly, at Whitehall. As it was, on arriving at Shrewsbury he set up as a linen draper with premises in the main street, known as Pride Hill.

They had five children on Pride Hill, the last to be born being our ancestor Francis (IV), in March 1781. Francis had an elder brother – ten years older – named William, who by 1806 was a burger in the town and ran a thriving wine lodge, also on Pride Hill; one of his boys (John Chance Salkeld) spent some three years at the famous Shrewsbury School.

Francis grew up, fatherless, on Pride Hill, until on 3 October 1797 he became apprenticed to Mr. Morrison of Runcorn, some forty-five miles to the north of Shrewsbury. But, with a third of his indentures yet to run, Francis married a young widow who already had a daughter two years old. The widow's name was Elizabeth Kirkham, daughter of Thomas Kirkham. She died in March 1849 and was buried in a table tomb in Daresbury churchyard, with both her husbands; her daughter Catherine died in January 1851, wed to a surgeon Thomas Case. By the kindness of my cousin Miss Elsie Guest, a coloured photograph of Elizabeth in a long gown and a mob cap is amongst my treasures.

In the 1861 National Census, Francis describes himself as a 'retired grocer' with one servant, but he was a man of many parts, owning a canal wharf and a number of canal boats, a brewery, a farmer and property owner. It was probably his canal boats which made Francis a rich man, plying as they did with china clay from Runcorn to the Potteries, and back with packed chinaware for export overseas, after transfer to ocean-going ships. All this brings a need for a study of Runcorn, from the canal age to the coming of the railways, and I have tried to pick out some of the highlights of those days.

Francis had seven children plus two stillborn, but the only male to reach double years of age was our ancestor William Francis, born at Runcorn on 3 August 1809 who on his thirty-second birthday married Elizabeth Hall of Latchford near Warrington. He died at Pool House on 28 April 1897 having been a widower for the last 16 years of his life. If – quite rightly – we dub Francis as a 'grand old man' when he died in October 1866 at the age of 85, we must coin a still grander phrase for his son William Francis; he lived two years longer than his father, had more children than his father, and expanded the business whilst adding new ones to it. Of the eight children born to Elizabeth and her husband at Pool House, I give details but in this summary have only room for one – our ancestor Arthur Salkeld, who was born on 15 February 1851. He had two wives – the first being Clara Ellen Morris, daughter of a silk merchant from Rainow near Macclesfield – and the second a farmer's daughter Jessie Tinkler Crosby; for details of the seven children of the second marriage I must refer the reader to a later chapter.

Arthur's wedding to Clara Ellen was on 28 July 1880, when he was 29 and she 34. He had thereafter two main problems to contend with – a not very robust wife, and a failing career for himself – this latter because of the declining nature of the canal business in the face of railway developments, and his own lack of personal business acumen. He later moved to a house in the Waterloo district of Liverpool, where he died in June 1920.

But to return to his first marriage, to my mother's mother Clara Ellen; their first child, Lilian, was born there on 20 May 1881, robust enough; but their second child, little Edith, survived for only 16 months and was buried in Runcorn cemetery on 2 January 1884; Clara Ellen herself did not live very long thereafter, being buried in Edith's grave in April 1890, leaving Lilian, motherless, to live with her father Arthur, until his second marriage. She got on very well with her stepmother Jessie, and later with the other half-brothers and sisters; went to the Queen's school in Chester, and in June 1905 married Joseph William Moore, son of a doctor from Middlewich. Two children (Denzil and Grange) were born to them at 13 The Holloway, Runcorn, whence in 1912 they moved to a larger detached house named Kinderton House, on Weston Road, still nearer to 'The Works'. Two more children, John and Joan, were to complete the Moore family. Lilian became a widow in November 1955 and a year later moved with her daughter Joan to a smaller house in Chester, where she died on 23 March 1973 and is buried with her husband in Runcorn cemetery. Lilian had two grandchildren, Gillian Elizabeth Ann born to Grange and Dorothy Moore on 14 February 1943, and Timothy Christopher born to John and Joan Mary Moore in May 1942. Gillian and Christopher each have children.

Starting about A.D. 1240 at Little Salkeld in Cumbria – a few miles east of Carlisle – the tale of my mother's ancestry turns and twists – at various speeds – from Melmerby to Corby Castle and to Rosgill on Shap, thence to Pardshaw, Winster, Broadgate, Mislet and Kendal and then leaves for Yorkshire. So too does the mode of life change – from Border warfare to hillside farming in Dentdale, and then, on leaving Yorkshire, to schoolmastering in the little shipyards of Woodbridge in Suffolk. But not for long – an unaccountable urge to live in Shrewsbury for a couple of generations leads to an apprenticeship in Runcorn, probably on work arising from the busy canals, and a growing success in other businesses in turn brings prosperity in Runcorn, until widowhood in Chester. From say A.D. 1240 to 1973, is a tale some seven hundred and thirty years long.

> Long rolling years have swept those scenes away
> And peace is on the mountain and the fell;
> And rosy dawn and closing twilight gray
> Hear but the distant sheepwalk's tinkling bell.

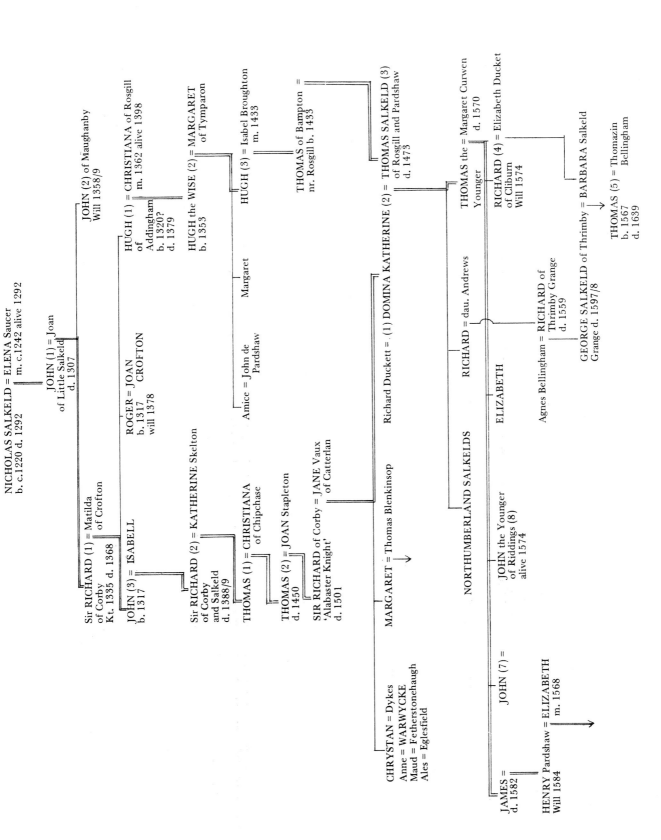

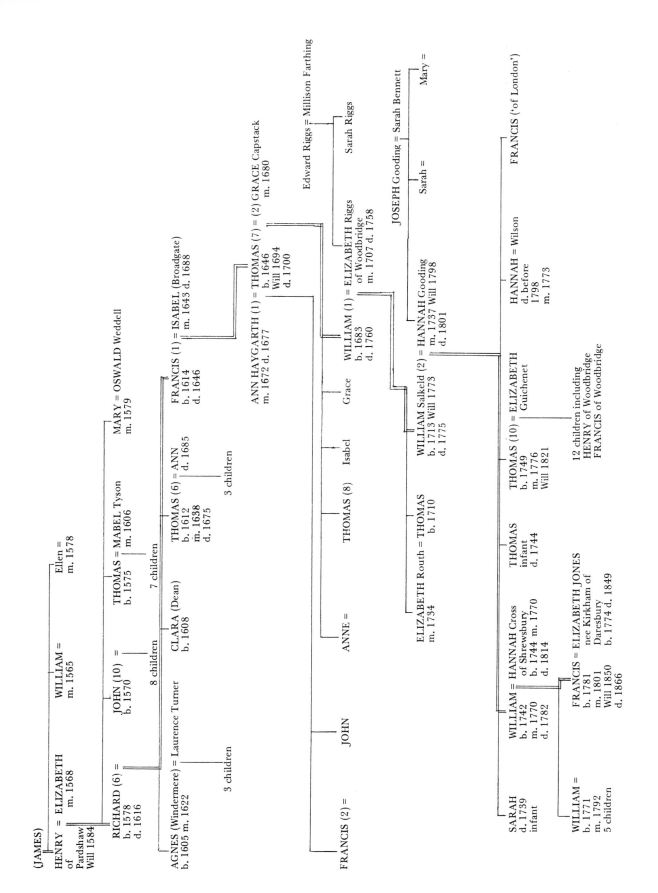

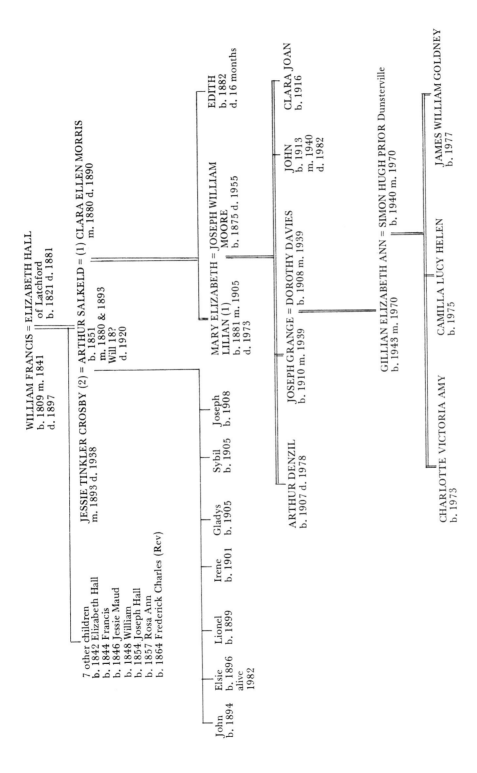

For details of children and dates not given above, please consult the main narrative.

Chapter One

Relatives and Sources

If one wishes to understand the varying fortunes and behaviour over the centuries of families such as the Salkelds, some regard must be given to the changing constraints under which they lived. For example, plagues decimated their numbers, famine and droughts influenced their fertility and death-rate, major and minor warfare continuously threatened, and took, their lives and their possessions, influenced the design of their houses and determined how they spent their time and energy; religious beliefs, persecution and civil legislation could depress or enhance their material standard of living and the effectiveness of their children's education, the very clothing they wore, and indeed were buried in.

Thus to a large extent they were the unwilling victims of their environment, and any study of them which omitted at least some mention of that environment would be but a skeleton jangling in the wind.

Two recent scholarly works[4,5] have distinguished no less than six branches of the Cumbrian Salkelds, from the parent stream of Little Salkeld and Corby (near Carlisle) to the five subsidiary streams of Rosgill (on Shap), Threapland, Whitehall, Brayton, and Ranbeck with Holme Hill. In their days these Salkelds provided England with High Sheriffs, Knights of the Shires, Members of Parliament, Commissioners for Royal Inquisitions, great landowners, gallant soldiers (two fought at Agincourt), learned theologians including Lancelot the last Prior and first Dean of Carlisle, and a pirate who called himself the King of Lundy. To this distinguished list may be added large numbers of yeoman farmers, 'statesmen' homesteaders, artisans, servants and ne'er-do-wells which it is not my intention to attempt to weave into one tidy tapestry.

The wealth of information available in the Record Offices, Archives and of course libraries of Cumberland, Westmorland, Northumberland, Lancashire and Yorkshire (into which counties many of these Salkelds later spilled) made it very tempting to flit from one Salkeld family to another, picking out the most intriguing anecdotes, much as a bee gathers its nectar from many flowers. Who for example could omit the following:

Inventory of Anthony Salkeld of Kirkoswald December 1593.

Imprimis   In mony xxvj^s viij^d [26s. 8d.]
Ite   One sele cape with foure silver buttons
               Tow clokes and tow shirtes and two shurt bandes
               Tow dubletes and tow pare of breches
               One payre of stockings and one payre of booutes
               One payre of shues and a sworde belte and dagger
               One griddle and bakebred a bowl and an Arrowbage with xviij shaftes.
By me Jane Salkeld.

She does not conceal that Anthony travels light – with no change of hose. She pens each word in a firm clear hand and signs it with her full name. One wonders who she was – sister, mother, widow, girl-friend? No matter, the tears are long since dry.

Or again, frugal old Thomas Salkeld of Winster, 'sick and weak in body', on 23 August 1667 directs in his will:

> Unto my son Thomas five shillings for a legacy to buy a girdle and brandiron . . . I give him all excepting a clack coat and a pair of black breetches which I give my sone Richard if he be pleased to wear them. I give two pairs of old breetches unto two sones of William Garnets . . .

No, we must deny ourselves the role of honey-bee, if we are to attempt the serious purpose of the book I have in mind – which is to trace as accurately as possible, within the limits of the available records and the writer's ability to use them – the saga of those related Salkelds which ended at the death of my mother Lilian Moore (born Salkeld), at Chester in March 1973, at the very respectable age of ninety-one.

From whence came they, by what route, and why? And what can be learnt from their lives? How far indeed do the records go back? At one time I became convinced that 1600 was the earliest but now, after a lot more work, I believe that there may be an unbroken line from her to Nicholas Salkeld who was born about 1220, in Cumbria, some seven hundred and fifty years or more before my mother's death.

The serious reader will ask 'How accurate are the facts presented?' Original sources including some 150 wills and inventories have been used wherever possible, but if a testator fails to mention all his children, or if a clerk mistakes a name or a date in compiling his parish register, or buries rather than baptises the entrant, these errors may inadvertently have crept into my text, though some I *have* been able to identify and eliminate. Thus each of the many Salkelds named in this book is a real one, in the sense that none has been invented! The worst that may have occurred is that, because of ambiguity especially in church registers, two Salkelds with identical names and similar ages and places of baptism may unknowingly have been treated as one; or that, despite many coincidences suggesting otherwise, a wrong Christian name may have been attributed to a wife or mother where her true name was not originally recorded in the register – as was so often the case on the distaff side.

It was the custom over most of the period covered by these studies to give only one Christian name at baptism, and to re-use that Christian name should the original owner die young, and certainly to re-use it in succeeding generations. This adds to the difficulty of differentiating between individuals with the same Christian names, and so I have added Roman numerals specific to particular individuals, wherever this appears to be helpful whether in the text, or in pedigrees or footnotes. This applies especially to the main Richards, Thomases, Johns and Hughs, but is not always used and is not confined to those names only.

Our curtain rises to reveal, as a backcloth, the old castle of Corby perched in the distance high over the valley of the River Eden. A few figures pass by, some with the accent of Scandinavians; a few pause to drink at a spring at the foot of a willow tree and one, called 'Saughkeld' because he lives near it, suddenly places an arrow in his bow, aims at the base of the tree, and kills a young fawn.

His father snatches it up and runs to a wattle-and-daub hut wherein sits old father Simon: Simon knows only too well that that unwanted burden belongs not to Robert but to King John of England, under the Forest Laws which are so rigorously enforced by the Forest Verderers; he has good friends in the vill, and quickly seeks their advice. And so, in the year 1208 His Majesty's Treasury records the receipt of no less than one hundred shillings from one Robert son of Simon of Salkeld, that his son may be 'quit of the fawn'; and he was so quit. Seven years later, that same king signed Magna Carta.

Amongst Simon's advisers was no doubt Adam, the Queen Mother's cook, who until his death in 1221 had held 'Saulhill' of King Richard and King John, by rendering each year to the king's bailiffs a pound of pepper; and Thomas the Vinor and Alice his wife, just now in trouble for 'alienating his sergeantry' by letting out his duties in the king's stores in return for one-twentieth of a military service. And there too might be Roger de Vaux, come to collect towards the £4 13s. 4d. yearly rental to be paid to the king for the two carucates of land, and a tan-mill, which was the Manor of Little Salkeld. And there also perhaps, Hugh son of Ranulf of Salkeld, still owing two and a half marks for an unpaid fine.

Next we learn a little, but not enough, of a tragedy which strikes one John Salkeld, an undertenant of the manor, who is killed: he it was who was a juror in the dispute over the rights of advowson for Appleby church, miles away. His alleged killer, one John de Castre, is later pardoned by the king.[6]

As we watch this scene, and the drinkers at the spring below the willow tree, we realise that though they are all *of* Salkeld, they may be quite unrelated to each other by blood; or perhaps more likely, some are blood-related, and others not. What of course we are sure of, is that *we* have undoubted blood-relatives and that where we have been able to relate these in a way we can prove – by birth, marriage, or burial entry for example in a church register, or by unambiguous mention in a will – we can fairly and truly say so in a pedigree chart. If this chart, so proven at each step, takes us in the end to one of these men or women 'of Salkeld', then clearly we and they *are* truly blood-related. And the evidence we can use for this is very extensive, including the records of numerous Heralds' Visitations, entries in county histories, official records ranging from tax returns (ship tax, window tax, hearth tax, etc.) to Guild lists of apprentices, service records from military and civil units, etc., not to mention records from schools, universities, professional bodies and the like. By using these sources, and many others, and checking as far as possible by cross-references, it has proved possible to work backwards from my mother Lilian née Salkeld to the Nicholas Salkeld already mentioned, born in Cumbria about 1220. It is a purpose of this book to demonstrate that this is so, but also to give in passing a factual and I hope interesting account of these Salkelds, their problems, and their times.

Now therefore we leave that shadowy stage with its random collection of men and women 'of Salkeld', to concentrate on the oldest known Salkeld *relatives-by-blood*, starting with Nicholas and his son John (I). Whether we ever get back to look again and in more detail at the others on that stage, remains to be seen.

There are over a hundred Salkeld wills and inventories in the Carlisle Castle archives, and others in Carlisle City Library, and in libraries in Preston, York (Borthwick), Newcastle, Leeds, Ipswich, Lichfield (for Shropshire) and Chester; these have been studied and the information incorporated into the text of this book. In many it has been necessary to translate from the original Middle English, or Latin, and this has kindly been done for me by Mr. Roger Pickavance despite his many other interests – at 67 Stanningley Road, Armley, Leeds, LS12 3NU. Clearly it is impossible to include more than a few in this book, but those of special interest have been given in full in the text.

Chapter Two

Early Salkelds of Addingham

Some Addingham Salkelds

If we were to follow the advice of the eminent Cumbrian genealogist T. H. B. Graham[8] we should trace our Salkeld ancestors back only to John (I) de Salkeld of Old Salkeld who, according to the Herald William Flower, Norroy King of Arms, in his official Visitation of Yorkshire in 1563-4[9] 'lived at the close of the thirteenth century and was dead by 1307'. But the equally well-known genealogist G. H. de S. Plantagenet Harrison (PH)[7] would have us believe that we can trace our ancestor Salkelds back nearly two hundred years further, to the reign of Henry I (1100-35) when a certain Nicholas Salkeld, Lord of Salkeld, begat a son Thomas in the reign of King Stephen (1135-54); exactly when, and where, we are not told.

According to Plantagenet Harrison,[7] the pedigree is as on page 14. However it is said[10] that he is not always reliable and assumed relationships which were not correct, though they might have been convenient.

A search of the early 'Pipe Rolls' – Treasury Accounts – conveniently summarised in the *Victoria County History of England*,[11] tells us that the first national document referring to Carlisle and its history was the Pipe Roll for A.D. 1130; 34 years later[2] 'Old Salehild' with Upperby, for two carucates of land and a tan mill, paid the Treasury £4 13s. 4d. for one year's rent. In later years (1166 to 1168) the tan mill is assessed separately at 25s. to 30s. and the land at £4, but by 1173 no payments were being made because of the 'wastage by war'. Things were back to normal by 1178, and by 1185 the accounts of 'Salechilla' as rendered to the Treasury by Roger de Vallibus were again £4 for the land (but only 20s. for the tan mill).[12]

The historian William Whellan,[13] says:

> The first possessor of the Manor of Little Salkeld subsequent to the Conquest, was one Walter, a Norman, who gave it to the [newly-founded] Priory of St Mary Carlisle as we learn from a deed [1292] of confirmation of Edward I in which Walter's gift is recited. The Manor continued to be held by the Prior and Convent till the period of the Reformation when it passed to their successors the Dean and Chapter of Carlisle. The village of Little Salkeld is situated near the Eden one mile south of the parish church and six miles north-east of Penrith . . . according to tradition the chapel was situated in a village called Addingham, on the east bank of the river, where human bones, crosses and other remains have been found. The old cross in the churchyard is said to have been brought from this place. . .

A casual reading of the literature – for example the *Transactions* of the CWAA Society – might lead one to imagine that the Salkelds in whom we are interested were *all* 'of Corby'. But King Edward II did not convey Corby to Richard (I) Salkeld, the son of John (I), until *after* the trial and execution of the Earl of Carlisle in 1323 (by which time Richard (I) was within two years of becoming an M.P.), so we realise that there must have been some earlier home or homes of the Salkelds.

The complaint of John (I)'s widow Joan, in 1307[14] of a burglary in 'her house at Old

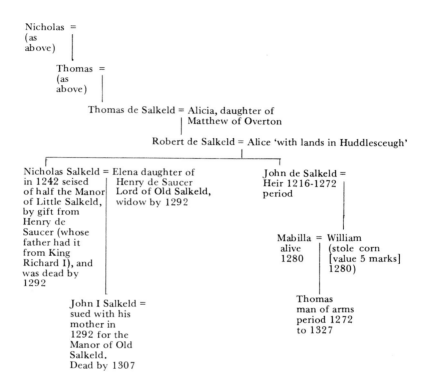

Nicholas =
(as
above)

Thomas =
(as
above)

Thomas de Salkeld = Alicia, daughter of
Matthew of Overton

Robert de Salkeld = Alice 'with lands in Huddlesceugh'

Nicholas Salkeld = Elena daughter of
in 1242 seised   Henry de Saucer
of half the Manor Lord of Old Salkeld,
of Little Salkeld, widow by 1292
by gift from
Henry de
Saucer (whose
father had it
from King
Richard I), and
was dead by
1292

John de Salkeld =
Heir 1216-1272
period

John I Salkeld =
sued with his
mother in
1292 for the
Manor of Old
Salkeld.
Dead by 1307

Mabilla = William
alive   (stole corn
1280   [value 5 marks]
       1280)

Thomas
man of arms
period 1272
to 1327

Salkeld' – is firm proof of where *she* lived. Her husband John (I) was one of 10 undertenants of the Manor of Little Salkeld, in 1292, and he was also a tenant of Hunsonby (map reference 5835) some two miles to the east of it. In the Manor he has the lease of half a mill, as well as land, from the owner's wife, for her lifetime and for 10 years thereafter. Today's O.S. map shows there to be two mills very near to, and immediately to the south of, Little Salkeld, and as these are dependent on streams they are probably on the site of John (I)'s half mill.

Years later (in 1332) Richard (I) Salkeld – John (I)'s son – acquired from William de Arthuret and Joan his wife a moiety of the Manor of Little Salkeld. At this stage Graham thinks that Salkeld Hall was probably Richard (I)'s home, for although he had only just been given Corby Castle, we know that Richard (I)'s second son Hugh moved in there – incidentally without the Royal Assent which later cost him a fine – and stayed for the rest of his lifetime. So although this Richard became Knight of the Shire and Lord of Corby, he lived apparently at Little Salkeld some twenty miles to the south of Corby – no doubt a safer place from the raiding hoards of Scots. From some date unknown, but probably considerably before 1300, 'our' Salkelds therefore had their main home not at Corby but at or near Little Salkeld, in the parish of Addingham.

They had other homes nearby – not only was John (I) Salkeld a tenant of Hunsonby some two miles to the east, in 1292 and perhaps well before that – but he in turn had a son John (II) who lived a little farther down the river at Maughanby (O.S. 572380); we know this from his will, dated 1359. In it he leaves detailed instructions about his funeral, which is to be at the little church of Addingham – St Michael's – whose rector is Thomas Salkeld and whose church is also the parish church for Little Salkeld. Although this Addingham is not shown on today's Ordnance Survey map, its location is given on a sketch map about Great Salkeld – over the other side of the River Eden – in an article in CWAA 25.[15] It was built on a bend in the river, at O.S. 566395, but being on the east bank where the river bent westwards, both the church – an old pre-Norman affair – and the village were in time eroded away. In the surrounding fields, which have names such as Chapelflatt, Kirk Meadow, and Kirkbank, one may find old stones, some with lettering, and monuments removed from the old church, the remains of which are now below the waters of the River Eden; so too, presumably, are the bones of John Salkeld of Maughanby, and perhaps also of his wife Margaret who came from Croglin (O.S. 5645) a few miles to the north.

John's nephew Roger, whose will of 1378 we are also lucky to have, left no instructions as to where he was to be buried, but as he makes a bequest to the rector of the next parish – Kirkoswald – we can guess that perhaps he lived near to Kirkoswald, with his wife and two daughters.

We know also that Alice, the wife of Robert de Salkeld, was grantee of land at Huddlesceugh[16] in the 13th century, and Huddlesceugh is but three miles up a little side valley from Kirkoswald. So Roger and his uncle Robert may have lived near to each other, and perhaps saw a good deal of John of nearby Maughanby. Roger's wife, Johanna, daughter of Thomas Beauchamp, also came from Lazonby, close by.

One can say therefore that a strip of land some two miles wide, running on the east bank of the River Eden from the bridge at Langwathby to a point about six miles northwards, would include most of the homesteads of these early Salkelds.

Certainly they were living within this strip before the beginning of the year 1300. We know from other sources that Little Salkeld Hall was not given up until 1640-4, when the Royalist George Salkeld (he who was baptised at Addingham in 1608, the son of Thomas)[17] was forced to sell it and the rest of his Addingham properties to Cromwell's Colonel Thomas Cholmley. It follows that this Hall was the home of the Salkelds for some three hundred and fifty years – longer even than Corby Castle was to be. Chancery papers suggest that at this time it was called Low Hall, or Salkeld Lowhall. Although its subsequent owners (pre-1688 Mr. Smallwood; about 1790 Colonel Lacy; and in 1826 Robert Hodgson) made large additions to it, the old mansion still bears many marks of antiquity; the walls of the eastern wing are three and a half feet thick, and in the centre part of the old house is a wall over ten feet thick, containing the chimney of what appears to be the original ancient hall. Nikolaus Pevsner, in his *Buildings of England – Cumberland and Westmorland*,[18] gives it the following brief mention:

> Salkeld Hall. The front is shortly after 1790. Five bays, two storeys, pedimented doorway, one-storeyed two-bay wings.

What it was like when the Salkelds lived there, we can but guess.

1. Little Salkeld Hall.

In its heyday, Addingham church was the parish church of a parish which included not only Little Salkeld, but Addingham village, Hunsonby and Winskill, Gamblesby and Glassonby. In the next parish was Kirkoswald – full of Salkelds as we shall see – and then Lazonby.

If we turn back to the three pedigree charts we shall see, at the top, the pedigree of these 'ancient' Salkelds.

Of Nicholas, little is known. He probably had several sons as well as John our ancestor, for although John was a juror in the advowson inquisition on Appleby church, and was an under-tenant of the Manor of Little Salkeld, there were at least two other Salkelds around of much the same age and background. These were Henry (who in 1271 gave evidence at Carlisle[19] regarding trespassing at Penrith) and Thomas, who was nominated in 1281[20] to be an attorney, and who, with John, was also an under-tenant of the Hall. But because of absence of proof that they were brothers (or at least related), I have not put them on the chart.

Of John, however, more is known. Firstly, he probably married Joan in 1242, and they had at least four children. Of his son John of Maughanby, who married Margaret from nearby Croglin, we know a lot, because his will of 1358-9 happily survived in Carlisle and is commented on at some length in a later chapter. Of his son Robert, we only know[26] that he was appointed a Baron of the King's Exchequer in Ireland, which must have been a pretty grim job. Of John (I)'s daughter Elena (named no doubt after her grandmother), all that has come down to us is that she was prosecuted for trespass in the Forest, in the year 1310. And that leaves only John (I)'s son Richard (I), soon to be Lord of Corby, of whom later we treat at length.

But there was more to John (I) than breeding sons; he moved in pretty distinguished circles. Nicholson and Burn in their famous *History*[22] draw our attention to his inclusion in the Inquisition held in 1292 on the ownership of Salkeld, wherein he sat alongside such eminent Cumbrians as Robert of Croglin, Adam of Ulverly, Robert of Tymparon, and Thomas de Lowther – and they found Salkeld belonged to John de Balliol, then King of Scotland.

Around John (I)'s death there is some mystery. We know that he died before 1307, for in that year his widow Joan lodges a very official complaint[14] that a neighbour, one John de Hoton, had broken into her house (in Little Salkeld) and removed a wagon laden with corn, and its oxen. We must not prejudge the issue – for all *we* know, they may have belonged to de Hoton – but the anecdote does help to put a date on her husband's death, and confirms also just where she was living. More serious however is the record that John (I) was killed in 1306[6] and that John de Castre was later acquitted of causing his death; why should he have been killed? We don't know.

We shall soon be leaving Addingham and its 'two by six' mile colony of early Salkelds, for the Castle of Corby, about twenty miles farther north, where the *family* of John (I)'s son Richard (I) held sway for several centuries. But before doing so, let us think of Addingham as a continuing Salkeld colony, and look at it briefly in the period of its existence when *church registers* can tell us some later facts, i.e. in the period starting not at 1300 but at 1600. Now we find that Thomas Salkeld is busily raising a family there, and is held in high esteem as 'Mr. Thomas'. In order of their appearance in the Addingham register his children are (with baptismal dates in brackets): Isabel (24 February 1604, a 'son' (10 February 1605), Frances (male, 10 April 1607), John (22 February 1607/8), George (22 March 1608/9) and Katherine (12 February 1612).

Further examination shows however that this Frances was buried, not baptised, and so must presumably have been born before that date. And George, of course, is the George already referred to who eventually sold the Hall at Little Salkeld to the Roundheads. Quite why it was in his possession, rather than in that of his elder brother John, is not obvious, unless John had died meanwhile. From these dates one can reason that his father Thomas was born about 1580 or before, and on my charts I have identified him as the Thomas given in the Morland church register as baptised on 6 May 1575, the son of Edward Salkeld and grandson of Richard (V) Salkeld of Thrimby and Mistress Agnes; there is enough information available to be quite certain of this relationship.

Another Salkeld on the Addingham register must be mentioned here: Henry, 'house-holder of Gamesby', who was buried there on 6 May 1609. A study of the register of the parish of Kirkoswald – next door to Addingham – reveals that this Henry was the son of Lancelot Salkeld who married Isabel and died in 1574; he was also the father of the bastard – Anthony whose pathetic little inventory, made in 1593 by 'me, Jane Salkeld', was mentioned in the Summary. Lancelot had three other sons, of whom this Henry is the most important because he and his wife Elizabeth (née Cowp) had a large family at Kirkoswald. In the 1600s, Kirkoswald was a colony still of Salkelds, and indeed had been for many years previously. Part of the evidence for this lies in the text of certain Kirkoswald-Salkeld wills, some of which bear dates thirty or more years previous to the parish register entries. One of these wills, with its accompanying inventory, is included to show also the range of monetary values assigned to Salkeld possessions in about 1576.

The two oldest-ever Salkeld wills are the subject of our next pages.

The great fire at Carlisle, in the year 1292, followed in 1628 by the burning of the seat of the bishops of Carlisle – Rose Castle – has left so few episcopal registers that all those from the years 1292 to 1561 can be contained in two volumes, and before 1292 nothing exists. But the Chancellor of Carlisle, R. S. Ferguson, in 1893 collected together the 157 wills and grants of probate which had been transcribed from these registers and edited them for publication in one volume;[23] they contain the two oldest Salkeld wills which I have found. The first, dated 1359, is that of John (II) Salkeld of Maughanby (O.S. 572380), *who was a brother of Richard (I) Salkeld of Corby*. The second is that of John's nephew Roger, son of that Richard, and was made in 1378.

Before considering them in detail, some of Chancellor Ferguson's editorial comments are well worth noting:

> The wills are mainly those of clergy and persons of the middle class. We are brought face to face with their lavish expenditure in wax lights and in feastings at funerals – the poor neighbours and hungry clerics crowding to the burials to secure their doles . . . large indeed was the toll taken by the priests from a dead man's goods. His best beast by way of mortuary, and legacies for singing innumerable masses for his soul, trentals, vigils and dirges. Little wonder that some . . . (clerics) were well endowed with worldly goods – several farmed to a considerable extent, to judge from the horses and cattle they dispose of, whilst bequests of clothes, beds, hangings, brass pots, brewing utensils and the like indicate that some of the beneficed clergy, poor as was the diocese, were well clad and dwelt in well-furnished residences, waited upon by numerous servants, more than their successors today would afford.

The will of John (II) Salkeld of Maughanby may have been made when he was at least sixty years old, for we know that John's father, John (I), was murdered in 1306

2. The site of the home of John of Maughanby.

whereas the will is dated 1359. The testator had married Margaret of nearby Croglin (O.S. 575472), whom he mentions at the end of his will; it would appear that they had no children of that marriage. It comes as a slight shock to find, sandwiched between bequests to the Vicar of Addingham and to the Prioress of Armathwaite and her Sisters, references to his two bastard sons John and Richard! Nor does he treat them alike – John gets 10 marks, but Richard only 40s. – less than a third as much. Both were later imprisoned in Carlisle for trespass 'of vert and venison in Inglewood Forest' on 3 July 1374, but we do not know their ages.

John pays much attention to the details of his own funeral; he is to be buried at St Michael's, Addingham (his parish church) and following custom he gives his best animal as a burial fee. Twenty shillings are to be spent on candles to be burnt round his corpse on the day of the funeral, and 40s. on various prayers and hymns for his soul – at the discretion of his executors. Many bequests are made to the church and its servants – 100s. each to the work of the Abbey at Carlisle and to the Priory and Convent; 20 marks to the friars, to be divided equally among the Augustinians, Franciscans, Dominicans and Carmelites living in Carlisle, Penrith and Appleby; 20s. to the Vicar of Addingham, 40s. to the Prioress of Armathwaite and her sisters, 20s. to his personal priest one Thomas Capellano, half a mark only to priest Remigo Capellano but 20s. to Henry the Rector of Hoton in the Forest, and then – a delightful touch – 6s. 8d. to John del Brigge of Penrith 'because he is poor'.

Nor is the fabric forgotten. Forty shillings to the making of a certain window in the chancel, 100s. to the repair of the Eden Bridge (Langwathby, 5633) and 40s. for the little bridge in the Forest of Inglewood 'near Wodermouth'. More personal bequests include his 'special shell' (probably a silver-mounted cup) to the Prior and Convent of Carlisle, 40s. to the sons and daughters of John Salkeld junior (this junior will be the John (III) who married Isabell and died in or before 1379); and with other bequests he disposes in all of no less than £101 3s. 4d., a very large sum in those days. He has a tenement in Carlisle, and leaves the remainder of his estate to his wife Margaret, his brother Richard (I) (later to be knight of Corby) and to the Vicar.

So much for John (II)'s will. The second Salkeld will (A.D. 1378), that of Roger his nephew, calls for less comment as it is of much the same pattern, but more modest. This Roger married Joan, a daughter of Clement of Crofton, in 1355; he died six years after making his will, and she outlived him by some thirty years. They had two daughters, Margaret and Alice (who married John de Crackenthorpe). Margaret gets 40s. and 20s. each goes to the 'two sons' of his brother Hugo (I) but this Hugo has three sons – Hugo (II) 'The Wise', Robert, and William of Flymby who was presumably the unlucky one. Brother Hugo (I) gets all the arms, and Roger's wife Joan the rest of the estate. In all, the personal bequests total £29 6s. 2d., or less than a third of his uncle's.

Readers of the Testament Karleolensia may note that other Salkelds are mentioned, and in particular one Hugh the son of Ranulph who is named as an executor and as a beneficiary in the estates of W. de Routhburg, Archdeacon of Carlisle in 1364. Elsewhere are named Thomas de Salkeld, Rector of Addingham, and William Salkeld, 'persoun' of Ayketon.

The best part of two hundred years must now elapse before Salkeld wills again become available as sources of information for our studies: the next is dated 1562 and consists of a modest nine lines, largely illegible, of William Salkeld's Maulds Meaburne estate. The wills of John (II) and of Roger, at which we have been looking, are relatively speaking priceless, in that they enable us to see back 600 years, and with precision. We see that these 'ancient' Salkelds were men of substance, wine-drinkers, farmers, carrying arms, mindful of the public needs for bridge and church repairs, on intimate terms with local churchmen for whose beliefs they had great respect and bade fair to comply with; used indeed to having personal servants and even their own private chaplains – and nevertheless not ashamed, it would seem, of procreating their own bastards! 'Colourful' might perhaps be an appropriate one-word summary.

Note – In 1360 the bridge at Salkeld was washed away, whereupon Bishop Welton of Carlisle issued an Indulgence of 40 days to all who should contribute to its repair. Roger Salkeld and Richard Hunter were appointed to receive the money, and any withholding were threatened with excommunication. Roger himself contributed 6s. 8d.[24]

Chapter Three

First Salkelds of Corby Castle

The events leading to the execution of Andrew Harcla, Earl of Carlisle, at Harraby on 3 March 1323 have been graphically recounted by Dr. J. Mason[40] (*CWAA* 29, p. 98-137). King Edward II had had help from de Harcla in holding the rebellious Scots and yet, on the pretext that treason lay behind his treaty with Robert the Bruce, Edward ordered de Harcla's arrest under conditions of trickery. It was carried out, while Andrew was dictating letters in the Great Hall of Carlisle Castle, by Sir Anthony de Lucy and three other knights with the aid of 'four men-at-arms of good mettle', one of whom was named Richard (I) Salkeld (*Chronicles of Lanercost*, p. 251).

Those charged with this arrest had been promised by the king a good reward, and in due course Richard (I) received the grant of the escheated vill of 'Great Corkeby'; the award was confirmed some ten years later (on 14 October 1335)[26] by the new King Edward III, Richard to hold the manor of Corby of the king by service of half a knight's fee.

This trick of fate set this branch of our family upon the path of wealth and power in Cumberland, more than six hundred and fifty years ago. Without it, Richard (I) Salkeld might well have ended his days with an arrow in his back, late 'man-at-arms of good mettle'. With it, he established powerful connections, married an heiress, and raised an excellent and able family to serve his country for many generations; his family occupied Corby Castle for over three hundred years, and branches of it moved to other Cumbrian centres where they dwelt for long periods.

The exact date of Richard's birth I cannot find, but various events, including his death in 1368, suggest that he was born about 1290, the son of John (I), 'Lord of Salkeld', as Richard is described in the first reference to him, as a plaintiff in a plea of warranty in 1310.[27] (Throughout these next few chapters, which have unfortunately to deal with many 'undated' individuals, I have judged it more helpful to estimate dates and to say so, rather than to forego any attempt at a time scale.)

Of special interest is an entry in Cal. Inq. 21 September 1316[28] that Richard (I) de Salkeld held land, rental 12d. (one carucate) on that date 'late of John de Wygeton', at Melmerby, only some three miles east of his brother John (II)'s home at Maughanby, source of the oldest will, as just described. Of special interest, because this suggests *where* Richard (I) may have lived *before* he was granted the Castle of Corby, and before he bought an interest in the Manor of Little Salkeld.

About this time he became an adherent of Thomas Earl of Lancaster, to whom no doubt his 'mettle' was useful, but in 1318 it became necessary for Richard (I) to seek a pardon for all felonies and trespasses 'committed up to 7 August' which pardon was granted 'by consent of Parliament'[29] except (intriguing qualification) for having robbed the Cardinal Legatee!

We do not know exactly when Richard (I) married, but from the activities of his

children I estimate that it must have been about 1315. There is no doubt that his bride
was Matilda, daughter and heiress of Clement of Crofton and his wife Johanna, herself
daughter and heiress of Hugh de Ulvesby (today named Ousby, just south of Melmerby),
in Cumbria. Their first child was John (III), born perhaps about 1317; who was, in
time, to marry Isabell and to succeed to Corby, but not until their second child Hugh
(I) had lived in it for his lifetime. Hugh (I) was, I estimate, born about 1320, and we
know that he died in 1379, at the age therefore of nearly sixty, and very much our blood
ancestor.

Richard (I) and Matilda had other children, of less interest to us, and of less certain
lineage. They include:

> An unnamed daughter, who married William le Vaux of Catterlen in January 1351;
> A son William, unhappily drowned in the River Eden in 1345;
> Thomas, rector of St. Mungo in Caldbeck in about 1370;
> Roger, who became a Commissioner in 1373 and was a Verderer until 1378; owned the Manor of
> Crofton and Ulvesby [Ousby], having in 1355 married Joan Crofton by whom he had two daughters –
> Margaret who married Robert Bellingham of Burneshead, and Alice who married John de Crack-
> enthorpe, both illustrious Cumbrian names. His will (proved 1378) left money (6s. 8d.) for the
> repair of Salkeld bridge.

The gift of Corby Castle to Richard (I) was in June 1323, and in the following year
he was summoned (through the Sheriff of Cumberland) to attend the Council of
Westminster as a man-at-arms. In 1325 he became M.P. for Westmorland, and again
in 1328, when he was also created Knight of the Shire. Nevertheless he was not immune
from punishment for trespass, for which he received a general pardon on 29 August
1330.

It is popularly supposed that Hugh (I) Salkeld (Richard (I)'s second son) lived all
his lifetime at Corby before it reverted to John (III) (Richard (I)'s eldest son); this
supposition arises from the fact that neither Richard (I) nor Hugh (I) had sought a
licence from the king to their Corby arrangements. Hugh (I) had to beg the sovereign's
pardon, and was fined £10;[30] this was in the year 1369, a year after Sir Richard (I)'s
death – which death no doubt brought the omission to light. What, one may fairly ask,
had happened at Corby between its being granted to Richard (I) in June 1323, and its
occupation by Hugh (I) who would only be aged about three at that time? Even the
eldest and heir – John (III) – was probably only five, and scarcely in need of a castle!

Richard had to fight a claim, by Richard son of Conan de Ask, to 12 acres and half
a mill, to which claim he replied tersely that they were part of the Corby Manor which
he had from the king.

In 1332, Richard (I) and his wife Matilda[31] increased their land-holding by buying,
from William and Joan de Arthuret, a moiety of the Manor of Little Salkeld. Only a
few years later, in May 1342, he received a licence from the king to settle Great Corby
upon himself and his wife Matilda in tail, with reversion to his heirs – all that is save
12 messuages, a mill, 160 acres of land, three acres of meadow and one-third of a mill,
which were specified as going to their son John (III) and his wife Isabell in tail. By
that date – 1342 – Hugh (I) would be about twenty-two and a highly marriageable
proposition, and indeed he did marry, and made a brilliant match, in the person of
Christiana, heiress of Sir John Rosgill, thus bringing to the Salkeld family further
estates at Rosgill, on Shap fells. But *when* did he marry? The eminent genealogist
T. H. B. Graham, whose paper on Old Salkeld[8] is a great source of information,

3. Corby Castle.

estimates that Hugh (I) married Christiana in 1362. If that were so, Hugh (I) would
have been living as a bachelor, in Corby Castle, until he was 42 years old – and as he
died in 1379[32] at age 59, would not have left himself very long to bring up his
considerable family. But it could have been done.

In 1342, by indenture, Sir Richard (I) grants the monks of Wetheral further fishing
rights in the River Eden at 'Munkwath', and in the same year he enters into an agreement

with a William Carter and his wife Isabel for a messuage in Carlisle. Later, he is again a Commissioner, in 1343 inquiring into the murder of William Newby, a chaplain; and in 1348 surveying the military requirements of Penrith with Roger Salkeld (probably the brother whom we mentioned earlier).

> To inform themselves of the bounds of Penrith, for the crenellation of which the King had granted licence, which need such defences and in what places of the town it be expedient that a wall be made.[35]

Sir Richard (I) died in 1368 and an Inquisition, for his son Hugh (I), took place.[33] Another was held on the estate of Hugh (I) in 1379,[34] but the most informative was that held in 1389 which showed that his descendants had inherited Corby Manor, half the vill of Salkeld, Thornished, Melmerby and Skirwith – each with a tenement – and a burgage in Carlisle (12 Ric. II, p. 134).

In 1372 Hugh became too infirm to continue as a Verderer,[37] he died in 1379,[32] being buried in Addingham churchyard. On his death, Corby was to pass to his elder brother John (III) and wife Isabell, and thereafter to John's son Richard (II) and his wife Kateran (Skelton) – in other words, Corby moved over from our male ancestors to our female ones![8] John (III) had died before Hugh (I), so that Corby passed from Hugh (I) to his nephew Richard (II) as confirmed also in the manuscript notes written by Lord William Howard, given later.

There is a special difficulty in distinguishing between the acts of Hugh (I) the son of Richard of Corby, and Hugh's own son, also called Hugh (II) who also had a son Hugh (III)! Some who have written of this period in the Salkeld history have failed clearly to identify to which of these Hughs they are referring; this doesn't alter the pedigree but it can give a distorted picture of the Hughs concerned. In what follows I hope I have avoided some of this, by consideration of the dates ascribed to their acts, and by thinking of the likely ages of the Hughs concerned.

There is no doubt (*CWAA*, vol. 7, p. 240) however that Hugh (I), the son of Sir Richard of Corby, in 1358 bought the mills at Fenton and Little Corby from Thomas de Malton for 20 marks of silver, Hugh (I) being then about thirty-eight years of age and his son Hugh (II) being but a child or – if, as some say, the marriage to Christiana was not until 1362 – still unborn. Similarly, in 1365 Hugh (I) bought 30 acres from Robert of Corby, and again this must have been Hugh (I) the son of Sir Richard (I). There is also no doubt that Roger, whose will of 1378 we have already seen, left his arms to his brother Hugh (I), both sons of Sir Richard (I) Salkeld. But from then, our troubles start.

The main hurdle is the bald statement by William Flower, Norroy King of Arms, in his Visitation of 1563-4:[9]

> Hugh (II) Salkeld the second was for his wysdom and lernynge called 'Wise Hugh'. Was steward and surveior to Roger Clyfford Lord of Westmorland, as appeareth by his Patent beryng date 22 July 1373 and of King Rychard the 2 the 2 yere.

This Hugh is clearly the *grandson* of Sir Richard (I) of Corby, because it speaks of Hugh (II) 'the second'. From now on, we shall give Hugh (I)'s son Hugh (II) the title 'Wise Hugh'! The post of steward to Roger, Lord Clifford was at Greystoke, and was a highly responsible one, of the type described so excellently by Mark Girouard[38] as 'Always a gentleman, sometimes a knight, traditionally a grave and respectable figure, with a gown, chain and white staff as insignia of his office' – and responsible directly for the running of the household and the entertainment of the guests.

If then, as Ragg would have us believe, Hugh (I) son of Richard (I) had married Christiana in 1362, Wise Hugh (II) could scarcely have been born before 1363, and so would only be 11 years old when appointed steward at Greystoke! Even were he not so appointed until '2 the 2 yere' which would be 1379, he would still be but 27 years old, young for this post? For this reason I believe Ragg's date for the marriage with the heiress of Rosgill, Christiana, as in 1362, should be, more probably, 10 years sooner – that is, in 1352; and I estimate that Wise Hugh (II) was born in about 1353, some twenty-six years before his father's death.

This estimate, furthermore, fits in much better with what we know of 'Wise Hugh's' career. For all the authorities say that there was a Hugh Salkeld who represented Westmorland in Parliament in each of the years 1377, 1381, 1388, 1390, 1392, 1397 and 1400; the Hugh (II) named in 1388 is marked 'jun.' which implies that this Hugh was Wise Hugh (II), whereas possibly the Hugh (I) of 1377 was his father who died in the following year leaving all the other entries to be of Hugh (II) the Wise. Were Ragg right, this second Hugh (II) would only have been about eighteen years old when attending Parliament in 1381, after his father's death.

On my charts, therefore, I show the date of the marriage of Hugh (I), the son of Sir Richard (I) of Corby, to the heiress Christiana of Rosgill as in the year 1352, and the date of birth of Wise Hugh (II) as 1353, both estimated.

Wise Hugh (II) was the eldest son of Hugh (I) and married Margaret Tymparon, but before describing his career it is desirable briefly to deal with the remainder of Hugh (I)'s family. He had a second son Robert who dwelt at Tymparon and married Joan who was a widow in 1378; a third son William 'of Flimby', and a daughter Margaret who married John de Cliborn. Of these children, Robert is responsible for the entire 'Whitehall' branch of the Salkeld family, through his son John (IV) of Goborro, and John's son Lancelot and grandson Thomas of Whitehall. None of the Whitehall Salkelds is therefore our own direct ancestor, which is a pity because that branch is a picturesque one.

Hugh (I) (the son of Sir Richard (I) Salkeld) died, as we have said, in 1379, surviving his father by only 11 years and being too infirm to be a Verderer in the last seven of those eleven. His wife Christiana was still alive in 1398[5] and her father Sir John Rosgill was alive in 1382; he was the son of Robert (d. 1358) the son of Sir William (d. 1339) and his wife Aline. Sir John had a brother Robert and sisters Joan and Christiana, but how many of all these Rosgills lived on at Rosgill after Christiana married Hugh (I), I have not yet discovered.

Ragg[31] gives evidence that Hugh (I) and his wife were in possession of Rosgill by 1372 (while still owning Corby therefore) and we know that they had the King's pardon, in 1369, for having taken over at Corby from Sir Richard, without the necessary licence. After Hugh (I)'s death in 1379, there is evidence that Christiana continued to live at Rosgill for there is an indenture dated 1398, witnessed by Remigi de Melmoreby (Melmerby), giving her rights so to do until her death, when the Rosgill properties are to pass to her son 'Wise Hugh' (II).

We know that, since about 1372, the Culwens of Shap (who also had lands at Ormside and Asby) had let certain grazing rights on Shap, to Hugh (I) Salkeld. The above-mentioned Indenture of 1398 perpetuated a somewhat strange and unexpected business arrangement between the two families, made in about 1390, which provided for the Culwen family to move into Rosgill and live there with the Salkelds.

This brings us to the end of our story about Hugh (I), the son of Sir Richard (I), and his heiress wife Christiana, and we now start to consider the adventures, in more detail, of their son and heir, and our blood ancestor, the redoubted Hugh (II) Salkeld known as Hugh the Wise, of Rosgill. We deal first with his seal.

F. W. Ragg in an article on seals found on manuscripts in the Lowther Archives,[36] says:

> Seals of three other families that bore the fretty and the chief occur amongst the Lowther muniments, and following up the description of the early Curwen shield it may not be out of place here to say something about these. Except for what might easily be differences in the skill and the style of the engravers the differences between these, where there is no hint of colour, are hardly to be told. Of each of two of these I passed only a single impression – de Thornburg of September, 1376; and de Salkeld of Rosgill, of Ascensiontide, 1407. These were seals of Rolland de Thornburgh and Hugh de Salkeld. Of the third family Clibborn (Cliburn), I passed five. These began with February 1436 (John de Clibburn), Lent 1440 (Margaret, widow of John de Clibborn, daughter of Hugh de Salkeld of Rosgill), February 1489 (a later John de Clibburn), March 1549 (Thomas Cliburn), and ended with October 1549 (Richard Cliburn). All these shields – Thornburgh, Salkeld, and Clibburn – are composed of fretty with four laths each way under and touching a chief. In the Salkeld shield there is a near approach to symmetry in the arrangement of the fretty on the field. Both the Thornburgh and the Clibburn shields, like the Curwen described above, have the arrangement a little too much to the left to be symmetrical. The latest of these Cliburn shields (of 1549) has both of the outermost laths starting not from the underside of the chief at the corners, but starting from the sides of the shield just below the points where the chief touches the edge, an attempt it would seem to place the fretty symmetrically on the field.

HUGH DE SALKELD OF ROSGILL (1250-1425/P)

For Arms of Hugh de Salkeld of Rosgill[57] see also *Transactions of Cumberland and Westmorland Antiquarian & Archaeological Society*, new series, vol. 14 and the 1975 edition of an *An Armorial for Westmorland and Lonsdale* by Boumphrey, Hudleston & Hughes, p. 259 – an extra series of the same *CWAA Soc.*, vol. 21, published by Northumberland Press, Gateshead.[8]

Arms of Hugh de Salkeld in 1391 were sealed with a shield bearing a caraton and thereon a cinquefoil. In 1407 however his seal bears fretty and a chief.

> The following were recorded for his descendants by Flower at the visitation of Yorkshire 1563-4. Arms Quarterly: 1 and 4 vert fretty Argent (Salkeld): 2 Argent fretty and a chief Gules (Salkeld): Argent a bend chequy or and Gules (Vaux). Crest a demi lion rampant vert (NUY) NB (1478) give the following arms: Vert a fret argent; and adds that the arms of Clifford and of Salkeld are in north-east windows of the quire of the church at Shap, which was noted also by Bishop Nicolson (Miscellany Accounts 75). The Salkeld arms are quartered with those of Sharp in Warton Church, William Sharp, having married Alice daughter of John Salkeld of Knock.[4,5]

SHERIFFS, KNIGHTS AND HIGH CONSTABLES

Knights

Though some say that John de Salkeld, son of Nicholas, was a Knight of the Shire before his death in 1306, I cannot find convincing evidence to support this. But there is

4. Rosgill Hall.

no doubt that his son Richard (I) *was* a Knight of the Shire, and we need to understand how this distinction differed from that of knighthood today.[40]

Before the Norman Conquest, the king himself maintained and paid for such bodies of troops as there were under arms, but William the Conqueror introduced into England the system of tenure by knight-service which operated in Normandy. To his selected barons he granted lands in return for one or more units of knight's-service which were the service for 40 days each year of 10 knights per unit, at their own expense. These units could be sub-contracted, and it became common for land to be granted for only one knight's service, or for a fraction of one, and even, by the knight paying 'scutage', to avoid actual personal service at all, the king using the scutage money to hire soldiers at good rates of pay and with the prospect of plunder.

Edward I laid down the numbers and descriptions of weapons to be kept by each man according to his land holding (Statute of Winchester 1285) and each army was raised for a particular purpose and disbanded at the close of it. Knights had also to attend at particular Parliaments, being summoned by the County Sheriff to do so, whereas barons were summoned directly by the king until such time as membership became an hereditary duty associated with land-tenure. Both knights and barons had also a legal status and much administrative responsibility for running their county; for example in the times of Edward III no less than 1,636 knights of the shires attended one or more of the 50 parliaments, of which 126 knights were escheators, 371 were collectors of taxes, 381 sheriffs, and 641 Justices of the Peace. The supply of suitable candidates was helped by the system of primogeniture (eldest male child inheriting) which left younger sons with little choice but the church or the army. However, in the 13th and 14th centuries the cost of the knight's equipment – horse, arms, armour and attendant squires – became so heavy that many squires failed to be able to meet it, and remained squires all their lives instead of being promoted to knighthood in due course. Many knights sought also to avoid knighthood with its cost and onerous duties away from home, and by the first quarter of the 13th century it became necessary to enforce the taking up of this 'honour', on pain of heavy fine. In 1278 Edward I directed the sheriffs to force knightly rank upon all holders of land worth £20 a year; in the time of Elizabeth this was raised to £40. The Tudor sovereigns conferred knighthood very freely and after a time the prefix 'Sir', at one time used indiscriminately, was by custom reserved for knights and baronets. The distraint of knighthood was abolished by the Long Parliament of 1641.

Edward III and Henry V discouraged tournaments, and the coming of gunpowder dealt a death-blow to knighthood as a military and political force. The respect for women, which had formed part of the knightly ideal, was often skin-deep – marriages in high life were generally business affairs – the woman 'went with the fief'. Wealth consisted of land, which became more and more subdivided, while the merchant class were extending their operations and attracting younger sons to their ranks.[41]

As we pursue our studies of the Salkelds, we shall not be able to avoid seeing these trends working, at least until about 1600, and to their advantage. There were other Salkeld 'knights of the shire', often men of considerable wealth, as we shall see. From 1430 to 1832 they were elected in the county courts on the votes of the '40s. freeholders' who were obliged to attend court to do so; at the close of the 18th century these freeholders represented two per cent. of the populace, so the process of electing such powerful knights could scarcely be described as democratic![41]

Sheriffs

In the time of King Richard II (1377-99), besides the heavily-armed and armoured knights, the light horsemen, and the archers, the king had a less important supply of soldiers because of the ancient principle that all able-bodied men were bound to arm themselves and serve to keep the peace and defend the realm, and by the Statute of Winchester (1285) as later modified, every free man between the ages of 16 and 60 had to provide himself with suitable weapons, according to the value of his lands and chattels. The men thus armed were organised into the various hundreds and linked up for the whole shire under the control of the sheriff. Until the appointment of lord-lieutenants under the Tudors, the sheriff remained the leader of the shire-levies; he was normally responsible for seeing that the men of the lower classes in his shire were organised in groups (called 'tithings') for police and surety purposes, and for the holding of the old local courts, the shire and hundred moots. It was his duty to arrest suspects and carry out the penalties adjudged by the courts. Royal writs were addressed to him, the prisoners awaiting trial were entrusted to him, and through his bailiffs he usually collected the Crown's older resources of revenue from the shire. The sheriffs had long been generally hated, for they had great opportunities for oppression and extortion (Myers, p. 51).[42]

The office of High Sheriff was held for one year and involved presiding at the County Court, being the keeper of the king's peace, commanding all (free) people of the county to attend, executing all writs, carrying out the punishments of the Court, collecting fines and imposing capital punishment. As bailiffs directly answerable to the sovereign, the High Sheriff must seize all lands devolving on the Crown, levy all fines, and take care of all waifs and strays. The Courts met monthly, every freeman was bound to attend; there the knights of the shire were elected, and outlawries were pronounced; very few people could then write, not even persons of the highest rank and eminence (Nicolson and Burn, p. 33 of vol. I),[22] and so documents were signed with a cross.

According to Whellan (pp. 68-70)[13] the following Salkelds were High Sheriffs for Cumberland – 1448 Richard, 1461 Richard, 1466 Richard, 1484 Richard, 1495 Richard, 1544 Thomas, 1576 Richard, 1579 George, 1587 George, 1596 Lancelot, 1599 Thomas, 1663 Francis, 1819 Thomas, 1850 Thomas – and the following were M.P.s for Westmorland (Whellan, pp. 706-7)[13] – 1377 Hugh (II) de Salkeld, 1381 Hugh (II), 1388 Hugh (II), 1389 Hugh (II), 1390 Hugh (II), 1392 Hugh (II), 1396 Hugh (II), 1400 Hugh (II) – but unfortunately Whellan does not give a list of Westmorland High Sheriffs. According to *CWAA* Old Series IV, p. 316-7[43] the Westmorland Sheriffs were – 1458 Richard, 1495 Richard, 1514 Thomas, 1579 George, 1587 George, 1596 Lancelot; and members of Parliament were, for Cumberland – 1328, 1381, 1467 and 1472, all Richard de Salkeld.

High Constables

These duties are described in *CWAA Transactions*, vol. 71, pp. 75-89.[44]

BORDER WARFARE AND THOMAS V

William Hutchinson wrote a two-volume *History of the County of Cumberland*,[45] in 1794, and in the Introduction to the first volume gives much detail of Border warfare (from about pages 16 to 32). It is clear that this was of two general types – the first comprising the major battles between Scotland and England in which tens of thousands of troops were deployed and which are described in general history books – and the second type, often a precursor to, or a consequence of, the first – an armed raid from England into Scotland, and vice versa. We deal here only with the second type, as more relevant to our task of presenting the essential background information behind our Salkeld study. These raids had their own pattern of behaviour and it will perhaps bring home the effect they had on living conditions on the Borders, and on the brutal education of these raiders, if we start with a precise example in which a Salkeld was personally involved.

On page 25 Hutchinson[46] lists the names of 'Gentlemen of the County called out by Sir Thomas Wharton' in 1543, a list of some 37 named individuals and giving also the numbers of horsemen and footmen which each brought along – totalling some four hundred horse and about as many on foot. Included is 'Thomas Salkeld, of the Whitehall, 4 horse'. Their 'glorious achievements' are listed as 192 towns, towers, stedes, barnekins (outward wards of a castle), churches and houses burnt down, 403 Scots slain, 816 prisoners taken, 10,386 horned cattle, 12,492 sheep, 1,296 nags and geldings, 200 goats and 890 'bolls of corn' stolen. Two years later another raid, under the Earl of Hertford, burnt seven monasteries, 16 castles or towers, five market towns, 243 villages, 13 mills, and three hospitals.

Hutchinson (p. 30) gives many examples of complaints made by individuals and small groups of people who had suffered loss of cattle, corn, furniture and even daughters in the period 1582 to 1587. Other examples are given in the *Calendar of the Border Papers* by Bain, vol. 1, 1560-94,[47] and again in vol. 2. These show that, although George Salkeld was a Commissioner for the Western Marches in that period, his efforts did not prevent Henry Salkeld from losing eight head of cattle, valued at £16, in 1593 at Kirkoswald; and Rowland and John had similar losses there, when Lord Scrope was the Lord Warden of the Marches.

More serious was Lord Scrope's report to Lord Cecil (July 1600) that the infamous Scottish rebels the Grames had stolen from his home near Carlisle the six-year-old son of sheriff Thomas (V) Salkeld, in broad daylight! They held him to ransom until Thomas (V) released the rebel Wattie, a brother of Jock of the Peartree who was to be tried at the last Assizes at Appleby for stealing a horse – a capital offence. Subsequently Thomas (V) and others petitioned the Privy Council for more soldiers – in 1600. Only a few years previously the notorious rebel Kinmont Willie had been rescued from no less than Carlisle Castle by his friends the Grames – leaving behind some very red faces! But the Grames had their own point of view, as is well brought out in *CWAA* 69, p. 129-51[48] which describes their mode of life and how in fact they feared the local gentry who they claimed were 'thirstening for their blood' and 'would cut their throats with their hands did they dare'. In particular they named Thomas (V) Salkeld who they believed was motivated by a desire to stand well with Lord Dacre. The king (James I) actively supported by his feudal landlords moved against those he regarded as lawless chiefs of clans; legislation, passed in 1587, was followed by many hangings at Carlisle, Newcastle and Durham in the years thereafter.

It is important to make clear the simple truth that those Salkelds, who took part in the sort of forays here described, did it partly to defend their own wives and families and possessions, but also because it was expected of them by their colleagues, the big landowners of the two counties.

To be effective in this sort of work required strength, courage, loyalty, good horseman-ship and the power of command, and the Salkeld who reached the high office of sheriff or warden or member of Parliament – or even indeed knighthood of the shire – was undoubtedly a physically tough hard-riding hard-working hard-drinking leader who acted first and thought about it later. That they survived even to middle age, in this environment, is one of the surprises of this study.

With the aid of my charts (p. 7) of Salkeld pedigrees, it is easy to identify the Thomas Salkelds mentioned above. The first Thomas named was born about 1515, and in 1543 – the year described – married Marie daughter of William de Vaux and Catterlen. He died in May 1573, aged about fifty-eight. The second Thomas (V) mentioned was of a very different branch, and is marked with a Roman (V) throughout; he was the eldest son of 'Gentleman George' and Barbara, was born 1567, married Thomazin Bellingham, was a sheriff in 1598, and had the sad task of selling the second half of Corby Castle to Lord William Howard in 1625. The boy who was kidnapped was undoubtedly his son Richard, who had been born in January 1592; it was this Richard who died without issue leaving his estates at Rosgill to his married daughter Dorothy; thus he and his father between them lost both Corby and Rosgill from the Salkeld estates. His father (V) had died in 1639, at the very reasonable age of 72, so that, despite their arduous life, these two sheriffs called Thomas averaged sixty-five years on this earth, between them.

HUGH THE WISE

We have, in the preceding chapter, already given some information on Hugh (II) the Wise – the eldest son of Hugh (I) the son of Sir Richard (I) Salkeld of Corby. But there is more to tell.

In July 1386 – when, I estimate, he was 33 years old – he was appointed Commissioner of the Peace for Westmorland – and again in July 1389, when he was already a member of Parliament for that county. Two years later he was appointed a sub-escheator for Northumberland by the king, with the fearsome order 'In pain of £500 to leave all else and be without excuse before the King and Council at Middlesex to answer what shall be laid against him'. He appeared to be able to comply, but his duties as member of Parliament were also considerable; for example, he was paid £40 on 25 February 1382 for 100 days service in Parliament; that is a considerable period, and the rate – of 8s. a day – continued without change to 1388 when on 17 October he was paid £19 12s. for 49 days, followed by £13 12s. on 3 December for 34 days, £24 on 2 March for 60 days, £18 18s. 6d. on 10 February 1393 for 46 days, and £15 4s. on 12 February 1397 for 38 days. Though this rate of pay is constant, at 8s. a day, it is significantly less than the rate of 9s. a day which his father Hugh (I) received for attendance in the year 1377 – that is, £27 4s. for 60 days.

So much for his public life. At home there was of course the substantial task of running the Rosgill estates and entertaining the Culwens and his own many relatives; the arrangement with the Culwens blossomed and on 2 February 1390 Gilbert de Culwen quitclaimed to Hugh (II) Salkeld lands in Ormeshed and Shap, and the 1372 grazing agreement, for only 7s. a year of 'good English money', continued to be regarded as a sound bargain. Indeed in 1402 Hugh did homage to Gilbert, at Thornthwaite, the Culwen property near Rosgill.

5. Thornthwaite Hall, near Rosgill.

Many years later – in 1429 – there was a quarrel between the two families, over the Culwens' desire to extend the park at Thornthwaite by enclosing waste land which the Salkelds had been using for grazing (land on west bank of River Lowther between Swindale and Tothemfield Dyke); settled for a while, trouble blew up again 44 years later and this time it needed no less a personage than Richard Redmayne the Abbot of Shap to restore peace (*CWAA*, vol. 9, p. 279).

However, before the turn of the century, Wise Hugh (II) had married Margaret, the sole daughter of Sir John de Tymparon, of Derwentwater, and they had two sons and three daughters. The eldest son, and heir, christened Hugh (III), was later to marry Isabell Broughton in 1433(?) and to die in about 1447. We will treat of the others later, but this third Hugh presents a special problem, regarding his date of birth. For on

4 December 1395 an order was issued for the arrest of Hugh (II) senior *and (III) junior*, on a complaint of Shap Abbey that they had threatened to burn the Abbey down; and that same year Hugh (II), who had been under-sheriff of Westmorland, was removed from that post. It is of course conceivable that the Hugh (III) 'junior' *was* the young son of Hugh (II) and Margaret, in which case it would appear that they had married *much* earlier than the turn of the century; for Hugh (II) the Wise, I have estimated, was himself born about 1353 and so might well have married at say age twenty-seven – that is, in 1380. If their first child Hugh (III) 'junior' was born the following year, he would have been a youth of 14 when the Abbey laid this charge against him and his father. I shall mark my charts with these assumed dates, in the absence of more precise information. We do not know what punishment was awarded for this threat of arson, but it is so out of character, at least as far as Hugh the Wise is concerned, that one hopes the case was dismissed and the Abbot given a reprimand for his petulance!

A few years later – in 1403 – Hugh (II) made a grant of Salkeld land to his widowed daughter Margaret, who had married Matthew Smyth, now deceased; the land was at nearby Bampton and he charged her 6s. a year for it, with reversion to Rosgill if she died without heir. However she re-married, this time to William Lawesit, and in 1407 her father Hugh (II) granted him lands and tenements in Great Asby, Maulds Meaburn, Bampton Patrick, Bampton Cundale and Barton – all in Westmorland – for an annual rental for life of 26s. 8d., and in exchange for rights on Shap and Ormeshed.

Of his other two daughters, Isabell married John de Dalston of Dalston, and Amice married John de Pardshaw, who though living in 1411 was dead by 1416. She didn't, as a widow, feel capable of handling his lands profitably, and traded them in to her father Hugh (II), for a half-yearly pension. What happened to these lands at Pardshaw is told in a later chapter – they come back to our ancestral line.

We must add a word about Thomas, the last remaining of Wise Hugh (II)'s children. According to P.H.[7] he married and produced, at Rosgill, no less than five sons, named John, William, Roger, Thomas jun., and Richard; all six of them were living in 1456 and described as 'gentlemen'. Judged by their military antecedents, and propinquity at Rosgill, one would expect at least one of these sons to get into trouble and so find immortality in the records. So far however I have not traced such an entry, though in my Appendix 'Salkelds at Agincourt' I show that possibly the above-mentioned John, together with Robert (a grandson of Hugh (I)) could conceivably have been the John and Robert Salkelds mentioned as present at that famous battle in 1415.

As the years went by and his family grew up, Wise Hugh (II) was much in demand. It may have been his earlier associations with the Cliffords (when he was their steward at Greystoke) which led to his appointment to a Commission which met at Skipton on 16 June 1422 to examine the vexed problem of what should be done with Skipton Castle. For the 7th Lord Clifford, born 1388, had been killed at the siege of Meaux, and his widow Elizabeth, daughter of Henry Percy (Hotspur), instead of passing the castle to the heir Thomas, insisted on living in it although it was sorely in need of repair. The estate included 235 acres of arable, and 200 of meadowland, with various mills – not exactly an easy inheritance for a widow to manage. No doubt Wise Hugh found a good solution.

Later – in 1431, Hugh (II) 'senior' was fined for having acquired, without licence, from Christopher Moresby, the Manor of Culgarth – but he was pardoned for that.

Born, as I think, in 1353 or thereabouts, Hugh (II) the Wise was now getting to be an old man, and it is not clear whether it was he, or his son Hugh (III), who got involved in 1433 in an attack on the Cliburn home of Margaret Salkeld's husband John, by William Threlkeld and Thomas Musgrave and others. Hugh, with fellow J.P.s Sir Christopher Moresby and Robert Crackenthorpe, tried to restore order but ended up being cited as witnesses in John's subsequent appeal to the Chancellor of England for redress. For a fuller account of this interesting feud, and of the death two years later of Crackenthorpe, see *CWAA*, vol. 63, p. 178.[49]

Lastly, a positive piece of information, to offset some of the estimating which I have had to do in the above paragraphs in order to establish some sort of time scale of the events therein described. For in 1436 there was compiled a list of all those living in Westmorland and who had lands worth 100s. or more. The list contains 52 names in all. Top of it, with lands worth £86, was Sir Thomas Strickland Kt.; next came Henry Threlkeld with £80, then Sir Christopher Moresby Kt. with £60, then Sir Robert Leyburn Kt. with £53, and then our Hugh (II) Salkeld with lands and tenements worth £46, on which a subsidy of 23s. was due. This Hugh (II) is happily marked 'senior' on the list, because there is a Hugh (III) Salkeld junior, with lands shown as worth 100s. and paying a subsidy of only 2s. 6d. So, born as I estimate in the year 1353, we know that Hugh the Wise was alive in 1436, a very respectable 83-year-old. We shall find, towards the end of our studies, that there were older Salkelds still – though for his times, perhaps, not wiser ones.

CUMBRIAN CHURCH REGISTERS AS A SOURCE OF INFORMATION ON THE SALKELDS

On 29 September 1538 Thomas Cromwell, then Vicar General, issued the following injunction:[50]

> The curate of every parish church shall keep one book or register, which book he shall every Sunday take forth, and in the presence of the churchwardens or one of them, write and record in the same all the weddings, christ'nings, and burials made the whole week before: and for every time that the same shall be omitted shall forfeit to the said church iij[s] iiij[d].

and by the end of that year no less than 812 parish registers had been started throughout the land; but in what is today Cumbria, only five – Kirkby Lonsdale, Lazonby Lorton, Morland and St Bees were included in that number. The oldest registers still extant are usually transcripts made in pursuance of later injunctions of 1597 and 1603, which laid down that each parish was to provide itself with a parchment book into which the entries from the old paper books were to be copied, and for further security a true copy was to be transmitted to the bishop of the diocese every year within a month after Easter, to be preserved in the episcopal archives. These latter, known as 'Bishops Transcripts', can today often be found in County Record Offices and may usefully cover years for which the Parish Register has been lost or defaced, all too common in Cumbria.

But for our present studies we have to remember that the leading Salkeld ancestors were often – anytime after about 1655 – Quakers, and though these parish registers will tell us much of interest about their friends who were not, they may contain little or nothing of direct ancestral interest after about 1700. We can pick them up again in Suffolk when the swing back to the Church of England was under way.

In a period of some hundred and sixty years only 60 Cumbrian parish registers start before 1600, and a further 91 before 1700, a total of 151 out of the 297 benefices now in Cumbria. Roughly half of the pre-1600 have been 'deposited', and roughly one-third of the pre-1700; those 'deposited' can be studied in comfort in County Record Office Search Rooms, but those not deposited are locked away in church vestries so that a request to see them may result in the vicar or rector offering to have a search made by perhaps a churchwarden, or perhaps by his wife – a nuisance to all concerned. Very recent legislation is intended to encourage local clergy to deposit at least their oldest records, so that they can be stored under suitable conditions of temperature and humidity; the damage done in recent centuries by careless storage in damp boxes is almost indescribable, and though the above figures would suggest that very many registers are available for study, it has also to be added that many of their pages are torn off or unreadable; quite often several years of entries are missing, for a variety of reasons.

Parish	Starts Year	Numbers of Salkeld:			Cumbrian Totals	Cumulative %
		Births	Marriages	Burials		
Penrith	1556	76	29	62	167	15.7
Brough	1556	73	30	58	161	30.8
Morland	1538	78	22	52	152	45.1
Kirkoswald	1577	63	21	31	115	55.9
Warcop	1597	33	24	19	76	63.0
Cr. Ravensworth	1568	31	16	15	62	68.8
Askham	1566	24	6	15	45	73.0
Lowther	1540	15	7	13	35	76.4
Dean	1542	19	5	6	30	79.2
Shap	1559	10	9	6	25	81.5
Crosthwaite	1562	9	4	7	20	83.4
Dacre	1559	10	5	4	19	85.3
Holme Cultram	1580	7	6	5	18	87.0
St Bees	1538	8	1	8	17	88.5
Knock/Marton	1586	11	3	7	21	90.3
Harrington	1603	8	3	2	13	91.7
Kendal	1558	5	5	1	11	92.7
Windermere	1611	7	0	4	11	93.8
Caldbeck	1647	4	3	1	8	94.4
Allhallows	1666	0	0	7	7	95.2
Totals		491	199	323	1013	100 = 1065

Fortunately, of the 1,065 entries of births or marriages or burials of Salkelds in the 200 years from 1538, which I have been able to collect from *Cumbrian* registers, 868, or 81.5 per cent, are from only 10 parishes, and if a further 10 parishes are included these 20 will contain 95 per cent of the Salkeld entries. They are tabulated below. It is certain that many more Salkelds lived and worked in these and other Cumbrian parishes but for many reasons their entries were never made, or have since been lost; as one example only, it is believed that the plague which swept Cumbria in 1598 and which according to Whellan (p. 596) caused 2,260 deaths in Penrith alone, so upset the administration that the burial of only 583 was recorded. It is best therefore to take the following figures as a sample of the whole, and to bear in mind that some of the registers started up much later than others, as the table shows, and would not therefore be expected to contain so many entries. Perhaps the greatest interest in the table is the way it brings to light just where the concentrations of Salkelds in Cumbria occurred, in 1538 to 1738. Not shown in the table, but of special historical interest, is Addingham, with five birth entries and one burial, in the 200 years.

Over the full 30 parishes – including the 20 shown above – the total of entries was: births 516, marriages 217 and burials 332, total 1,065, and showing a ratio of births to marriages of 2.38, and of burials to births of 0.643, which latter figure is low. But the main point of interest is perhaps the fact that there were some five hundred births of Salkelds in the 200-year period represented above, in Cumbria; an analysis of these births shows that 48.5 per cent of them were girls, and that there were very few twins, and no triplets nor 'quads'.

Except therefore for the parishes of Penrith, Brough, Morland and Kirkoswald (which four accounted for over half of all Salkeld births in Cumbria in this period), the birth of a Salkeld in any other parish was, on average, a fairly *rare* event in any one year. Shap for example had 10 Salkeld births in the 50 years between its first and last birth registration of a Salkeld – one every five years; a Salkeld wedding was about twice as rare. In the latter half of the 200-year period, entries per year were reduced by transfer from Church of England to Quaker beliefs, but this effect is not apparent in the above table because it is totalled for the whole period.

Chapter Four

Hugh the Third

In the last chapter are given my reasons for believing that Hugh the third, son of Wise Hugh (II) and of Margaret Tymparon, was born about 1381 and that at the tender age of 14 he had, possibly with his father's support – or possibly on his own – threatened to burn down the Abbey of Shap; he was living at Rosgill at the time, and the Abbey is quite near.

Hugh the third is stated to have married Isabell Broughton in 1433, by which date, on my reckoning, he would have been aged 52, rather surprisingly old for a first marriage; he is also said to have died about 1447, only 14 years later and aged, I estimate, 66, which I find quite believable; so I would suspect the date given for his marriage, believing it to have been earlier. And if so, the birthdate of their firstborn child Thomas – our direct ancestor – might well have been before 1433.

Their only other child was a girl, Christiana, who married Thomas Lancaster of Sockbridge and produced no less than six sons for the Lancasters. Other activities with this famous family are mentioned later. How far the marriage of Christiana and Thomas Lancaster was a love-match, or how far she was prevailed to marry him because of their respective estates, would prove an interesting study but not one for which there is room here. The relationship between the Lancasters, and the Salkelds of Rosgill, was at this period a close one.[51]

I think that Hugh (III), perhaps as a reaction to his wise (II) father, was a bit wild; apart from the threat to burn down the Abbey, we find that Hugh (III), together with two of the Lancasters, a Hoton, and two Fetherstanehalghs, in 1439 (October) raided the home of Thomas Baty at Brougham, and stole 37 oxen worth 40 marks. They then tricked Baty into believing that they had had nothing to do with this theft, and persuaded him to sign a bond of 100 marks agreeing that he would accept their arbitration; they then found against him, and proceeded to sue him through no less an authority than the Chancellor (the Earl of Salisbury), for payment. But Baty was made of sterner stuff, and petitioned the Bishop of Bath to intercede and cite Salkeld and the others to appear in Chancery, which is how the whole action came to light – through the Chancery records. Unfortunately, the result of the proceedings is not known – at least to me – but it must be regarded as unlikely that such a theft would go unpunished. Hugh (III) would then, I reckon, be about fifty-eight years of age.

At Lowther, the antiquarian F. W. Ragg found a deed dated 1447 under which Hugh (III) hands over all his manors – including Rosgill, Ormished and Gnype and Newbiggin, to a group of executors including his wife's father John Broughton, Robert Salkeld, and the three Lancasters, William, Roger and Christopher, presumably in trust for his wife Isabell and their son Thomas Salkeld (of Bampton), then only some thirteen years old. It would be very interesting to examine this deed in more detail.

No doubt Hugh (III) died soon thereafter, for another deed dated 4 July 1452 gives

6. Shap Abbey today.

his widow, for the rest of her life, the lands at Little Salkeld 'given to her husband by his grandfather Hugh (I)'. This sounds very much as though Isabell, tired of life at Rosgill after her husband's death, returns to the Little Salkeld of her husband's family. But of course Rosgill is still the main family home of this branch (Corby now being the home of the Salkelds descended from John (III) the son of Sir Richard (I)) and three years later – in 1455 – there is an entry that the heirs of Hugh (III) Salkeld hold the hamlet of Rosgill by military service – no doubt headed by young Thomas, just of age and the son and heir of Hugh the third.

This entry is mentioned by F. W. Ragg in his important paper 'Shap and Rosgill and some Early Owners'.[3] He then goes on to say ·'In 1473 a Thomas [III] Salkeld was in possession, probably the son of Hugh [III] and Isabell Broughton; this last Thomas [III] appears to have married his kinswoman Catherine, one of the co-heirs to Richard [III] Salkeld of Corby'. This, as written by Ragg, would imply that the son of Hugh (III) and Isabell married Catherine. And yet at the end of the pedigree chart which Ragg gives (facing p. 62) we find an extra Thomas inserted, saying that there was a Thomas son of Hugh and Isabell who married – no wife's name given – and whose marriage produced *another* Thomas (III) who then married Catherine. What does William Flower, in his Visitation[9] as Norroy King of Arms, in 1563-4 say about the problem? He comes firmly down on the side of Thomas (III) son of Thomas – that is, he follows Ragg's pedigree chart rather than Ragg's written text. So in my own chart I shall show both Thomases.

What then can be said about the Thomas who was son of Hugh the third and who himself had a son Thomas (III) (who later married Catherine)? Extremely little. There is every reason to suppose that he was born at Rosgill, and was only about thirteen when his father died, as explained above – based that is on the belief that young Thomas was born in 1433. There is an interesting reference in *Cal. Pat. Rolls*, vol. 8, Ed. IV[52] – to a deed of lands at Ormside to 'Thomas Salkeld junior Lord of Rosgill', when he would be 36 years old, but not too much significance must be attached to the epithet 'junior' for as we show later there was a perfectly good Thomas (I) son of Richard (II), called Thomas (I) the Elder, alive in 1438, though *his* son Thomas (II) the Younger died in November 1439. And according to PH,[7] there was the Thomas 'of Rosgill' alive in 1456 with his five sons (already mentioned) including a Thomas junior, all of Rosgill. One must therefore conclude that a great deal more research would be needed to produce a reliable pedigree of all these Salkeld Thomases of Rosgill and of Corby, but in the belief that Norroy King of Arms should be the supreme authority, my charts show my preferred solution; who Thomas the son of Hugh III married, we do not know, but we can reasonably assume that the marriage took place in the period 1450-60 and that Thomas (III) of Rosgill, the important product of it, married Catherine the co-heiress of Sir Richard (III) and Jane Vaux, after 1475. As the descendants, respectively, of the brothers John (III) and Hugh (I) (the sons of the first Sir Richard (I) Salkeld of Corby), Catherine and Thomas (III) were kinsmen before their marriage, and of course their marriage brought together again the estates of Corby and of Rosgill and indeed many others which meanwhile had become attached – such as Pardshaw. For the immediate purposes of our study, it matters not whether there were one or two Thomases between Hugh the third and the husband of Catherine – in either case they are blood ancestors.

7. The Salkeld Tomb in Wetheral church.

And now that we have reached as far forward in our pedigree as Catherine who married Thomas (III) Salkeld her kinsman, we must, before proceeding with that lady, go right back to *her* ancestors John (III) (the brother of Hugh (I) and his wife Isabell and say something about Catherine's great-great-grandfather, John's son Richard (II), and then about his son Thomas (I) the Elder, and his son Thomas (II) the Younger, and finally his son the great Sir Richard (III) of Corby who was Catherine's father, and who, with his wife Jane Vaux, today lies buried in an alabaster tomb in Wetheral church. Having done that, we can then more meaningfully return to Catherine and her husband (and kinsman) Thomas (III) and their very important family, from whence we came. It would no doubt make these complex relationships a little clearer to our readers, if at this stage the charts which I have compiled were studied for a few moments.

As earlier pointed out, these charts are far from complete, and no doubt omit many worthy Salkelds who ought to have a rightful place; but at least, within the limitations above described, I believe they fairly represent the main streams and the main individual relationships and thus enable us to select which parts of this complex we must study as our objective, and which parts, however interesting, must be relegated as being outside our blood-ancestor lines.

We therefore now turn back to John (III), the eldest son of the first Sir Richard (I) Salkeld of Corby – the John (III) who one would have expected to have inherited, and lived in, Corby when his father died, but who – perhaps because John's family was apparently small – found it to be the home of his younger brother Hugh (I), father of Hugh (II) the Wise.

THE DESCENDANTS OF JOHN (III)

As the eldest son of Sir Richard (I) Salkeld and his wife Matilda, John (II) was no doubt born in about 1317, many years before his father had been knighted, and before the family had been granted Corby Castle as their home. As already explained, it is probable that Richard (I) and his wife were living in the village of Melmerby, where we know he had land and a messuage, and from whence they later moved to Little Salkeld Hall, before finding their resting place within the walls of Corby Castle. But at this stage – 1317 – it was Melmerby, for it was not until 1332 that a moiety of the manor of Little Salkeld was acquired, and by then John (III) would be a lad of about fifteen; indeed the first we hear about his exploits (as distinct from being the son of his father) is in February 1330, when on his behalf a pardon was requested from the clerk in Chancery, one William de Inglis, for John (III)'s crime against the Forest Laws of taking and killing a hind in the Forest of Inglewood.

Many years later – in May 1351 – when John (III) was earning his living as lieutenant of William Langley, the Chief Forester of Inglewood Forest, he was fined £20 for trespass,[53] for which he was pardoned. But less than two years later – in February 1353 – he was charged with 'trespass of vert and venison', and this time lost his job, an order being issued on 10 February to elect a Verderer vice John (III). We also know that about that time – in July 1351 – he had been in debt to a John de Gray of Rotherfield to the very substantial tune of £40, and as at that time he was employed as a forester it is not very obvious how he hoped ever to repay such a burden.

We do not know the surname of his wife Isabell, nor in which year they married, but their eldest son Richard (II) was born in 1355, when father John (III) would be about thirty-eight and so perhaps they married about 1353 – the year he lost his steady job as a verderer. But our authority William Flower, Norroy King of Arms, records[9] that John (III) was dead before 1379, the year when his brother Hugh (I) died. Whether John (III) and Isabell had other children than the Richard (II) mentioned above, is not recorded, but it is clear that it was Hugh (I) and his family who took over Corby Castle from Sir Richard (I) and Matilda his wife, when the time came, and it is unlikely that John (III) and Isabell lived in the castle for any significant period. As Sir Richard (I)'s eldest son, we can imagine that John (III) was not too pleased about being denied Corby; had he lived longer than his brother Hugh (I), he would probably have had it – but in the event it was John (III)'s son Richard (II) who inherited Corby Castle, when Hugh (I) died.

8. Melmerby church.

Adding together all we know about John (III) – which is mostly that he was prone to trespassing – and perhaps not very good at it either – we do not get a very impressive picture of this eldest son of the brave and gallant Sir Richard (I) Salkeld. But this is, to some extent at least, because we live in a very different age and can easily make the mistake of thinking that standards then were much as they are today – which is quite wrong. For this reason I have studied the series of papers on Inglewood Forest, which appeared in the years 1905 to 1911 in the *CWAA Transactions*,[54] and selected a number of points which together throw considerable light on the matter of trespassing, and on the forest staff and the regulations under which they had to operate. To my mind, this helps to put John (III) into a less unfavourable light.

However that may be, John (III)'s importance to our present study lies entirely in the fact that he sired this son Richard (II) – not to be confused with his grandfather the first Salkeld (I) of Corby – nor indeed with his great-grandson Richard (III) who married Jane Vaux and rests under the alabaster effigy in Wetheral church. John (III)'s Richard (II) inherited Corby Castle when his uncle Hugh (I) died in 1379, when Richard (II) would be about twenty-four years of age. Three years later he represented Westmorland in Parliament, and was a Knight of the Shire. Six years after that – in 1388-9 – he was dead, aged well under forty. His wife Katherine (née Skelton), survived him by some fifty years, dying in November 1438-9. She was the daughter of Thomas Skelton of Braithwaite in the parish of Dean, where lay the Pardshaw lands owned by the Salkelds and which are discussed in a later chapter. As far as is known, the widow Katherine did not remarry, and no doubt lived out her life at Corby, with her son Thomas (I) (later known as 'The Elder') and his wife Christiana (née Chipchase), and in later years with her grandson, also Thomas (II) ('The Younger') and his wife Joan, née Stapleton.

Though there is no doubt about the pedigree described above, the precise dates of the births, marriages and deaths of these Salkelds are, I am sad to say, uncertain. Many church records, if kept at all, have disappeared since; wills seem rarely to have been made, and if they were made, have vanished into the tummies of mice and rats or disintegrated into dust on the vestry floor. And there is confusion amongst the few records which do exist. For example, there is one entry which states that this Richard (II) – to whom I have, above, attributed a birthdate of 1355 – 'was a forester in 1351'; this would mean that he was born in about 1330 and therefore unlikely to have married before 1350; in 1350 his bride would be perhaps eighteen – and therefore might have been born in about 1332; but we know that, as a widow, she died in 1438 – over a hundred years later; whatever assumptions of this sort are made, it seems highly unlikely that her husband Richard (II) was a forester in the year 1351. My own estimate of his birthdate therefore remains at 1355.

We know also that Richard (II)'s son Thomas (I) the elder, was alive in 1438, and that Thomas's wife Christiana was the daughter of Heron of Chipchase; that their son Thomas (II) died on 2 November 1439, and that the date of his death was 'in the lifetime of his grandmother', the Katherine mentioned above. When Richard (II) died, we know too that he was found seized of Corby Castle and a moiety of Little Salkeld Manor. That was in 1389.[55] When the Manor was more fully valued, in 1449-50, amongst the items specified were a messuage called 'Langthwaite', three messuages called 'Riddings' at Corkeby, and four messuages and two cottages at Little Corkeby (ibid. 28 Hen. VI, p. 240). These 'Riddings' comprised a one-tenth part of the Manor of Corkeby, and we shall find a reference to them again, when we study the Pardshaw Salkelds.

In view of the doubts there are, at times, about the exact dates of some of the acts described above, it is comforting to be able to quote the following precise confirmation of this part of the Salkeld pedigree:

Richard (III) Salkeld filii Thomae (II) filii Thomas (I) filii Richardi (II) Salkeld defuncti, ac consanguinei et heredis ejusdem Richardi (III) probatae aetatis.[56]

That a Thomas Salkeld owned Corby and these other properties at Little Corby, in 1451, is also confirmed in a list of 'Sheriffs Seizures' 30 Hen. VI; why they were seized is not told, but they were returned in due course. If this seizure implies that Thomas (II) the Younger was alive in 1451, he cannot have died in November 1439 'within the lifetime of his grandmother Katherine', as stated above. Graham, in his very informative paper,[57] notices this discrepancy but offers no explanation of it. Clearly, one of all these assertions must be wrong, but *exact* dates are only important if they alter a relationship, which these do not. An alternative explanation, of course, is that the Thomas Salkeld whose property the sheriffs seized, was not Thomas (II) the Younger, but his father, Thomas (I) the Elder, whom we know to have been alive in 1438 – some fourteen years before the seizure. Thomas (I) the Elder was born the eldest child of Richard (II) and Katherine, whom I have argued above married in perhaps 1375-80, so that Thomas (I) the Elder would be born perhaps in 1376-81, which would make him between 62 and 67 in the year 1438 (when he is known to have been alive) and somewhere between 71 and 76 when the sheriffs acted in 1451. This explanation seems to me to fit the available information better than any other so far proposed, and I shall use it in this book. In short, it means that Thomas (II) the Younger died before his father Thomas (I) the Elder, so that Thomas the Younger's son and heir – the famous Sir Richard (III) Salkeld of Corby Castle, who was born in 1425 – had a grandfather but no father, from age about fourteen until he was about twenty-seven or more – that is, when grandfather Thomas (II) the Elder finally did die. What arrangement Thomas (II) the Younger had made about his inheritance before he died, I have not yet discovered. It may be, of course, that Richard (III) did not inherit Corby until his grandfather Thomas (I) the *Elder* died – sometime after 1451. But we deal with this famous Richard (III) in a later chapter.

Let us however re-capitulate, to bring Richard (II) the son of John (III) rather more into the limelight. That he was born in 1355 is refreshingly certain, as the records show that he was aged 24 in the second year of the reign of Richard II, PH[7] records that Richard (II) was heir to his grandfather and to his father, and was Lord of Corby and of Salkeld in 1379 and a knight of the shire in 1382. Nicholson and Burn add, and in 1384.[58] He was a juror on at least two occasions – in April 1380 at the Inquisition on the death of William de Stapleton of Edenhall[24] (father of his son's wife Joan Stapleton), and again in 1383 on the death of William de Hoton.[59] We have already spoken of his lands at Corby, Little Salkeld, Melmerby, Thornishead and Skitwith, each with a tenement, which he had King Richard II's permission to settle for life on his wife and children – referred to again in 18 Hen. VI, p. 38, with lands at Aglionby added (this is 1460, after Katherine's death). Before his own death in 1389 he obtained a licence (for 40s.) to enfeoff two men of Corby Manor with regrant to himself and his wife

Katherine and their heirs. A shrewd and wealthy Salkeld, who died at the youthful age of 34, leaving his son Thomas (I), whom I estimate was born about 1379, to succeed him – a lad of but 10 years old; this lad was certainly alive in 1438 and on my reckoning died in about 1451, at the respectable age of 72 or thereabouts.

LORDS OF THE MANOR OF CORBY

Elsewhere the sale of a moiety of Corby to Lord William Howard, by Blenkinsop in 1605, and by Thomas Salkeld in 1625, is discussed, but the following summary entitled 'The Lords of the Manor of Corby' was in the *handwriting* of Lord William, of Naworth Castle, in 1625. It was communicated to the editors of Hutchinson's *History of Cumberland* by Mr. Henry Howard, from the original manuscript preserved at Corby, and published in London in 1794[45] (vol. 1, pp. 170-3). It was in Latin and Mr. C. N. Richardson, Head of Classics at Cranleigh School, very kindly translated it for me, as follows:

Richard (I) Salkeld, by the gift of the lord king Edward III (1336/5), in the ninth year of his reign: from a petition dated 14th October.

The king to all the usual recipients. Know ye that whereas my father the lord Edward late king of England, in recognition of the excellent service which Richard of Salkeld had rendered to my father, gave him the manor of Corby in the county of Cumbria which had belonged to Andrew of Harcla, and which as a result of his forfeiture had come into my father's hands as his escheat, to be held by the same Richard I and his heirs; and whereas my father also provided to the same Richard I and his heirs 20 librates of land in some suitable place; we wishing to pay a more generous debt of gratitude to the same Richard do grant to him and his heirs the aforesaid manor of Corby with its appurtenances as equivalent to the 20 librates of land in perpetuity. As witnessed by the king at Berwick on Tweed.

From this Richard (I) Salkeld the aforesaid manor, which was hereditary, passed to Richard (II) his son, and so on from son to son to a certain Richard (III) Salkeld, soldier, who died without male heir of his body in the sixteenth year of the reign of Henry VII (1485-1509: = 1501) leaving six daughters as his heirs. A division of the whole estate of the aforesaid Richard (III) Salkeld, soldier, was made by a deed dated 12th March at Penrith in the twentieth year of Henry VII (1504), as a result of which the aforesaid manor of Corkby was assigned to Mistress Katherine Duckett, the eldest daughter, at that time wife of Thomas (III) Salkeld of Rosgill, and to Margaret, the second daughter, widow of Thomas Blenkinsop Esquire of Hallbeck, to be held by her and her heirs as her full share of the total estate of her aforementioned father.

To this Margaret Blenkinsop was born Thomas, and to him a second Thomas, to whom was born a third Thomas, from whom came Henry Blenkinsop Esq., who on the 22nd November 1605 made over his whole moiety of the aforesaid manor of Corkby to Master William Howard, as is shown by his charter of the date aforementioned.

And to the aforementioned Katherine was born Thomas (IV) Salkeld; to him Richard (IV), to him Barbara, his sole daughter and heir, who married George Salkeld, the son of Richard (V) Salkeld Esq. of Thrimby, brother of the aforesaid Thomas, the grandfather of the aforementioned Barbara, and to them was born Thomas (V) Salkeld Esq., who on 10th February 1624 made over his whole moiety of the aforesaid manor of Corkby to the same Master William Howard, who now holds the manor of Corkby in entirety, by virtue, as explained above, of the two distinct perquisitions. A.D. 1625.

This Lord William Howard of Naworth was brother to the Earl of Arundel (1557-95) and son of the 4th Duke of Norfolk (1538-72) Earl Marshal of England. William (1563-1640) was Earl of Carlisle, and bought the Corby estates for his son Sir Francis Howard (1588-1660) who passed Corby on to his son Francis (1635-1702). The 4th Duke was educated to M.A. at Oxford and Cambridge, but his son William (according to my translator Mr. Richardson) in this manuscript 'contains many examples of dog-latin and . . . some definite errors in the Latin'. I believe also that he has omitted two Salkelds in the chain he describes – John (III) the son of Richard (I), and a Richard the brother of Thomas (IV) and the father of Richard (V). (It is certainly very easy so to do.) Nevertheless, Lord William's manuscript is a unique document and one central to our pedigrees and to the Salkeld-Corby relationship.

Chapter Five

Rosgill and the Children of Sheriff Thomas the Younger

Whilst it may well be argued that the wealthiest and most powerful Salkeld was Sir Richard (III) of Corby (1425-1501) – who had the great good sense to marry Jane Vaux the sole heiress of Roland Vaux of Triermain and Catterlen – yet Sir Richard (III) and Jane between them did not produce a male heir (though some say he did have a bastard son John). All their efforts resulted in a procession of daughters, numbering no less than six. He thereupon made surely the greatest mistake a Salkeld ever made – he nominated the *two* eldest daughters Katherine and Margaret as co-heiresses.

Katherine, determined to keep the Salkeld succession alive, married her cousin Thomas (III) Salkeld and produced at least two perfectly good male heirs, including Richard the father-to-be of Richard (V) of Thrimby Grange, and Thomas (IV) who married Margaret Curwen. Fine. It was her sister and co-heiress Margaret who inadvertently let the side down – she married Thomas Blenkinsop who sired – some generations later – the Henry Blenkinsop who sold their moiety of Corby to Lord William Howard, thereby starting a series of squabbles and law-suits which so impoverished the Salkelds that they had to sell their remaining moiety to Lord William also.

This Thomas (IV) Salkeld, husband of Margaret Curwen, was a sheriff who, like his ancestors, played a prominent part in the defence of Carlisle and its environs from the regular and remorseless attacks of the Scots from over the Border.

Thomas was a big landowner, his estates at this time including his mother's half of Corby, the family inheritance of Pardshaw and adjacent Mosser (near Cockermouth) and his father's lands and mansion at Rosgill on Shap fells, about which we must now speak.

Rosgill is a hamlet within the parish of Shap, high up on the windswept fells some sixteen miles from Kendal and about eleven miles from Penrith by the old A6 trunk road. Shap has an ancient parish church in the Norman style, of about thirteenth-century origin, dedicated to St. Michael. The manor of Shap was originally in the possession of the Curwens of Workington, and then of the nearby Abbey of Shap, and after the dissolution was granted Lord Wharton, eventually coming to rest in Lonsdale hands. Within the parish boundaries lay the hamlet of Rosgill and Rosgill Hall, sitting right down on the north bank of the River Lower and about two and a half miles north-west of Shap village.

It was on the marriage of Hugh (I) Salkeld to Christiana, daughter and heiress of Sir John of 'Rossegyll' in 1352 *or* 1362, that this Manor of Rosgill passed to the Salkelds. From then on there are references (Nicholson and Burn, vol. 1, p. 478)[22] to its occupation by various Salkelds – in 1469 by Thomas junior, in 1512 by Richard, in 1535 by Thomas, in 1556 and 1566 by Richard, until in 1631 on the death of the current Richard it passed, for lack of male heir, to his sister Dorothy who was already married to William Warmsley; on his death she married into the family of Christian of Unerigg Hall in

9. Catterlen Hall.

Cumberland; later it was sold to the Lowthers, having been in the possession of the Salkelds for some two hundred and seventy years. The Manor House today has stained glass recording these ownerships, and I have used a painting of the two windows as a basis for the cover of this book.

Thomas (IV) Salkeld of Rosgill unfortunately left no will, but his pedigree has been well documented (Nicholson and Burn, vol. 2, p. 59)[22] and we know, not least from

10.   A view of the country above Rosgill.

the excellent will of his son and heir Richard (IV) dated 30 January 1574-5, that he had sons James, Jhon and Jhon, and a daughter Elizabeth, all alive in 1575. The curious naming of two sons 'John' or 'Jhon' was apparently deliberate, though unusual, and indeed one finds that the epithet 'Younger' occurs at times to differentiate one from the other.

The son Richard (IV) – brother of James and the Jhons – lived at Cliburn until Thomas's death, and when Richard died we find inventories for the contents of Rosgill, dated 6 February 1574-5, and another, dated 10 February, for the contents of their moiety of Corby. Transcriptions of both of these inventories give fascinating insights into the lives of these Salkelds.

Richard's will, witnessed by John 'Crakenthropp', John Rigg, and his brother John Salkeld the Younger, after certain minor bequests leaves the entire estate to his wife Elizabeth, and then to his son-in-law George Salkeld and his wife Barbara – who was of course Richard's one and only daughter. This George is the 'Gentleman George' of Thrimby Grange some three miles only from Rosgill; as he is not our *direct* ancestor, a short monograph about him, which I wrote in 1978, has to be relegated as an Appendix to the end of this book.

In his will Richard (IV) leaves the not very princely sum of £6 13s. 6d. to each of his three brothers. The inventories are well worth study and comparison, and give a picture of life at Rosgill and at Corby some four hundred years ago. My impression of Corby is that it had become a 'Salkeld satellite' of Rosgill – not so comfortably furnished, bedroom furniture confined to little more than beds and bedding, a working kitchen, brewhouse and buttery, certainly with table linen and pewter vessels – sometimes even silver utensils – but nothing extravagant, and outside, four 'worke nagges'; whereas at Rosgill there were 'worke nagges' but also four riding horses with saddlery. Oxen at both sites, but at Rosgill no less than 442 sheep – a large flock for those times. Hay and corn at both sites, but at Rosgill, a bull. And inside at Rosgill, in the high loft, a 'standing bedd with taisters and curtains' and a particularly well-equipped 'great chamber'.

We can readily envisage Richard's three brothers visiting their father Thomas (IV) at Rosgill, changing horses for fresh ones from the Hall's stables, riding out over the Shap fells, sampling the produce of the buttery and brewhouse, perhaps sleeping there for night after night. James, who lived mainly at Pardshaw Hall (some thirty miles away as the crow flies) was buried at the parish church at Dean on 29 December 1582, and would perhaps have seen less of Rosgill than would John the Younger his brother, who may have had his main home there, although we know that he had, at Corby, a home in the 'Riddings' as well. Perhaps it was the other John who lived mostly at Rosgill with his father, until Thomas died in 1573, when brother Richard (IV) moved in from Cliburn, only a few miles away. A thorough search of all the parish registers in this district – including those of Bampton, Shap, Askham, Lowther and Morland, has failed to find an entry concerning this James, of whose existence we know only from Richard's will; and yet, as we shall show later, James was our direct ancestor. Only when we come to examine the registers of Dean (the parish church of Pardshaw), do we find a record of James' burial. Why Pardshaw? Because, as our reader may recall, extensive lands at Pardshaw came into the Salkeld estates when Amice married John de Pardshaw, and, outliving him, traded (in 1416) them to her father Hugh (II), our ancestor.

No doubt a man likes to be buried where his heart is, and the fact that in his will Richard (IV) says that he is to be buried at Shap – not at Corby – completes this comparison. Today Rosgill is dominated by modern silos, smelling of the treacle which oozes from their base. No doubt many times more productive than in Thomas (IV)'s time – silage having so largely replaced traditional meadow hay – we find there tractors, rather than riding horses, spanners rather than saddlery. By contrast, Corby is now a splendid mansion, which has not housed a Salkeld for 300 years. Why? – too many daughters!

After James's death at Pardshaw, his son Henry took over there; Henry in his will referred with affection to his uncle Richard (IV) and his uncle John the Younger, and understandably does not mention his father James, by now dead. To follow Henry's fortunes, we must take the same roads and tracks from Rosgill as would James have done to go home to Pardshaw, over the hills in a westerly direction.

ADDINGHAM AND KIRKOSWALD RECORDS

Preceding chapters have shown that many of the earliest Salkelds lived and worked in a strip of villages about two by six miles long, running north from Langwathby up the east bank of the River Eden, to Kirkoswald, and that they were familiar figures within that strip, long before King Edward III presented Sir Richard (I) with Corby Castle, some twenty miles to the north.

We can pick up the story of Salkeld activities in the same strip, *some two hundred and fifty years later*, by using the several wills and inventories which have survived in Carlisle, starting with the oldest dated May 1574; and adding to them the entries, such as they are, in the registers of baptisms, marriages and burials for the parishes of Kirkoswald and Addingham.

Sadly, the information on the wills and inventories rarely overlaps that in the church registers; this is because the will had often been written before the registers had started – or at least, before the registers were being properly kept; and also because many of the Salkelds in the registers did not make wills, or if they did, later lost them. Nevertheless, information on the Salkelds in this far-off period is so hard to obtain that it seemed well worth recording what there was, and so the inventories have been given in full wherever their interest seemed to warrant it.

The Little Salkeld will which now follows with inventory, throws a good light on living conditions in the Kirkoswald/Addingham area. It was transcribed for me by Mr. Pickavance.

[Will
Lancellot Salkeld
of Little Salkeld 3 May 1574] (son of John, son of Richard III)

Item in primis I make and [ ] my executores Isabell salkeld my spous & my chyldren lawfully begottin of hir body of all my goods moveable & vnmoveable all legacyes & dettis Discharged Item first I geve & bequyeth to my bastard sone Antony one quoye stirke quhyte higgyt & one yowe & a Lamb to go for vand to his vse And I gewe to my brother mychaell salkeld one pair of new bootes, And I geve all the leses & lands that I have ryght of or orght to have ryght of to my sone hendry and yf the said hendre Do chance to die that then the saide Lands & Leses to come to my sycund sone thomas and yf the said thomas die that then the said Landes & lesies to come to my thrid sone Williame, And yf it chance that my eldest sone hendry do die without yshev of aires male and his two youngest brotheren to die without yshev of aires male sycklik them I geve all my goodes wall of my Landes & Leseis to my brother Jhon and his aires male, And yf it pleis god that my brother John Die without yschew of aires male that then all the saidis Landis & leseis to come to my brother mychaell & his aires male lawhfully gottin And yf fortune that all my said chyldren & bretheren to die without yshev of aires male lawhfully to be gottin of thare bodeis that the all the said Landes & leseis to come to me & my aires, And I will & [ ] my weilbelovit wyf Isobell Salkald to Delyver or carse to be deliverit all my leseis & wrytyngs that sche hath in Kepyng or knoveth of to my weilbelovit cosyng & assurit frend Rychart warvicke to be in his Kepyng & custody to the weill & proffett of my said chyldren & as my whole trust is that he will maynteyne thame in all there ryghtis, also I ordane that my wyf shall have the whole proffett & vse of my Landes and leseis Duryng hir wedorhead to the vpbryngyng of my chyldren wnto my sone come to full yeares & then my said wyf to have ryght according to the laves of thus realme, Item co[n]cernyng the mariages of my Daughters I ordayne that my vyf shall marye theme or any others that shall have my dawhteres In custody with my goods reservand my Landes & leaseis to my aires male [ ] where there is certane Landes in ower knyipe of the yearly rent of thretene shillyngs four pennes beand nov in travys betnix William salkeld & duellyng at hilltovn in vestmvyrland & as doeth appear by our obligation to be sene which both the parteis was bound to byid ord[e]r and as not yet performed Therefor I crave & desyre that my trusty & weilbelovit maister rechart Levder & m^r george salkeld that they vill be so good maisters & frendes wnto me as to make one end of same by the motione of maister rechart warvicke m^r lanselot salkeld of quhyte [white] hall & my breatheren. And also where as there is one Tenement in tytill salkeld not in the occupation of Lansellot hogivne of the yearlye rent of twelf shillyngs sax pens which I have by exchange for other Lands of my maister rechart salkeld as doth appear by my lese thereof for many years to ru[n] which tennement I will that lanselot hosune [?] shall take the same by lease for terme of xiiij yeares and yf the said Lansellot hoggin do refuse so to take it then I will desyre my trusty frendes m^r rechart warvicke m^r lansellot salkeld of whyte hall and my breatheren John & mychaell to maynteyne my vyf & chyldren that thare said ryght & all other ryght tveathyng my said wyf & children Also I desyre my good maister m^r rechart salkeld for the good trust I have in to him and maiser george salkeld his sone in law that they will suffer my said wyf & chyldren to inioye all suche Landes as I have by exchange of his vorschipe specially with his good will & favor which I harttely crave at your hands both co[n]cernyng Landes & Leaseis which I have frome my good maister by grant as doth appere, And also I do appoynt my super visers of thus my Last will & testament my maister m^r rechart salkeld m^r rechart warvycke & m^r lansellot salkeld of Whytehall & george hvdson trustyng that they will see it performed . . .

Some other Addingham-Kirkoswald Wills and Inventories – oldest first.

Thomas Salkeld of Lazonby; will dated 5 November 1575. Unmarried? Yeoman. Leaves only a small sum £3, all to a 'stranger', but interest is that his four 'appraisers' were Christopher, Henrye, Oswald, and Rowland Salkeld.

Christopher Salkeld of Kirkoswald; will 7 May 1576. Wife Eleanor, children Rowland, Thomas, Christopher, and four girls. Inventory team included Henri, Oswald, Rowland, and Robert Salkeld; and Henri, George and Anthony mentioned as debtors. Inventory given in full.

Rowlande Salkeld of Harskeugh, Kirkoswald. Will 8 June 1577. Wife Elsabethe, child Margaret. Mentions John, Matthew, Oswald, Henry and Roger, all Salkelds.

There is then a gap of 16 years, when the next will is that of young Anthony – not really a will, an inventory 'By me, Jane' dated 21 December 1593 – see Summary to this book for details.

Roger Salkeld of Kirkoswald – short inventory, probate on 27 February 1596; and in register.

Oswald Salkeld of Overhaskeye, Kirkoswald. Inventory dated 15 December 1614. Probate suggests wife's name Elizabeth. The second of these wills to correspond to the parish register – buried six days before date of Inventory. Mentions John Salkeld's wife.

Even with others added, I cannot account for more than half the Salkeld entries in this period, entirely for lack of detailed information. The same problem arises when attempting to interpret the entries in the registers of other parishes, and so it will be appreciated that the charts of Salkeld pedigrees, though checked and cross-checked, can only represent some fraction of all the Salkelds whose names would, in a perfect world, be on it. This does not mean that these charts are wrong; it means that they are incomplete.

A particularly interesting feature of the above records is the frequency with which a 'team' of Salkelds seems to have been assembled to act as appraisers and/or witnesses of wills of other Salkelds. Notably for instance we find the names of Henry, Oswald and Rowland Salkeld recurring in these roles, as might be expected perhaps in a closely-knit family. One can at least deduce that they trusted and respected each other, more often than not!

As the years go by, the Kirkoswald registers become rather more informative, by including against an entry some hint of the individual's occupation. The first entry records the burial of the Vicar on 10 May 1577, and between then and 1760 some sixty entries are so qualified. An analysis of these reveals that the most frequent occupation *recorded* is, perhaps understandably, that of clerk or cleric (18 entries), then miller (10), Excise Officer (six), fuller or surveyor (four each), mercer (three) and then in ones or twos we find militia, brewer, carpenter, dyer, smith, mason, shoemaker, tailor, farmer, baker, sweeper, cowper, parish apprentice, and maid-servant. It is not obvious why there should be so many 'surveyors' – nor indeed exactly what they did – and the incidence of so many Excise Officers – the first being recorded in the year 1715 – calls

[Inventory
Lancelott Salkeld of lytle Salkeld
21 May 1574]

In primis ij kyen & ij calfes pr[i]ce		xl^s
It[e]m	a qwye pr[i]ce	xiij^s iiij^d
It[e]m	iiij ews iiij lambs, iij sheap shepe	xx^s
It[e]m	xij bushels of byg pr[i]ce	xlviij^s
It[e]m	viijth bushels of Rye pr[i]ce	xxxij^s
It[e]m	han[e]r sawn by estimac[i]on	xij^s
It[e]m	iij con[e]rletes pr[i]ce	viij^s
It[e]m	x pare of sheates pr[i]ce	viij^s
It[e]m	iij pare of blanketes pr[i]ce	viij^s
It[e]m	ij old bed con[e]rynges pr[i]ce	vj^s viij^d
It[e]m	a Fether bed pr[i]ce	vj^s viij^d
It[e]m	ij blewcottes ij dubletes ij) pare of hose, ij lyn shertes a) hatt, and a pare of buttes)	xvj^s
It[e]m	Fyare vessell as potes & pans	xiij^s iiij^d
It[e]m	in pud[e]r vessell pr[i]ce	iij^s iij ^{d}
It[e]m	plow geare, Cart geare) and Conp[er] geare pr[i]ce)	vj^s
It[e]m	a Crossbowe of sceale pr[i]ce	v^s
It[e]m	one old Cupburde & a chist	ij^s
It[e]m	one Iron Cruke pr[i]ce	vj^d
It[e]m	m^r John Thryrlkeld of) melm^{r}bie ys awynge me) for a crosbowe)	xiiij^s
It[e]m	will[ia]m Rige ys awynge) for a hand goone)	v^s

S[um]m[a]   xv^h xj^s x^d

The debitary of the said Lancelott Salkeld att the day of his deathe

Fyrst I awe vnto nycoles newton of borowed money		xxxvj^s viij^d
It[e]m	to John hodgeson of [?P] onsonbie for) suche lyke)	xiiij^s viij^d
It[e]m	to the house of Karliell for Rent	xvj^s iij^d
It[e]m	to Ric[hard] Sowrebie of Langwathebie	iiij^s
It[e]m	to Sr John Anston	ij^s vj^d
It[e]m	to Thom[a]s Warwicke	xij^d
It[e]m	to hew Lambert for) the drawght of one ox)	iij^s iiij^d
It[e]m	to John gowling for his waige	xvj^s
It[e]m	ought to Thom[a]s loweraine of) stassil ij b[ushel]s of hau[e]r or)	iiij^s
It[e]m	ought to Ric[hard] lowerlaine for a bute) hyad pr[i]ce)	ij^s vj^d
It[e]m	ought to John hodges of) vnsonby of lent money)	iij^s
It[e]m	ought to John nycolson	iij^s

S[um]m[a]   v^h vj^s xj^d

11. Kirkoswald church and tower.

for some explanation. No doubt they changed posts frequently, and probably there was only one Excise Officer using Kirkoswald church for the baptism of his children, at any one time. The only Salkeld entry to have with it a record of occupation is that on 7 October 1701, when William Salkeld, 'a miller', has a son baptised.

There are other sources than wills and church records from which one can catch a glimpse of these Salkelds of Addingham and Kirkoswald. For example, Bain in his two-volume book on the *Calendar of the Border Papers*[47] 1560-1594, p. 49 says that in 1581 Robert Salkeld was a bowman for Kirkoswald and that at a muster (with Robert) Matthew, Henry and Oswald Salkeld were present, 'without furniture' – meaning of course, unarmed. Others in the 'Strip' were John Salkeld of Little Salkeld – a bowman – and Richard but 'unfurnished'. At nearby Renwick, George mustered without 'furniture' but John Salkeld of Renwick failed to appear and was marked 'absent'. Bain gives details of other Salkelds who mustered elsewhere, some with 'nagges' and some with 'bowes'. And we remember that poor Anthony who died at Kirkoswald in 1593 was, according to 'Me Jane Salkeld' the possessor of 'An Arrobage with xviij shaftes' slung over his 'sele cape with foure silver buttons'.

[WILL OF RICHARD IV SALKELD OF ROSEGILL, WESTMORLAND, ESQUIRE]
[dated 30th January 1574/75]
[to be buried in the parish church of Shapp]

An important link between Corby and Rosgill.

> Also I ‹g›ive and bequyethe to Thomas (V) Salkeld, sonne and heyre apparent of George Salkeld and barbareye my daughter, one standing c[up] w[i]th a cover double gylt, one goblet w[i]th a cover double gylt, one cuppe of silver w[i]th a cou‹er› all my silver sponnes, and all my beddstockes, cubbertes, tables, bourdes, stoylles & counbers, & the sayme to remayne at my houses of Rosegill & Corkbie as heyrelumes to the sayme houses. And also I geve and bequyethe to my godsonne Rycherd Salkeld brother to the said Thomas one horse called graye thomson. It[e]m I geve and bequyethe to my thre brethere‹s› James, Jhone & Jhone, everye one of theime vj^li xiij^s iiij^d to be payed at suche reasonable‹e› dayes as my executors & they can agre vpon. It[e]m I geve and bequyethe to Madlayne Salkeld and Fraunces hir sister, Daughters to my doughters Barbarye eyther of theyme one hundrethe markes towards theire pr[e]ferment of mariedge. It[e]m I geve and bequiethe to Thomas myres, Thomas Salkeld & Leonard Salkeld my servantes everye one of thei‹m› twentye shillinges by yeare duringe theyre lifes ou[e]r and besydes theyre payes vpon condition that they shalbe towardes & serve my heires at my houses of Rosegill & Cor‹kbie› and other whare convenientlye It[e]m I geve and bequythe vnto Anthony Cragell my servant xxvj^s viij^d by yeare during his life and he to be banckman for the sayme and further to have wages for his other service as my heyres and he can agre. The residew of all goodes and cattelles not legasyd my debtes payed and funeral expenses discharged I do geve to Elezabethe Salkeld my wyfe, George Salkeld my sonne in Law and Barbareye his wyfe being my Daugher w[hi]ch thre I do mayke my executores of this my last wyll and testament

[witnesses: John Crakinthropp, John Rigg, John Salkeld the Younger (see Henry's Pardshaw Hall will), Thomas Myres, John Lambert, Anthony Crayel, & others]

> N.B. 'James John and John' were *alive* when this will was written in January 1574/75.

Enough of wills! What of the buildings which housed their owners?

The following extract from William Camden's *Britannia*, published in London in 1789, is taken from vol. 3, p. 174.[61]

[Inventory of Richard Salkeld's goods at Rosegill and Corkbie]
[dated 6th February 1574/75]

Rosegill
    In the halle

First j table, j counter of Joynyd)		
worke w[i]th buffettes, chares;)	xl^s	0-40- 0
and fourmes & a payre of playnge tables)		
In the kytchinge		
It[em] a greyte cawdran, iij brase pottes w[i]th)		
other brase and Iron vessels & other gere)	iiij^{li} iiij^s viij^d	4- 4- 8
perteynynge thereunto)		
It[em] w[i]thin the said Kytchinge xlj peace)		
of puder vessell, ij aulmeries & a barrell)	xliiij^s	0-44- 0
In the Larder		
It[em] in woode vessell	xviij^s	0-18- 0
In the brewe house		
It[em] A massefatt & other wood vessell	xij^s	0-12- 0
In the butterye		
It[em] iij saltes of pnder ij basonnes & [ ])		
w[i]th candlestickes Trenchers drinking)	xlvj^s	0-46- 0
glasses &c hobbes & barrelles)		
It[em] in napperye w[i]thin the sayme	xl^s	0-50- 0
In playte		
It[em] a silver salte w[i]th a cover gylt weyinge)		
xij ou[n]ces It[em] a standinge cupp gylt)		
w[i]th a cover weyinge xlij ou[n]ces It[em])		
a goblet gylt w[i]th a cover weinge 30 ou[n]ces)	xxv^{li} ij^s viij^d	25- 2- 8
It[em] a silver cupp w[i]th a cover weing viij)		
ounces It[em] xx silver sponnes weing xxiij)		
ounces)		
In the grete chamber		
It[em] A longe table A cupberte A sware table)		
A standing bedd A truckle bedd A chayre viij)	iiij^{li} xiij^s iiij^d	4-13- 4
buffet stoylles & A clothe of arras for the table)		
In the hie lofte		
It[em] ij counters Fes a cupbord ij buffettes)		
A chare A standinge bedd w[i]th taisters &)	iij^{li} iij^s iij^d	3- 3- 4
curtins A truckle bedd)		
All the beddinge belonginge to the chambers)		
before naimde & to all other about the house)	xxiij^{li} v^s iiij^d	23- 5- 4
w[i]th furniture for the syme dothe amounte)		
to the sume of)		

In Corne at Rosegill & Slegill

Bothe in the garner, barnes & sowne vpon the)		
ground priced to ye valew)	xxj^{li} iij^s iiij^d	21- 3- 4
It[e]m in Haye there	iij^{li}	3- 0- 0
It[em] husbayne gere	xxx^s	0-30- 0
All the quicke goodes at Rosegill as horse, noyte,		
shepe & swyne		
It[e]m iiij horse for the saddle & saddles	xx^{li}	20- 0- 0
It[em] iiij worke nagges	iiij^{li}	4- 0- 0
It[em] the number of shepe is iiij^c)	xx v^{li}	
xlij shepe priced to the valew of)	iij	x

It[em] viij oxen priced at 33ˢ iiijᵈ a peace xiijˡⁱ vjˢ viijᵈ 13- 6- 8
It[em] xviij kyee & a bull pr[iced] xxvˡⁱ xiijˢ iiijᵈ 25-13- 4
It[em] ix younge noyte called twynters pr[iced] iiijˡⁱ xˢ 4-10- 0
It[em] xiiij calves pr[i]ced iijˡⁱ xˢ 3-10- 0
It[em] iiij swynes xvjˢ 0-16- 0
It[e]m in apperrel to the valewe of xˡⁱ 10- 0- 0
                                                            ——————
                                                            107- 9- 8 + x

S[um]ma totalis at Rosegill is ijᶜ xlijˡⁱ xviijˢ vijᵈ 242-18- 7?

Corkbie
Priced there the xᵒ daye of februarye aᵒ 1574[/5] by these foure men, viz Simon Skelton, Rolland Salkeld, Robert Shaparowe & Wyll[ia]m Halle, sworne before Jhone Welthe Jurat of Wetherall
    In the Halle
First ij flanders counters one cupbord ij fourmes)
  a close priss   ) xlˢ 0-40- 0
        In the Kytching and brew house
It[e]m all the vessell & other gere belonging iijˡⁱ 11- 0- 0
All the quycke goodes there
It[e]m iiij oxen priced at vjˡⁱ xiijˢ iiijᵈ 6-13- 4
It[em] ij kine priced at xlˢ 0-40- 0
It[em] viij quies pr[i]ced at vˡⁱ vjˢ viijᵈ 5- 6- 8
It[em] vj young stottes pr[i]ced at iiijˡⁱ 4- 0- 0
It[em] ij worke nagges priced at xxˢ 0-20- 0
It[em] husbond gere xxˢ 0-20- 0
                                                            ——————
                                                            26- 0- 0

The whole sume at Corkbie xljˡⁱ vjˢ viijᵈ £41- 6- 8
It[e]m more for chattell realles viz. leases
  for yeares
It[e]m his p[ar]t of wetherall baye xxˡⁱ 20- 0- 0
It[em] the tythe corne of Corkbie)
It[em] the tythe corne of Slegill) xˡⁱ 10- 0- 0
Su[m]ma totalis iijᶜ xxxiiijˡⁱ vˢ iiijᵈ 334- 5- 4
    In the Kytching and brewhouse
It[e]m all the vessell & othe gere belonging)
  to the sayme houses is pr[i]ced at   ) iiijˡⁱ xxᵈ 4- 0-20
    In the butterye
It[e]m A silver peace xxvjˢ viijᵈ 0-26- 8
It[em] iiij bourdclothes & iiij napkinnes w[i]th)
  two towelles & a cupbordclothe   ) vjˢ viijᵈ 0- 6- 8
It[em] ij latten candlestyckes ij puder saltes)
  A bason of puder iij standes A masfat &   ) viijˢ viijᵈ 0- 8- 8
  A gilefatt   )
    In the chambers
It[e]m iiij standbeddes xiijˢ iiijᵈ 0-13- 4
It[e]m viij bedestockes & two whelebeddes viijˢ 0- 8- 0
It[e]m iij fedder beddes & iij matresses w[i]th)
  bolsters & pillobres & all other furniture for) viijˡⁱ viijᵈ 8- 0- 8
  the sayme   )
Corne in the garners & barnes and sowne vpon ye ground
It[em] all the corne priced at xxijˡⁱ xijᵈ 22- 0-12
It[em] haye in the barne xlˢ 0-40- 0
                                                            ——————
                                                            39- 5- 0

The Eden runs by Kirkoswald ... formely the property of Hugh Morvill ... thence by Armathwayte, a castle of the Skeltons; Corby, a casle of the Noble and antient family of the Salkelds which received great addition of wealth by marriage with the heiress of Rosgill ... thence by Warwick ...

The Virosidium where the 6th cohort of the Nervi was formely stationed on the wall against the Picts and the Scots, and in the last age a strong stone bridge was built at the expence of the Salkelds and Richmonds.

[p. 190] Kirkoswald castle SSE 12 miles from Carlisle and four from Naworth, stands almost on Eden. It was much improved by Sir Hugh Morvell who got the town a market (time of King John) and finished and moated by Thomas Dacre who married the heiress of Greystock but is now ruined ...

Northward from Ousby on the River Eden stands the capital grand castle of Kirkoswald and a very fine church there and quondam college now the noble mansion house of the late Sir Timothy Fetherstonehaugh colonel of the King's side taken at Wigan [Nicholas Fetherstonehagh married Maud, daughter and co-heiress of Sir Richard Salkeld, in 1461], ... and executed by beheading at Chester by the command of the unworthy Col. Mitton after the said knight had quarter given him. This great castle of Kirkoswald was once 'the fairest fabrick that ever eyes looked upon. The hall I have seen 100 yards long' and the great portraiture of King Brutus lying in the end of the roof of this hall and of all his succeeding successors Kings of England portraid to the waist, their visage, hats, feathers, garbs and habits in the roof of this hall now translated to Naworth castle ...

[p. 191] The church of Kirkoswald was turned into a college of 12 secular priests 1523 ... the choir is so apportioned to the body that Bishop Nicolson supposed it was rebuilt by some of the lords of Dacre when the church was made collegiate, as their arms and those of the Cliffords are painted in most of the windows.

The belfry is placed without the church on the top of the hill to the east ...

THE PARISHES AROUND ROSGILL, 1500-1650

The Salkelds held Rosgill from its coming into their hands by the marriage of Christiana daughter of Sir John Rossegyll in 1352 or 1362 to Hugh Salkeld of Corby; they lived in it until 1631 when the death of her Salkeld brother with no male heir put it into the hands of Dorothy who had married William Warmsley – some two hundred and seventy years in all. Rosgill has no parish church of its own, but there are several nearby churches which could have been used by the Salkelds and it is therefore desirable to study the registers of *all* those still in possession up to say 1650. This leaves six churches near to Rosgill and between them their registers contain some two hundred and fifty Salkeld entries, up to 1650.

Bampton (p. 61), one of the very nearest churches to Rosgill, has no Salkeld entries within the period 1500 to 1650. (It has about twelve in the next 100 years.) Furthermore, the round journey by horseback to the most popular of the churches – Morland – from Rosgill Hall would, by the tracks available in those times, be little short of twenty miles (or perhaps three hours' ride) there and back. But went they did, especially for baptisms, marriages, and burials; we will now examine their records, starting with the most populated, to see what more we can learn of the Rosgill Salkelds.

Morland

The Morland registers prove to be goldmines, especially if read alongside the few wills which have survived. They show that at least four different groups of Salkelds were using Morland church in the 150-year period, often indeed at the same times; they are the 'Rosgill group', the 'Morland group', the 'Thrimby-in-Morland' group which

Church	Distance from Rosgill Hall 'by crowfly'	Church Register starts	Number of Salkeld entries (b., m. and bur.)			Total
			Pre-1550	1550 – 1600	1600 – 50	
Shap	2½ miles	1559	0	22	3	25
Bampton	2¾ miles	1638 or? 1652	0	0	0	0
Askham	6 miles	1566	0	12	23	35
Lowther	6½ miles	1540	18	12	1	31
Morland including Thrimby	7+ miles	1538	20	70	30	120
Crosby Ravensworth	7 miles	1568	0	13	22	35
Cliburn	8 miles	1565	0	0	5	5
Totals			38	129	84	251

sprang from it, and a small group headed by a William. Of the first three groups, none contains our direct ancestors though the first gets very close. It has the will and inventory of the John (d. 1563) who headed the 'Thrimby-in-Morland' group but who must not (despite the fact that his address included the word 'Thrimby') – be confused with the Salkelds of Thrimby Grange. This John, I believe, may have lived in Thrimby *Hall* – only a mile away by road from Thrimby *Grange*.

Askham with Lowther

The next most important parish church was Askham with Lowther. I have joined these two registers together because it is obvious that Lowther fades out over the years as Askham increases its importance as a Salkeld shrine; indeed one entry (the marriage of Henry in 1661) occurs in both registers, for good measure! But the 35 Askham entries are composed almost entirely of members of four Salkeld groups – led by William (buried 1602) leaving seven children, then Thomas and Christopher both from nearby Helton, and their children, and finally Henry (d. 1660) with four children. The 31 Lowther entries are mostly of the family of Henry (who d. 1567) and his wife Grace Brougham who between 1541 and 1604 had 10 children (eight boys and two girls) of whom no less than five of the first six died within the first two years. Of the remainder, I cannot account on any of my charts for Richard buried April 1555, Henry buried 1567, or another Henry buried 1615. But none of these, I am confident, affected our own ancestral lines.

Crosby Ravenscroft

With very few exceptions the entire Salkeld entries are of the family of James of Maulds Meaburn and his wife Marion Winter (married 1579) and these cover the longer period 1575 to 1709, with many 'James' in the pedigree (an unusual Christian name for a Salkeld in this period). Many were long lived, and there is every sign that the isolation of these small farming communities led to their having their own compact and complete pedigree tree. One James married Grace from the nearby Dryevers, and I have copies of three Dryever wills which help to support these conclusions. But these Crosby Ravenscroft Salkelds do not contribute to our knowledge of our own Salkeld ancestors. Three entries which I cannot fit into the charts are Thomas (son of John) buried February 1570; Barbary (daughter of Richard) baptised 16 July 1571, and Edward marrying an Elizabeth Willan on 9 July 1573.

Bampton

Some of the entries quoted, when read alongside copies of Salkeld wills – in this case from the Record Office at Carlisle – enable a small pedigree chart of 'Bampton Salkelds' to be constructed:

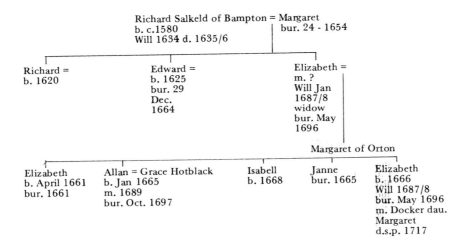

This small and secluded branch of the Cumbrian Salkelds was probably an off-shoot from the Rosgill Salkelds – geographically so near, and with the key Christian name 'Richard' – but branching before perhaps 1550 and therefore some one hundred years before the Bampton register starts. Moreover it will be noticed that nearly all the register entries are burials (all that is save two baptisms), there being no weddings of Salkelds recorded until 1768. The sad conclusion is that Bampton Salkelds used their local church for disposal of their dead – transport of bodies being a real problem – and perhaps for jolly events like weddings were prepared to ride over to Morland or Shap or Askham or Lowther where they would meet their Rosgill and their Thrimby namesakes.

That this branch died out soon after 1700 may have been due to the plague which raged hereabouts in 1696-7, and also to a quite common Salkeld trait, of producing many more female than male children.

Shap

The Parish *Church* [for a detailed description of the history and architecture of the *Abbey*, see *CWAA* Old Series, vol. X, pp. 286-314].

As would be expected from its proximity to Rosgill, there are numerous Rosgill entries in the Shap register but, as this only starts in 1559, the bulk of the 25 Shap entries about Salkelds occur in the 50 years from 1550 to 1600. The largest single set of entries contains the names of the children of 'Mr. George of Rosgill and Thrimby, namely Allan (baptised Shap, June 1566), who was buried at Morland in 1568; Dorothy (January 1571), Jane (March 1577) whose marriage at Shap in 1590 is also recorded (suggesting some delay between birth and baptism); Mary (October 1579) whose marriage 20 years later to Mr. Henry Dacre is important and was at Shap church; Frances (buried February 1582 at Shap) and Thomas (baptised April 1590). 'Mr. George's' step-daughter Madelon is also recorded as marrying 'Mr. Robert' of Thrymby on 3 February 1579 and so is her burial at Shap only five years later (13 April 1584).

Other interesting entries include that of the burial of Richard of Rosgill on 3 February 1574-5 and of his wife Elizabeth (née Duckett) on 11 March 1586. A Rowland Salkeld of Rosgill – whom I cannot with certainty place on the chart, for lack of detail – is recorded as being buried on 1 February 1573, and his wife Agnes on 11 May 1588.

The daughter of John of Rosgill was baptised Tomazin on 22 February 1590. The two sons, Richard and George, of 'Mr. Thomas', were baptised on 17 January 1593 and 15 September 1594, and George the son of 'Mr. Hugh', on 26 July 1600. And we end with repeating the entry of the marriage of 'Mistress Mary' on 7 November 1599, to Mr. Henry Dacre of Lanercost, an event recorded also in Nicholson and Burn's *History*.

Did 'Mr. George' marry again? His wife (and cousin) Barbara Salkeld had, by my charts, her last child (this Mary) in October 1579, but 10 years later the Shap register shows that a George Salkeld married an Elizabeth Short of Rosgill (on 12 May 1589) and that they had a son Thomas in April 1590. 'Mr. George', we know, died in the plague year 1597-8, but I can find no record of the burial of his wife Barbara, which could of course have occurred any time after Mary's birth in 1579. That this George and Elizabeth should have christened their only son Thomas in 1590 – when a Thomas by Mr. George's first wife Barbara was still very much alive – rather steers me into thinking that this second marriage was to some other George Salkeld, and I have not shown it on my charts.

It must be emphasised that these pages are dealing only with those Salkelds who used – for baptisms, marriages or burials – the named churches near to Rosgill. There are other large groups of Salkelds – for example in and around Penrith, Brough, Warcop, or around Whitehall near Cockermouth – who used their own local churches and whose names would not therefore be expected to appear in the above.

Chapter Six

Pardshaw and Winster

The Pardshaw Salkelds

Pardshaw (sometimes spelt Pardsay or Perdyshowe) is a hamlet in the parish of Dean some four miles south-south-west of Cockermouth in Cumbria. A Pardshaw Hall today stands some half a mile from the hamlet (Ordnance Survey Sheet 89, 1025) to the east of Dean and to the west of Mosser but this hall, though some hundreds of years old, is not the original hall in which we are interested. This is some hundred yards away, and has been largely rebuilt as a dwelling house but on the upstairs floor is still visible a fine mullioned window in what the present owners call 'Old Pardshaw Hall'. Inside are the remains of a stone staircase to the first floor, but little else to bear testimony of past glories.

Going back to 21 February 1321 there is a record[62] that Thomas de Pardshaw witnessed a bond on that date, and his widow Joan (Eglesfield) on 24 February 1349 rented out 12 bovates of land and six homesteads for the rest of her life for 20 marks plus 10d. and some bushels of oatmeal a year; earlier John de Pardshaw witnessed various charters in 1320 and became a proctor in 1332; a later John gave evidence in Carlisle in 1397 on the value of some property[59]. But of much more interest to us is the comment by the eminent antiquarian F. W. Ragg that one Amice de Salkeld, who looks like the daughter of Hugh (II) Salkeld, married John de Pardshaw on 14 September 1411. Hugh and other tenants received from Robert the Abbot of Shap a grant to pasture 200 sheep in the open fields of Rosgill. Not though for long, for on 7 July 1416 Amice 'lately wife of John de Pardshaw gent' grants to Hugh (II) 'all my estate which I have (or had) in the manor of Pardshaw with its belongings (a hamlet in the township of Dene)' and continues:

> Also other lands rents and services etc. within the township of Dene aforesaid, to be held by the aforesaid Hugh (II) and his assigns etc. of the chief lords of the fee by the service thence owed etc. by giving to me the aforesaid Amice yearly and to my last assigns while my life lasts at two terms of the year namely St Martinmass and Easter by even portion 10 marks of lawful money of England etc. And if it so happen that the aforesaid rent of 10 marks should be in arrears in whole or in part for a whole quarter of a year then it shall be lawful for the said Amice to distrain and this document is dated at Pardshaw on Wednesday the feast of the Translation of St Thomas the Martyr 1416.

In short, on becoming a widow, Amice was pleased to pass her late husband's lands to her father Hugh (II), having none to work them for her. Thereafter these Pardshaw lands remained in Salkeld tenure and we find several references to them in later years. For example, in 1544 they, with 1,000 acres in the adjoining hamlet of Mosser, were held by Thomas Salkeld of Corby[63] 'of the King as of his manor of Dean' by the service of 'the moiety of one knight's fee, 2s. 8d. cornage, the puture of the sergeants, 8d. free rent, homage and fealty' (Whellan[13] p. 354). And in 1578 George Salkeld in the right of his wife Barbara (born Salkeld) held lands at Pardshaw under practically the same terms except that the free rent had risen to 10s. 8d. a year.

12. Old Pardshaw Hall.

It is against this background that must be read one of the important documents of our study – the will of Henry Salkeld of Pardshaw, dated at the Hall on 28 November 1584 – of which a copy follows. In this will Henry leaves everything to his wife Elizabeth and to his children Richard (VI), Thomas and Mary, with the proviso that his wife is to continue to live at the Hall until his eldest son John reaches the age of 21, 'for the upbringing of my poor children' according to the lease and Interest heretofore granted 'by my dear Uncle Richard Salkeld as it doth appear by the said lease . . . I make surprised of this my present will and testament to the Right Worshipful Sir Henry Curwen of Workington, Knight, Mr. Edward Haylenbie of Carlisle, Esquire, Thomas Layther clerk and parson of Dean and my Uncle John Salkeld younger of the lowe Ryddings . . .'.

Rarely indeed is a will so helpful as to identify not only wife and children but the identity of two uncles, and other eminent figures. These two uncles were Richard (IV) who married Elizabeth Duckett and who had died 10 years earlier (in 1574) leaving a will nominating his sole child Barbara as heiress; and John the Younger, his brother, a witness to that will, whose other brothers were another John, and James, all named in Richard's will and all therefore alive in 1575. It follows that the father of Henry Salkeld of Pardshaw Hall was either this (elder) John, or James, and in either case that Henry's grandfather must have been Thomas (IV) the Younger who married Margaret Curwen and died in 1573. Although the will of this James is catalogued in the archives at Carlisle, it cannot now be found – it was dated 1565 though James lived on to at least 1575. However, I have little doubt that Henry's father was James rather than John, for James lived at Pardshaw and was buried at Dean, as was Henry. James was buried on 29 December 1582, and registered as 'Gent'. We also notice the reference to the Curwen family in Henry's will, for of course Margaret Curwen was his grandmother. As to the reference to John the Younger, this is also how this John is described when witnessing his own brother's will. Moreover, Henry's will describes John as to the 'lowe Ryddings', and T. H. B. Graham[64] records that in 1450 – some one hundred and thirty-four years previously – an inquiry into Thomas Salkeld's lands at Corby listed 'three messuages called Riddings' which formed no less than a tenth part of the Corby Manor.

Will of Henry Salkeld of Pardshaw Hall in the Parish of Dean
1584 – 28 November

I Henry Salkeld of Pardshaw Hall within the parish of Dean Sick in body but in good and perfect Remembrance praised be God do make this my present Testament containing herein my last Will in manner and form following. First I give my soule to Almighty God my maker and Redeemer, and my body to be buried in my parish Church or quier of Deane aforesaid, my duties and mortuaries thereto belonging due and accustomed paid and discharged according to the Laws of this Realm. Item I constitute ordain and make my wife Elizabeth Salkeld and my three children that is to say Richard Salkeld, Thomas Salkeld and Mary Salkeld my true and lawful executors of all my goods moveable and immoveable after my debts be paid, and my funeral expenses discharged. Also I will that my wife shall have the occupation of the Demesne or Tenement of Pardshawe Hall unto such time as my son John come to the full years of one and twenty for the upbringing of my poor children according to the Lease and Interest heretofor granted by my dead Uncle Richard Salkeld as it doth appear by the said Lease. Item I give and bequeath unto my said wife Elizabeth Salkeld all my 'Eitreste' Title and Tenentright of one Close called Skinner Close in as ample and large manner as

I can by and with the licence of the Lord. Item I make suprised of this my present will and Testament the Right Worshipful sir Henry [?Curwen] of Workington, Knight, Mr. Edward Haylenbie of Carlisle Esquire, Thomas Layther clerk and pason of Dean and my uncle John Salkeld younger of the [?Lowe] Ryddinges Witnesses hereof James Skelton, Henry Porter, Oswald Weddall and Henry Atkinson with others

The only other mention of a John Salkeld of *Pardshaw* occurs in a list of 'all the gentlemen of Cumberland' in 1526[64] – this may be the John of Pardsay who married Jane Curwen in 1530.

And so, having established a direct descent from Thomas (IV) Salkeld the Younger, who married Margaret Curwen, to Henry Salkeld of Pardshaw Hall – and thus through to his children and grandchildren – in theory we have but to consult the parish register of Dean, their parish church, to establish the next two generations; only a few of them will directly concern our pedigree studies, the dates against each name being dates of baptism unless otherwise indicated. Henry is shown in the register as marrying Elizabeth in 1568, and as dying at Pardshaw and being buried at Dean on 28 November 1584, 'a yeoman'. Of course there may well be other Salkelds descended from him but not shown in the Dean register because their parents had meanwhile moved elsewhere; as we shall show later, this is true of Richard (VI), the third son of Henry.

Much criticism can be directed at the Dean registers which, though they started in 1542 (only shortly after registers had become a legal requirement), were I believe lost some time in the years 1629 to 1657; moreover, the year 1623 saw an abnormal number of burials at Dean – 53 between Easter 1623 and Easter 1624, compared with but four in 1618 and 11 in 1629 – but how far this was due to the plague and how far to starvation – or both – is debatable.[65,66] Certainly there were no Salkeld entries in the Dean register after April 1625, though the register continued in use for another four years before being lost. Nor, when it resumed in 1657, is there a single Salkeld entry for very many years thereafter although the records of other Pardshaw families continue, apparently normally – and some of whom, interestingly enough, are shown as now living in Pardshaw Hall – the Ulacks and the Hutchinsons for example. For some twenty members of a family to disappear so quickly and completely, calls for an explanation which I have so far failed to find. (Bouch would suggest it was plague.)[67]

As to details of Henry's family, his eldest son John was born at the Hall about 1570 and was not yet twenty-one when Henry made his will nominating John as his heir. John married but we do not know his wife's name; their first child was Richard, born *c.* 1607 but buried in May 1614. Next came Lawrence (September 1609), John (August 1611), Henry (August 1614), Christopher (December 1616), Katherine (1619), Dorothy (1621) and Elizabeth (April 1625); if there were any more they may have been born after the register was lost.

Henry's second son was Thomas 'of Pardsay', born at Pardshaw Hall about 1575, who married Mabel Tyson about 1606 and appears not to have lived at the Hall thereafter; their first child was Jane (December 1606), then James (December 1608), Edward (March 1612 but buried January 1623), then Agnes (September 1615), John (November 1618), Richard (April 1622 but buried May of that year) and Elizabeth (September 1624). It is this James whom we mention again shortly. In passing we may note that Henry's will was witnessed by Osward Weddall or Woodall, who later (June 1579) became the husband of Henry's only daughter Mary.

This leaves Henry's third son Richard (VI), baptised at Dean on 13 February 1578 and marked in the register as 'of Pardshaw'; but it tells us no more about him than that he has a daughter Clara, baptised at Dean 15 December 1608, and mentioned in Henry's will. My identification of this Richard (VI) of Pardsay, as being none other than the Richard Salkeld who later in our story appears at Winster and dies there in 1616, is without doubt the weakest link in pedigrees here presented, for there is only a one-page inventory – no will – for Richard (VI) of Winster, and no will nor inventory for Richard (VI) of Pardsay. Though both Richards (VI) are recorded – at Dean or at Windermere – as having children, their *marriage* dates are unknown, although the birth dates of the children fall into the pattern one would expect if they had had a common father: the likelihood of that happening if they had been the offspring of separate fathers is low.

In December 1978 I was searching through the records at Kendal for information on the 17th-century 'Salkeld Tenement' which had been located at Winster – as described later – when I came across deeds relating to the establishment at Bowness of the first school and a quitclaim witnessed by three well-known Winster locals – Robert Philipson, Miles Dixon and Myles Fisher, and lastly, by a 'James Salkelt': other related deeds had been witnessed by two equally well-known Winster men, the yeoman Edward Robinson and the shearman George Atkinson. Now James, though a common enough name today, had been but rarely used by the Salkelds of Cumbria – in my records only eight times in 150 years including the two already mentioned in this book. As to dates, if this James were the James who was a grandson of Henry of Pardshaw, from his date of birth at Pardshaw he would have been just $21\frac{1}{2}$ years old when the Bowness deed was signed – perhaps why he signed last; that he was in the area at all *could* be because his uncle Richard (VI) of Pardsay was living nearby at Winster – was in fact Richard (VI) of Winster! No proof of course, but just enough to make one wonder. Both were Salkelds.

Now why should young Richard (VI) of Pardsay leave for Winster – with his wife – more than a full day's journey on horseback? Perhaps because his two elder brothers and their families could just about eke a living there, but leaving no room for Richard and his growing family? That he leaves Pardsay – and incidentally the Dean register – is fact; and of all the other Richards of whom I have a record in this period, not one qualifies on age to be both the father of young Clara of Pardsay (b. 15 December 1608) and a resident of some other nearby Cumbria township – and Salkeld we must remember is not, even in Cumbria, a common surname. James Salkeld is a very rare one, and Richard Salkeld, of the right age, relatively so.

But this is not a matter only of parish entries, for Richard (VI) is mentioned in his father's will, and it is I think highly significant that, whereas Carlisle produced 112 wills for my study and Preston only 11, before 1700, all the Winster wills including that of Henry came from Preston, and none at all from Carlisle; in other words, the will which mentioned Richard (VI) of Pardsay came from the same 'stable' as the will which mentioned Richard (VI) of Winster; had a Carlisle will been found between that of Henry in 1584 and his immediate descendants down to Thomas the joiner of Dent in 1694, that find might well have been construed as evidence contrary to my belief that Richard of Pardsay and Richard of Winster were one and the same man – but none has been so found. We know that the Lancashire Record Office 'suffered considerable vicissitudes in the past, in which much was lost',[68] and perhaps if that had not been so, further Salkeld wills would have been forthcoming to prove or disprove my contention.

To summarise; all the facts known to me support my belief that the Richard (VI) Salkeld, who died intestate at Winster in 1616, could be the same Richard (VI) who was born at Pardshaw to Henry and Elizabeth Salkeld on 13 February 1578. Further studies may disprove this but until they do I shall use this as part of the pedigree of my mother Lilian Salkeld.

And so this Richard (VI) of Pardsay and Winster, born 13 February 1578 (Dean register and will of Henry), is credited with the following children:

> Agnes,   b. *c.* 1605 – Windermere register
> Clara   1608 – Dean register
> Thomas VI   1612 – Windermere register
> Francis I   1614 – Windermere register

but no more, because (Windermere register) Richard (VI) died in 1616, at the early age of thirty-eight.

Let us now look at this Richard (VI) from the Winster end, and follow his progress down the years.

Richard and Thomas at Winster

Winster is a scattered township, its centre being three miles south of Windermere town and a mile and a half east of the lakeside. On the one-inch map most of Winster lies in square 4193.

The main feature to interest us is the group of buildings called 'Salkeld Tenement', practically unaltered since the earliest map of 1898; the Tenement buildings have been modernised, in some cases out of all recognition, but their outline on the ground is substantially unaltered; the old and no doubt muddy farmyard is now a pleasant place of well-kept lawns with trim paths and a profusion of flowering shrubs. Richard (VI) Salkeld, who died here in July 1616, would certainly have recognised the foundations of the old farmhouse placed centrally and facing south, though in his time the house was probably thatched.

Across the front door today is a lintel stone with the words 'Salkeld Tenement' carved upon it. Opposite is the old Great Barn, now two residential flats, the lower of which has the words 'Salkeld Barn' over the entrance. This barn at one time, I am told, contained the dairy; beyond, the large field beside it is reputed to have been a tannery. Another large barn, to the east of the Salkeld Barn and now converted into another two large flats, reaches right up to the main road through the village; probably the main entrance to the farm was near this barn, although today it is a few hundred yards north. Just before the new drive reaches the farmhouse, there is a drive to the right which leads down to a mill house where once a waterwheel driven by the River Winster turned a sawmill, only dismantled a few years ago to make way for residential improvements.

To the west, the ground rises away from the river to a hillcrest just below which is the old packman's road. Further over the hill lies Windermere Lake. It is a peaceful spot, and my thanks are due to the late Mr. Cave Brown Cave for identifying this Tenement for me. Today's inhabitants include no Salkelds, but they proved as anxious to know who the Salkelds were, as I was to study their Tenement.

13.   The Old Farmhouse, Winster.

Richard (VI) Salkeld, who lived here, left no will, but the Lancashire Record Office was able to produce an Inventory of his goods and chattels, a copy of which is included together with a transcript. The inventory says it was made in July 1615, but as the Windermere parish register clearly shows that he was buried on 2 July 1616, and as the inventory would have been taken a few days after the burial, it would seem that the local appraisers may have forgotten that the year 1615 had ended the preceding March, as was then the custom.

Richard (VI) had sheep, a horse and the apparatus needed to manage them, and some very modest indoor furniture. He owed for some hay which he had not yet used, and was owed for a bushel of oats, and some cash loans he had made. The total of the inventory was nearly £22 after paying 10s. for funeral expenses – a modest and respectable total and he had two sons who would no doubt find a use for it. Included in this were his animals, which I estimate were one good riding horse, about three cows and perhaps eight sheep. In those days the sheep were small and their fleece would average only about two pounds in weight each, so that Richard (VI) would expect only to get about 4s. 9d. from James Strickland the local packman when he called to take the year's clip to the central wool warehouse – of which there were two within a few miles of the village.

Richard (VI) grew crops, particularly oats which he would need for his porridge and his oatcakes, and barley for brewing his ale; he had sold some of this (about twenty gallons or a bushel) on the understanding that he would get it back again before the winter. He also grew hemp and flax, from whence came his stock of linen and 'harden' (sacking). And he grew hay, but here he was a bit short and had to buy some for the winter.

Indoors, his life was pretty spartan. He appears to have had no bed of his own (these are usually included as 'bedstocks and bedding') though this may be because the family bed – like the family spinning wheel – was regarded as his wife's possession. He had an arke in which he could store his oatmeal, a chest for his things, and a chair to sit on, but no table. Cooking utensils, unless his wife had some, were scarce.

All this could add up to a mature and benevolent man, just pulling his weight but no longer striving.

Two years earlier he had had a son Francis (I), but there is no record, since this birth, of the mother's death; we can perhaps assume that Richard (VI)'s wife was still alive, busying herself with the dairy work from the cows, the spinning of the wool and of the flax and hemp. There would be hens to feed and eggs to collect, because although these are not shown in the inventory this is only because hens, valued only at a penny each, were often 'rolled-up' with the other bits and pieces in the totals.

Our last picture, perhaps, of Richard (VI) alive, is one of an outdoor man, riding his horse over the hills, lending a little money here and there to his friends, and leaving the 'inke horns' and the 'moustrapp' of the inventory, for his wife to use. But the burial ground at Winster was not to be consecrated until 1721[13] so Richard (VI)'s body had to be conveyed from the Tenement to Windermere church. As Thomas Machell, making practically the same journey 75 years later, pointed out in his diary

> Cartmell Fell . . . may more truly be called Cartless Fell, for there is not a cart used in this country,

nor, we can add, was there a cart in Richard (VI)'s inventory. Probably the body would be wrapped and fastened across the horse's back for the rough but not long journey. Behind would follow, on horse and on foot, his relatives and friends from the Tenement and the farmhouses around.

But not all his relatives, for some would be too young for the funeral procession. To us, the most important one left behind would be young Francis (I), whose almost unreadable baptismal entry in the first volume of the original Windermere register, on 11 November, shows Richard as the father. From the sequence of the sheets and the dates on the remainder, it is highly probable that this undated sheet precedes one clearly marked with the year 1615, and thus the year 1614 may reasonably be assumed as the year of Francis' birth and baptism. From this we can deduce that the body being carried over the hills to Windermere was that of a man under forty.

Amongst the followers, however, there might have been a young girl of 11 – his eldest daughter Agnes, who later was to marry Laurence Turner of Winster and Kendal. His daughter Clara would perhaps be judged too young to go. As the procession winds down the hill to the church, they all pass out of our sight; we put back our hats lifted in deference to the dead, and return to the Tenement. The year is 1616.

There we find Richard's eldest son Thomae (VI) playing with his baby brother Francis; baptised before the Windermere register has started – perhaps in 1612 – he was recorded, by those making the inventory of his own possessions, many years later, as Thomae not Thomas, and this 'nickname' Latin version will be retained for ease of identification.

Who, though, would run the Tenement for the fifteen or twenty years which must elapse between Richard's early death, and the attainment of manhood by Thomae? There were plenty of candidates, and had Richard left a will as well as this inventory – and this he may have done – the problem would be solved.

Those years pass, and we next find Thomae, in the Tenement still but at age 26, marrying Ann, perhaps of Winster, perhaps not. Their first child was baptised at Windermere on 29 April 1638. Later they had two more daughters, and at least two sons, all at the Tenement. From these records, one can trace how the population of Salkelds in the Tenement averaged about four in the years 1610 to 1620, rising to a peak of about ten in the years 1640 to 1655, falling again to about four in 1670 and possibly to none by 1680. No doubt non-Salkelds also lived and worked in the same Tenement, their daily round being much the same as had been that of the late Richard (VI), with his sheep and cows and crops and dairy work, and a trip on horseback to market as the highlight of the week.

Fortunately Thomae, unlike his father Richard, did leave a will; so did his wife Ann. Thomae's was dated 23 August 1667, and it, apart from when he is disposing of his innumerable 'breetches', is rather dull. It gives instruction to his eldest son Thomas on the need to pay various sums to the other children, and the fact that this will was apparently made some eight years before his actual death suggests to me that poor Thomae was far from well towards the end of his life; indeed he may have allowed his son Thomas to take some of the stock before his death in August 1675. But nevertheless, Thomae does not forget his friends – the gift of breeches to the two sons of his friend William Garnett – his shoe repairer, is described more fully later.

But he was not a literate man, as the large 'T' with which he signs his will testifies. Nor perhaps was he a very good manager. His inventory shows that when he died he had little more than half his father Richard's cash balance after all debts had been paid. But certainly old Thomae had two, or possibly three, good horses, and plenty of fodder for them. He had wool but no sheep – perhaps he had already bought his little stock of wool for his wife to spin and weave in the winter nights by their peat fire.

Indoors, he might have been a little less spartan than his father. That however he was not a Quaker is suggested by the money he owed to the church – or rather the 'Chappall of Winster'. The pattern of burial costs which probably applied is discussed later.

[Richard Salkeld
Inventory
4 July 1615]

The Inventorie of all the goods and Chattelles w[h]ich were Richard Salkeldes of Winster deceased: prised the iiij^th day of July 1615 by James dickson James Atkinson Edward Robinson and will[ia]m Garnett Jnr.

Inpr[imis]	his apparrell	xxj˙ viij^d
Ite[m]	in sadles and a sadle garth	v˙
Ite[m]	Cordes	iiij^d
Ite[m]	a bottle ap[ar] of sheares w[i]th inke hornes))	vj^d
Ite[m]	in linen and harden and thred	xlj˙
Ite[m]	anarke w[i]th other implem[en]tes	ij˙
Ite[m]	in yron geare	xvj^d
Ite[m]	a handle w[i]th some other smale geare	ij^d
Ite[m]	a womble a moustrapp and an old boale	x^d
Ite[m]	a Chare	iij^d
Ite[m]	a Chist	xvj^d
Ite[m]	a harrowe	vj^d
Ite[m]	a horse	iij^li vj˙ viij^d
Ite[m]	in sheepe	xxvj˙
Ite[m]	Kine	iij^li xiij˙ iiij^d
Ite[m]	in money	vj^li viij˙
Ite[m]	in hay grasse taken of Nicolas Robinson	v˙
Ite[m]	in woll w[hi]ch was Sould to James strickland	iiij˙ x^d
Ite[m]	in lent money to robert Harrison wife	xij^d
Ite[m]	in money w[hi]ch is owne by allexander Layton))	xxv˙
Ite[m]	more owne by the said Allexander a bushell of oates w[hi]ch must be payed at martinmas)))	
Ite[m]	in money w[hi]ch is owne by Edmund Sewart	xl˙

Suma   xxj^li xiiij˙ ix^d   after paying
funerall expencis x˙

And so the years pass, until on 23 August 1675 yet another funeral procession winds its way from the Tenement to the church at Windermere. For the first time for 60 years, there is no male Salkeld left to take over the Tenement's management. After the funeral, widow Ann decided to let her home there, to Alice Hickingson, and to live instead with her own widowed daughter Ann Harrison and her little grand-daughter, another Ann, up the hill to Gilhead in Cartmel. It is from Gilhead that widow Ann the granny makes her will – with its glimpses of kindliness and prejudice. Her son Thomas, now farming at Mislet, returns there after the funeral, and his younger brother Richard, who lives at Kendal, makes his way home – we shall however meet him again.

Estimated numbers of Salkelds at Winster in Salkeld Tenement

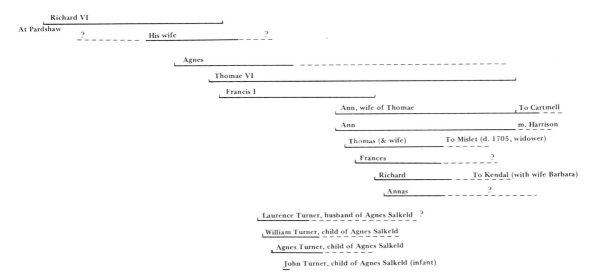

Numbers of Salkelds and their relatives in the Salkeld Tenement at Winster

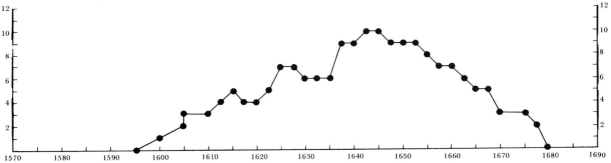

In an upstairs room at the Farmhouse in the Tenement, is a wooden cupboard with on it the letters RBM and the date 1689. There were both Braithwaites and Birkets living around, to account for the 'B'. *Our* task now is to leave the Tenement buildings to their new owners, whoever they may be, and to try to follow the fortunes of their late occupants the Salkelds, whose footsteps are no longer to be heard therein. They leave only their name behind.

But one of the principal characters, the widow Ann, is not far away – at Gilhead. Although she too was illiterate, her will shows her determination to have her modest possessions distributed to the best advantage. Thus the brass pot she had inherited from her husband Thomae was to go to her grandchild Ann, who would appreciate it most. This little Ann – now about six years old – was also to get her granny's best gown, her cloak, and her little red chest.

August 23 — Anno dom 1667

In the name of god Amen — I Thomas Salkeld
being Sick and weak in body yet perfect in mind and
memory praised be god for the same doe Ordaine &
make this my Last will & testament in manner & forme
following — ffirst I bequeath my Soule vnto the hands
of Almight god my maker and redeemer and my body
to be devoutly buried in windermer Church yard It
I giue vnto my Son Richard the first payment of
that Some of money wth my Sone Thomas is to pay
out of mine estate mentioned in a deed poole made
at the time of his Marriage It I giue the Second
payment of that deed poole vnto my Daughter Ann
Item it is my will that if either of them shall
Die the Surviver of them shall haue both payments
Item I giue the third and Last payment of that deed
vnto my three Children if they be all Liuing to be
Equally Deuided amongst them and if either Richard or
Ann die the Surviver shall haue foure pounds and my
Son Thomas fortie shillings Item I giue vnto my
Son Thomas fiue shillings for a Legacie to buy him
a girdle and brand Iron Item I giue him
Excepting a black coate and a pair of
black breeches wth I giue my son Richard if he be pleased
to wear them It I giue two pair of old breeches
vnto two sons of Will garnets Item I giue
vnto my son Richard and my Daughter Ann if they
be both Liuing either thirtie shillings to be paid
out of my goods after my debts be Discharged Item
I make my wife Ann my whole Exequtor Item I
Apointe Antony Garnett and Myles Brown to see y
this my will be performed and to either of them I giue
two shillings and sixpence and soe I rest desiring god
of his great merty to remitt my sins

Witnesses of this will
William Atkinson
William Tunnall
Anthony Rockliff

Thomas Salkeld T

6 Day of August 1675

A true and perfitte Inventory of all the goods Cattells
and Chattels depts Credits moveable and immoveable
with was thomas Fallows of winster in the parish
of Kendall lately deceassed Apprised the same
day by Anthony garnwett of linth John garnwell
of bartomelsell — James Jackson of bartome
lsell and James dicon of winster

	l	s	d
Imprimas his Apparrell	0	16	0
Item brass — powder	1	7	0
Item wood vessell	0	5	0
Item bedding	0	6	0
Item Iron gear	0	6	6
Item peate — sope	0	2	0
Item studles — Chaires	0	3	4
Item Chests Cuppord bed forkes tables	1	3	0
Item garner	0	6	8
Item wool	1	0	0
Item husbandry gear	0	14	0
Item in fuell	0	6	0
Item beas — horses	5	10	0
Item big oats — hay	5	10	0
Item manure — pooles	0	1	6
Suma bonar	17	17	0

Exhibet sub protestac

depts owen by the deceassed

	l	s	d
Imprimas to the Chappell of winster	3	4	8
Item to Robert tomson	0	5	0
Item to william Robinson	0	10	0
Item funerall expences	1	8	0
Item to James birkett	1	0	0
Suma depits	6	7	8
Suma dedlaryd	11	9	4

Inventory of Thomae, 1675.

April the 1st: 1683:

In the Name of God, Amen. I Ann Salket of Gill-head in Cartmelfell,
in the Countie of Lancashire, being in sound and perfect memorie, praise be
be God, doe make and ordain this my last Will and Testament in manner
and form following. First I committ my Soul into the hands of Almighty
God, trusting fully through the merits of Jesus Christ, to have my sins washed
out, and my Soul eternally saved; As for my body I committed to the ground
to be decently buried in the Church of Windermire. As for such temporal
goods as the Lord hath blessed me withal, I bequeath them in manner
and form following. Imprimis. I give to my Son Thomas Salket the A
Garner in the barn, and the bed in the Low Chamber in my house at
Winster; and with them two Shillings of mony. It I give my best hat and
a Red under=coat, which is my best Red Coat to my Grand=daughter Ann A
Salket the daughter of Thomas Salket. It I give to my grand=daughter Margaret
Salket the daughter of Thomas Salket my best Napkin and a Pinner. It I
leave foure Shillings to be equally distributed among the three children
of my Son Thomas Salket, which is every one One Shilling and foure
pence. It I give my Son Richard Salket two Pounds in mony out of
my goods or personal Estate. It I give the Same my Son Richard Salkett
one paire of Harding Sheets and two blankets with a Bolster, a Coverlet
and a Caddie. It I give the Same my Son Richard a Chest that stands
in the Low Chamber in my house at winster. It I give my grand=daughter
Ann Harrison my Brass pot and my best Gown and my Cloak. It I give to
Alice Birkinson of winster my now tenant an old Wastcoat not my worst.
It I give to my daughter in law Barbary Salket of Kendal and her foure
children five Shillings to be equally distributed among them. It all
my Cloaths linnen and woollen that remain, with all the rest apparrell
with all my bedding and houshold stuff, bills, bonds and personal
Estate whatsoever that remaineth I give and bequeath to my daughter
Ann Harrison widdow living at Gill head in Cartmelfell, whom I make
whole and sole Executor of this my last will and testament, paying
all my debts, Legacies and funeral Expenses. Supravizers hereof I make
and appoint Henry Bateman of the beetside in Crooke and George Birkett
Junior of the Same Crooke, whom I intreat for Gods sake to see this my
last will and testament well and truely performed, allowing to either of
them for their pains one Shilling and Six pence. In witness whereof
I have put to my hand and Seal the day and year above written.

Sealed in the
presence of us: to wit;

Henry Bateman jun
Agnes Garnel mark
George Birkett jun

Ann Salket her
mark

Will of Ann Salket of Cartmel (Winster).

In contrast, the four grand-children at Kendal had to be content with 5s. divided among them; at least their mother Barbara would not have to face the task of making Granny's coat, gown, and cloak fit a little girl of six.

Strangely, there is no mention of the other two daughters of Thomae and Ann – who had been baptised in December 1642 (Frances) and in February 1648 (Annas), both so shown in the Windermere register. Had they survived their mother's death, they would then have been aged 43 and 37 respectively. Perhaps they had married and moved away. Maybe they had died. Their mother forgets them – so therefore perhaps may we.

A Note on Thomae's Friend, William Garnett, of Winster

Thomae Salkeld in his will of 23 August 1667, at Winster, says 'I give two pairs of old breetches unto two sones of William Garnetts'. Thomae was 55 when he made that momentous decision, for he could have left them to his own sons – as indeed he left Richard a pair of black ones. There is so little known about Thomae and his home at Winster that one is tempted to explore even such a small matter as a gift of 'breetches', in the hope that a little more light may so be thrown on both.

A search of the Preston archives reveals that there are no wills existing for a William Garnett of Winster, though there is one for a William Garnett of Towns End in the next-door parish of Crosthwaite. It was made on 20 May 1650 and it leaves all to wife Margaret and then to their son James; there is a splendid inventory made on 13 June of that year, which from the stock of leather reveals that this William Garnett was a saddler and had a saddler's shop, and also sold shoes and boot-trees. Of most interest is a list of customers owing the shop money, and there on the list is our friend Thomas (VI) Salkield (*sic*) who owes 1s. 8d. If this, as is almost certain, is our Thomae, he would have been 38 at the time this inventory was made.

In the Record Office at Kendal is a parcel of deeds relating to the Garnett tenement at Winster, including a deed which records the sale by a William Garnett, of the 'tenement at Woode Close Winster' (known as the Garnett Tenement), on 7 November 1622, some twenty-seven years before the saddler William Garnett died. Other deeds show that this Garnett Tenement was held by the Atkinsons until 29 December 1718 when they sold it to William Hodgson, a carpenter in Winster.

Unfortunately, no similar and revealing deed can be found for the Salkeld Tenement at Winster, which must have been fairly close to the Garnett Tenement, as Winster is not a very large place; certainly small enough for a Thomae Salkeld of the Salkeld Tenement to know a William Garnett of the Garnett Tenement, to shop at William's saddlery shop, and to owe him 1s. 8d. Thomae would be a younger man than William, and indeed William died 17 years before him. Thomae left an inventory totalling £11 9s. 4d. and William one of £73, including debts owed to him by customers from Crooke, Cartmell, Underbarrow and Winster, etc.; but let us hope that his two sons accepted old Thomae's gift of breetches with a good grace. They may well of course have been friends of Thomae's sons Thomas and Richard Salkeld, in the days at Winster before these two set out for pastures new.

Chapter Seven

Mislet and Broadgate

Thomas and Francis leave Winster

In the preceding chapter the main theme was of old Richard (VI) and his elder son Thomae (VI), both of Winster. It would be logical next to treat of old Richard's other and younger son, Francis (I), but before doing so there is a little more to be said about the children of Thomae.

It has been noted that Thomae himself left little, and indeed had little to leave. When he died in 1675, his elder son Thomas would have been 35 years old. In the next eight years Thomas is on record as having got himself not only a wife but also three daughters, two of whom were married. Though the exact date when Thomas left the Salkeld Tenement is not known, the evidence suggests that it might have been when he was still quite a young man, and that as an elder son he *may* have taken with him some stock from the Tenement at Winster.

His will, written on 20 April 1705 at the age of 64, establishes very firmly that he then was 'of Mislet' and no longer of Winster, and that when he died he was a yeoman and a wealthier man than his father Thomae had been. He had no sons, but his daughter Ann had married William Satterthwaite, a tanner from Crofthead of Claife, in Lancashire, and they had a boy Thomas Satterthwaite, to whom old Thomas now left his estate in trust. Ann's sister Margaret had also married, this time a Mislet man named Thomas Kinge, a glazier; whether they had children is not known. Thomas appointed both Kinge and his son-in-law William Satterthwaite as trustees for this grandson, charging them to pay the Richmond fee rental of 4s. 11d. a year, and £20 to his aunt Margaret. The main interest of this will is that he also appointed a third trustee, one John Braithwaite, a fellow yeoman and 'my neighbour' of Mislet. Of this John we shall hear more.

On the one inch O.S. map (of Windermere) Mislet is marked in square 4399, less than two miles north-east of Windermere town, and some four miles, as the crow flies, from Winster. Apart from a closely neighbouring farm called Broadgate, it is isolated, with sheep-grazing fells all around. The layout, and its relationship to Broadgate, can better be appreciated from the larger-scale plan S.D. 4299-4399.

Mislet

What is notable about Mislet, and about the Salkelds and Braithwaites who lived in it or nearby, is their association with the new Quaker movement. Its founder, George Fox, first visited Sedbergh in 1652, and subsequently spent much time preaching in these parts; through his influence, many of the local folk became Quakers, some, very prominent ones. These in particular included the local Braithwaite families.

Broadgate farm, only 300 yards away, was also the home of a few Braithwaites. So was the farm known as High House, built by a Robert Braithwaite in 1652, but a mile north of Broadgate, and having in earlier years, in the front downstairs window, the arms of both families. From all this information, a local pedigree of the Braithwaites can be built up. It shows a Robert who *could* have built High House farm. It shows a John who *could* have been the third trustee of Thomas Salkeld's will – John would have been 42 years old at the time; he may have lived at Broadgate, or at Mislet. Both farms – as can be seen from their plans – had plenty of accommodation. The Mislet farmhouse is in at least two blocks, the main one having on the first floor a very long room, spanning three large windows, panelled all round, with a fireplace at each end – the living room, in short, of a gentleman's family.

John Braithwaite's father was Richard, and he died in April 1679; John's mother's name was Ann; she took part in local Quaker meetings, especially those at Mislet. As for Thomas Salkeld, there is no evidence that before his death in 1705 he had become a Quaker, but in John he had certainly appointed one as a trustee of his will. Furthermore, Thomas's younger brother Richard, born at Winster in 1646 and now a family man in Kendal, certainly was a Quaker. As far then as we know, though there were no Salkeld Quakers in the Winster Tenement, there were several of the next generation, at Mislet and a few at Broadgate.

We now turn back to Winster, to see what had happened to Francis (I) Salkeld, the younger son of old Richard (VI) and the brother of old Thomas (VI). We do not know exactly when he decided to leave the Winster Tenement; after his nearly indecipherable baptismal entry in the Windermere register we have to wait until page 27 of Volume II to find the next reference about him. It is

Thomas filius ffrancisci Salkeld de Hugill baptizate fuit April die vicissimo sexto A.D. 1646

Splendid – Francis has had a son Thomas (VII). Then, within a month, the entry

Franciscus Salkeld de Broadgate sepultus fuit maii vicissimo quinto A.D. 1646.

Francis is dead.

On that day in May Francis left behind an un-named widow with an infant child, having been living, says the register, at Broadgate, some three hundred yards only from Mislet, and surrounded by Braithwaites.

Why, in 1646, had he died so suddenly? We can but guess – perhaps a quarrel, perhaps an accident on the farm – probably not the Plague, as this would almost certainly have meant many more casualties. Serious, too, for our studies, for there is no record of Francis having been married before that baptism in April 1646, nor of his having had children before that date; so we can reasonably suppose that Francis' marriage had taken place – if at all – in about 1643 or 1644, at age about thirty. This infant Thomas, mother's name unknown, now had neither father, brother nor sister. He had, we may remind ourselves, a lusty young cousin in Richard Salkeld of Kendal, son of old Thomae, and baptised within days of each other.

This infant Thomas may well be the author's direct ancestor, so the question of his legitimacy is of more than passing moment! The problem lies in identifying the infant's mother.

There are at least two solutions, and each may be wrong – at best, only one can be right. But to discuss each in detail at this point in our narrative would interfere with its continuity and would involve considerable duplication; so the arguments have been collected together and it is suggested that the reader does not look at them until the main tale has unfolded. Meanwhile, the preferred solution is given now. See p. 85.

Her name was Isabell Braithwaite, until her marriage with Francis Salkeld; she was born at Broadgate, baptised on 29 June 1619 at Windermere parish church, and was the daughter of William Braithwaite of Broadgate and – possibly – of Elizabeth whose surname before marriage is not known.

I can find no register entry of the marriage of Francis Salkeld and Isabell *Braithwaite*; but thanks to the excellent Quaker records we know that an Isabel *Salkeld*, widow, of *Broadgate*, died a Quaker at Broadgate on 4 September 1688, some sixty-nine years after the baptism of Isabell Braithwaite at Windermere.

On becoming a Quaker the Church of England parish registers may contain thereafter no records of births, marriages nor deaths. It is especially interesting to note, for example, that Thomas Salkeld the joiner of Dent (West Yorkshire), a direct ancestor who died in 1700, does not exist as far as he or his family are concerned, in the Dent Church of England registers, yet his first wife Ann Haygarth is shown as having been christened, and her parents and relatives are named in detail, in the Church of England register. After his and his second wife (Grace's) death (in 1702), one of their sons – Thomas – presented himself for Church of England baptism at the age of 17 years (i.e. in 1709) but that is the only Church of England record of Salkeld in Dent in the period! Quaker records are however held centrally at the Society of Friends, Euston Road, London, and in the Public Record Office in Chancery Lane, and also at selected county centres (although York said they had no records for Dent).

Broadgate

We have briefly described Mislet as the farmstead home of Thomas and his three Salkeld daughters. We have established that this Thomas's uncle Francis (I) had, like Thomas, left Winster in the hands of Old Thomae and sought pastures new. For Thomas, those pastures were at Mislet. Now we have just learnt that Francis, for a brief period up to 1646, found *his* new pastures at the adjoining farm called Broadgate. We must say something about this farm.

The plan shows that, today, Broadgate is a slightly smaller farmstead than Mislet, as far as buildings go; but this may not always have been so – it is said that there are remains of old buildings in the Broadgate fields. The *largest* barn is only 100 years old – its centenary was celebrated in June 1979, and it is a specially fine building of great internal height. The farmhouse has of course been much modernised but the hollow lath walls are still to be detected by tapping; there is a spice cupboard against the main fireplace – let into the wall; and in the garden are relics of the old stone beehives whose honey was such an important source of sugar long ago.

Up to 1638 it had been farmed by William Braithwaite; the entry on 31 March of his burial 'in templo' in Windermere Church specifically shows that he was of Broadgate. On 1 November 1618 there is a record of the burial of an Elizabeth Braithwaite, also of Broadgate, and also 'in templo'; this lady may have been William's wife, or a daughter. (If she were his wife, their child Isabell, who was baptised on 29 June 1619, may possibly have had her baptism postponed from the previous October because of her mother's death.)

The only other record, in this period, of the Braithwaites of Broadgate, occurs in Part 2 of the Kendal church register, page 185, where the burial on 22 July 1578 of 'Mabell widow of Thomas Braithwaite of Broadgate' is recorded. These may have been the parents of William. If so, and if Elizabeth were his wife, William would have been in his sixties when he died, and at least twenty when his daughter Isabell was born. She became the wife of Francis Salkeld, and Francis had their child Thomas (VII) baptised at Windermere in April 1646, and then died a few weeks later. The widowed Isabell stayed on at Broadgate, her parents' home, and indeed lived there all her life, dying in 1688 after pressing her Quaker beliefs to her own peril and to the extreme annoyance of those who saw otherwise. As a widow she could of course help in the farm's work, but there were others living at Broadgate to run the farm. Near to Mislet and its Meeting House, Isabell could conveniently take part in Quaker activities but, as we shall see later, she did not confine these activities to Mislet.

Richard Braithwaite and his wife Anne were staunch Quakers. He had been born in February 1627 (Windermere register), so when George Fox first visited this area Richard would be little more than twenty-five years old. As the movement developed, Richard often lent his house in Mislet for the monthly 'Women's Meetings' at which his wife seems to have kept the minutes (these are well-preserved by the Kendal Society of Friends who kindly made them available to me for study, in the rooms of the Kendal Record Office). Those for 9 October 1677-8 record that the meeting was being 'holden at our useuall meeting place' – Richard Braithwaite's house – and that the main item for discussion that night was the resistance which should be offered to demands for the payment of tithes. The Quakers argued that as Christ had preached without payment – 'teaches freely without mony' – all 'hirling teachers' should 'be denied'. Those statements were made by Anne 'Breathat' – so she signed her name – and appear on the left-hand quarter at the top of the page. By good fortune the bottom left quarter is occupied by a testimony from 'Isabell Sokelt', whose name appears at the bottom of it, but in the same handwriting. Isabell's testimony is not too easy to read in places and so is transcribed below. The term 'steeplehouses' was the Quaker's name for a church – they preferred to hold their meetings under God's good sky.

> As concerning tythes and steeplehouses I am cleare and have paid none as for tythe eggs they sometimes have got them by wile or somewhat through feare but I do disowne and deny payment of any such things and hope in god to keep my conscience cleare and to stand witness against all dishoneste gaine by these hirelings being resolved to keep unto the true shepherd Christ Jesus my saviour and redeemer and to harken to his voice and so deny all other priests and strangeires for his sake and this is the testimony of Isabell Solkelt the 9 of the 10 month 1677.

This is the first evidence we have that Isabell *Salkeld* was attending Quaker meetings in Mislet in 1677, some thirty years after the death of her husband Francis. In the Quaker records of her death at Broadgate 11 years later she is also described as a widow. Meanwhile she speaks of 'feare'. Below are some examples of punishments meted out to nearby Friends for persisting in practising their beliefs.

So vicious became the scale of punishments for organising or for attending Quaker meetings, that the Mislet group built a separate Meeting House for their activities, to relieve Richard Braithwaite from being punished for using his home for this purpose. This Mislet Meeting House is a few paces from the main farmstead and takes the form of a small cottage, now smartly whitewashed, consisting of a single upstairs bedroom and a large downstairs meeting chamber. Immediately behind and to one side is the

ye 21 of ye 8 month our
wemans meeting holden
at our eusouall meeting
place

1678
ye 18 of ye 9 month our
wemens meeting at Wind
er moor

as for ye payment of tithes I am
cleare knowing a free teacher
yt is come Christ Jesus who
teaches freely without mony
or price & hath taught me so
to deney all hirsling teachers
& therefore of tithes & ment
ainse I am cleare & may be
leiue in god is foreuer shall
be keept cleare

anne breathat

as conserning tyths & steeple hous
dews I am cleare & haue payed none
as for tyth egges they somtimes hai
ne got them by will or som is haue
through feare but I do disowne & de
ny ye payment of any such thing
& hopes in god to keepe my consain
ce cleare & so stand u witnes again
st all these dishonest gaine of these
else hairlings being resolued to
keepe unto ye true sheepherd Chr
ist Jesus my saui our & re deem
er & to harken to his voyse & to
deney all outher priest & to euang
nony for his sake this I test
Isabell sokell
ye 9 of ye 10 month oun

Deare frinds this is my testi
mony for ye Lord against tyt
els & their maintainante as
I was conuinced of gods pouer
truth I was allso conuinced
of ye euell of ye prests wayes &
of ye great euell of paying of
tythes or up holding them an
y way & for ye uery cauleth
ey we haue suffered much
& ye Lord hath made me will
ing so to do for ye truth sake
& I am of ye sam mind at th
is day for they are enemys
to god & his truth & to our
immortall soulls they stand
ing in ye ready way
to disstruction drawing as many
way as they can & will not
follow them they preuare war a
gainst them but I haue met with
ye liueing god which will neuer
deceue me euen ye bread of life
which keepes me aliue to god
& his truth & ye more I eat ye m
ore I long for ye sam for I cannot
liue without it & our god is a god of
infinit wisdom he knowes how to fee
his children in due time for they ye hun
gers after this bread of life he
will satisfy as they ye truly thir
steth after ye streames of his loue
he will superall refresh & so my
deare frinds ye desire of my hea
it is for you as for my selfe ye
we may be keept & preserued
close unto this fountayne of
fullnes which can neuer be

14.   Coffin rest in the Quaker burial ground, Mislet.

Friends' Burial Ground, quite a small patch devoid of headstones (because these were not permitted until after 1850). A large slate resting horizontally on stones at the side of the entrance to the Burial Ground was used as a coffin rest and is still there, though much of the once six-foot high surrounding wall has gone.

This is probably the last resting-place of Isabell Salkeld, mother of Thomas (VII) and longtime widow of Francis the younger son of old Richard (VII). We close this chapter with one of her escapades, extracted from *Records of Kendale*, vol. III, p. 166; the place concerned, Underbarrow, is some five miles from Broadgate. The expedition, which she made with her Broadgate friends the Graves, cost each of them 5s. in fines for unlawful congregation. They were lucky.

Underbarrow

1671 – 7 October. Memorandum that upon the 20 July, 22 Charles II, John Phillipson of Calfgarth, yeo. came before Robert Phillipson, esq., at Calfgarth and gave information upon proof of the oaths of witnesses that Christopher Birkett of Underbarrow and his wife, Henry Hewert and Mary his wife, John Pepper, Miles Halhead and Thomas Cowper all of the same. Miles Bateman of Tullithwayte, younger, and Miles Hubersty of the same, Richard Judson of Crooke, John Thompson, Geo. Thompson, Peter Bateman and Dorothy Bateman all of the same, Rob. Thompson of Milnebecke, Geo. Dodgson of Strickland Ketle, Jas. Dodgson and his wife, John Helme, Randle Williamson and Ellis Kitchin all of the same, Roger Bacchus of Kendall and Jas. Newby of the same, Thomas Grave of Hugill and his wife; Elizabeth Grave, widow, and *Isabell Salkeld of the same*, did each on 4 July last assemble and unlawfully congregate in the house of the said Christopher Birkett of Underbarrow with other evil doers and disturbers of the king's peace unknown to the number of forty persons besides the family of the said Christopher at the assemblage of a conventicle and gathering under colour and pretext of exercising religion otherwise than allowed by the Liturgy of the English Church and against the king's peace, his crown and dignity, and against the form of the Statute in such case made and provided, wherefore the said Christopher Birkett and the other evil doers are convicted, Christopher Birkett's fine of £20, Miles Bateman's fine £20, for taking upon himself to (concionari) in the meeting and upon each other person five shillings for their consent, according to the form of the Statute, etc. (K. Indictment Book, 1669-1692).

Other Anti-Quaker Activities[70,71]

1662 – John Grave of Torpenhow (a village with Salkeld connections), having already been imprisoned for 22 weeks in Carlisle for reproving a priest in 1657, is reimprisoned in 1662.

1662 – Francis Howard, a papist of Corby (which castle for 300 years was in the hands of the Salkeld family before passing to the Howards) sued three Quakers for non-payment of tithes, totalling £3 4s. 0d. He was allowed to take cattle worth £39 5s.0d. in retribution!

1663 – On 22 November John Salkeld and four others were removed by force from a Quaker meeting and imprisoned; in the following January (the next session) they were fined and their goods distressed.

On 27 March 1675 the magistrates issued warrants against those who abstained from attending the church services on Sunday – and 134 prosecutions followed.

1676 – On 8 February Thomas (VII) Salkeld and his friend Francis Lund, of Dent, were prosecuted in the Ecclesiastical Court for refusing to pay 1½d. yearly for an Easter offering. The case was brought by Leonard Barton the vicar of Sedbergh (who died in January 1680) and as a result a writ of *de Excommunicato capiendo* was issued and they were committed to prison, for how long is not recorded.

1678 – On 15 September Thomas Grave of Hugill (Broadgate) had goods worth 12s. seized, and again in 1684 he and four others had £1 10s. 10d. worth of wool taken, for being absent from Sunday service.

By 1684 no less than 279 Quakers were imprisoned in Yorkshire for their faith, but

Cumberland with 22 and Westmorland with only five were by this date relatively fortunate.

By 1697 the position had much improved for the Quakers, and some groups were even licensed to hold Meetings, though the Test Act (which directed that all officers of Government must receive the sacrament) still operated to prevent Quakers holding public office.

Who was the Mother of Thomas Salkeld?

That there was an Isabel Salkeld living in the Mislet-Broadgate area cannot be doubted, for in July 1671 as we have seen she was fined 5s. for taking part in 'breaking the King's peace' in a Quaker meeting at Christopher Birkett's house (*Records of Kendale*, vol. III, p. 166).[71] The Quaker records in London – book 1216, p. 336 – show that an Isabell Salkeld 'residence Broadgate' was buried, a widow on 4 September 1688, as reported at the Kendal meeting; this is confirmed in book 1596, p. 152[73] but the word 'widow' is not included in that second entry. Her testimony to the Quaker Monthly Meeting in October 1677 or 1678 specifically mentions her full name including the word Salkeld (Sokelt) – that meeting was at Richard Braithwaite's house in Mislet; the local Quaker minutes record her attendance at another Mislet Monthly Meeting, also. But unfortunately there is no record of the marriage of this widow to a Salkeld, nor can her will be found.

There is however a perfectly good record in the Windermere parish book of the baptism on 29 June 1619 of an Isabell Braythat (*sic*) of Broadgate, daughter of William Braythat, and a further record of William Braithwaite of Broadgate being buried 'in templo' on 31 March 1638, when Isabell would have been nearly nineteen.

We also know, from the Windermere register, that Francis Salkeld of Broadgate christened a son Thomas on 26 April 1646, and most important of all, we know that that same Thomas, having lost his first wife Ann Haygarth in childbirth at their 'mansion' of Blandsgill in Dentdale, brought his second wife Grace the 26 miles to Broadgate when she was expecting *her* first child; that child, Ann, was given a Quaker baptism on 2 May 1682, as is recorded in the London Quaker registers; Grace's remaining children were however registered as born in Dent. There seems little doubt, from the above, that the Isabell Braithwaite who was baptised 'of Broadgate' on 29 June 1619, had married this Francis Salkeld there sometime around 1645; their first child Thomas was then born in April 1646 (as recorded), but Francis died the following month (as also recorded in the Windermere register) leaving Isabell a widow, in which state she remained until her death in September 1688. Finally, one of Thomas's children was baptised Isabell.

The attached table shows some of the varied population of Broadgate, over these years, including the other few Braithwaites who from time to time lived there. But the real centre of the Braithwaites was a few hundred yards from Broadgate – at the farm of Mislet, where they greatly outnumbered the few Salkelds. Both these farms are large, and offer plenty of accommodation.

It will be seen that Isabell Salkeld (née Braithwaite) would have been 26 years old when she married Francis Salkeld, having lost her father when she was nearly nineteen; she was 27 when her first and only child Thomas was born, and still 27 when her husband died. She was 69 when her widowhood came to an end. A sad life.

SOME RESIDENTS OF BROADGATE

Date	Surname	Christian name	Relatives	Entry for	Source of Information
22 Jul 1578	Braithwaite	Mabell	widow of Thomas Braithwaite of BROADGATE	buried	Records of Kendal p. 185
9 Dec 1579	Jopson	Thomas	—	buried	Records of Kendal p. 192
1 Nov 1618	Braithwaite	Elizabeth	of Broadgate	buried in templo	Windermere (W.P.) Parish Records
29 Jun 1619	'Braythat'	Isabella	daughter of William Braythat	baptised	Windermere (W.P.) Parish Records
4 Feb 1623	Smith	Nathaniel	son of Mr James Smith	baptised	Windermere (W.P.) Parish Records
31 Mar 1638	Braithwaite	William	of Broadgate	buried in templo	Windermere (W.P.) Parish Records
4 Dec 1642	Field	Christopher	son of William Field	buried in templo	Windermere (W.P.) Parish Records
17 May 1646	Field	Robert	son of William Field	baptised	Windermere (W.P.) Parish Records
26 Aug 1646	Salkeld	Thomas	son of Francis Salkeld	baptised	Windermere (W.P.) Parish Records
25 May 1646	Salkeld	Francis	—	buried	Windermere (W.P.) Parish Records
22 Apr 1649	Field	Elizabeth	daughter of William Field	baptised	Windermere (W.P.) Parish Records
22 Apr 1650	Sawrey	James	son of John Sawrey	buried 6d. paid	Windermere (W.P.) Parish Records
22 Apr 1652	Grave	John	'of the Broadgate'	buried	Windermere (W.P.) Parish Records
6 Sep 1659	Grave	Mary	daughter of Thomas	buried	Kendal Meeting Quaker Records
21 Sep 1661	Baxter	Hugh	—	buried	Windermere Parish Records
1 Sep 1661	Baxter	Jane	—	buried (Windermere)	(BB p. 27)
1 Apr 1665	Field	Margaret	wife of William Field	buried in templo	Windermere Parish Records
4 Jul 1670	Grave	'widdow'	'widdow'	buried Kendal	Kendal Quaker Records
(1682 Visit of Thos. Salkeld and Grace his wife, to Isabel at Broadgate)				—	London Quaker Records
18 Nov 1686	Grave	Jane	wife of Thomas Grave	buried	Kendal Quaker Records
31 Oct 1687	Grave	Sarah	daughter of Thomas and Jane	buried	Kendal Quaker Records
1688	Salkeld	Isabell	widow of ? Francis Salkeld of Winster	buried	Kendal Quaker Records
2 Nov 1688	Grave	Margaret	—	buried	Kendal Quaker Records
18 Jun 1694	Braithwaite	Edward	son of Bryon and Elizabeth of Broadgate	buried Kendal	Kendal Quaker Records
15 Sep 1698	Grange	Joseph	son of Thomas Grange, married Sarah Burkeat Lambrigg	wedding	BB p. 10
22 Nov 1701	Braithwaite	Margaret	wife of Edward Braithwaite	buried Kendal	Kendal Quaker Records

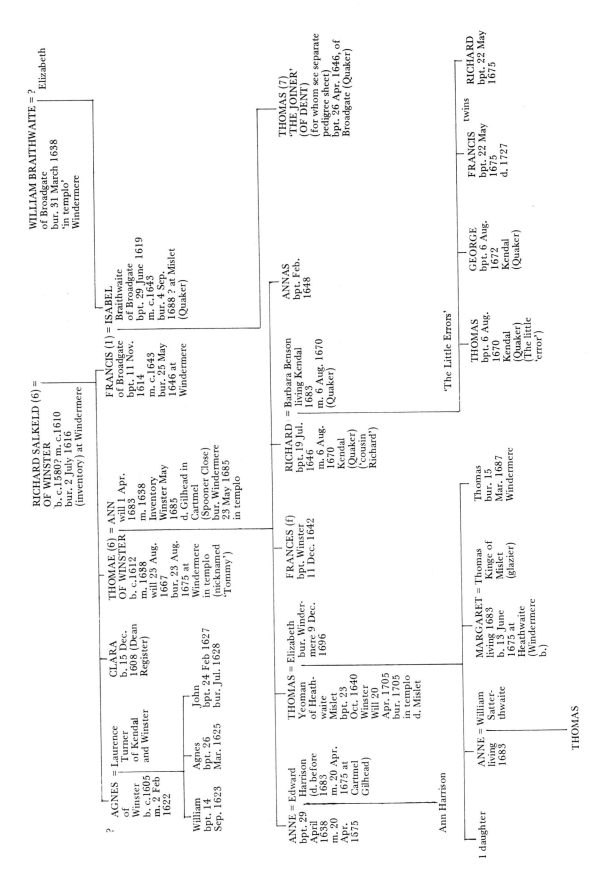

WILLIAM BRAITHWAITE = ?
of Broadgate   Elizabeth
bur. 31 March 1638
'in templo'
Windermere

RICHARD SALKELD (6) =
OF WINSTER
b. c.1580? m. c.1610
bur. 2 July 1616
(inventory) at Windermere

?   AGNES = Laurence
           of   Turner
           Winster of Kendal
           b. c.1605 and Winster
           m. 2 Feb
           1622

CLARA
b. 15 Dec.
1608 (Dean
Register)

THOMAE (6) = ANN
OF WINSTER   will 1 Apr.
b. c.1612   1683
m. 1638   Inventory
will 23 Aug. Winster May
1667   1685
bur. 23 Aug. d. Gilhead in
1675 at   Cartmel
Windermere   (Spooner Close)
in templo   bur. Windermere
(nicknamed   23 May 1685
'Tommy')   in templo

FRANCIS (1) = ISABEL
of Broadgate   Braithwaite
bpt. 11 Nov.   of Broadgate
1614   bpt. 29 June 1619
m. c.1643   m. c.1643
bur. 25 May   bur. 4 Sep.
1646 at   1688 ? at Mislet
Windermere   (Quaker)

THOMAS (7)
'THE JOINER',
(OF DENT)
(for whom see separate
pedigree sheet)
bpt. 26 Apr. 1646, of
Broadgate (Quaker)

William   John
bpt. 14   bpt. 24 Feb 1627
Sep. 1623   bur. Jul. 1628

Agnes
bpt. 26
Mar. 1625

FRANCES (f)
bpt. Winster
11 Dec. 1642

RICHARD = Barbara Benson
bpt. 19 Jul.   living Kendal
1646   1683
m. 6 Aug.   m. 6 Aug. 1670
1670   (Quaker)
Kendal
(Quaker)
('cousin
Richard')

ANNAS
bpt. Feb.
1648

'The Little Errors'

THOMAS = Elizabeth
Yeoman   bur. Winder-
of Heath- mere 9 Dec.
waite   1696
Mislet
bpt. 23
Oct. 1640
Winster
Will 20
Apr. 1705
bur. 1705
in templo
d. Mislet

MARGARET = Thomas
living 1683   Kinge of
b. 13 June   Mislet
1675 at   (glazier)
Heathwaite
(Windermere
b.)

Thomas
bur. 15
Mar. 1687
Windermere

THOMAS
bpt. 6 Aug.
1670
Kendal
(Quaker)
('The little
'error')

GEORGE
bpt. 6 Aug.
1672
Kendal
(Quaker)

FRANCIS   twins
bpt. 22 May
1675
d. 1727

RICHARD
bpt. 22 May
1675

ANNE = Edward
bpt. 29   Harrison
April   (d. before
1638   1683
m. 20   m. 20 Apr.
Apr.   1675 at
1675   Cartmel
          Gilhead)

Ann Harrison

ANNE = William
living   Satter-
1683   thwaite

1 daughter

THOMAS

Windermere Records

The registers of St Martin's church, Windermere, now in the custody of the Archivist at Kendal Record Office, contain eight Salkeld entries over the periods 1613-16 and 1638-48; no doubt had they been properly preserved, and those for the years 1628-37 had not been lost, this study of the Salkelds would have been much improved. As something of 'a quid pro quo' however many of the entries do include a mention of the location of the individual. One can say without fear of contradiction that:

1.   The population of Winster in the 15 years between 1613-28 included two Braith-waites, and at least ten Birketts, 17 Willans, nine Atkinsons, 11 Dixons, two Salkelds, and 20 others, a total of 70 named individuals.

2.   The Broadgate population included only two Braithwaites, out of a total of three named individuals.

3.   In contrast, the Mislet population included at least seven Braithwaites, out of a total of eight people.

It is also possible to show that the year 1623, which is included in the above figures, was a disaster year for some families. Thus, averaged over the whole period, the Willan family lost one member every other year – but in 1623 it lost seven. Similarly the Birketts lost six members in the period, but five of these were in 1623. The few Salkelds at Winster seemed to have escaped whatever it was – plague[65] or famine, or perhaps both.

Chapter Eight

The Youth of Thomas the Joiner

The stage is now set for a main theme of this book – the career of Thomas (VII), the son of Francis (I) Salkeld of Winster and Broadgate and of Isabell née Braithwaite of Broadgate. Baptised on 26 April 1646, an only child, and bereft of his father a few weeks after birth, his mother living in her late parent's lonely home, young Thomas could be pardoned had he sometimes wished that the Fates had dealt him a better start in life.

At some young but unknown age he would have to go to school; at Mislet a barn was set up as a Quaker school, and by 1702 its Trustees were receiving capital sums from local testators, the interest from which sums was to pay the £5 to £8 per year which was the cost of a master. William Williamson of Common in Applethwaite in 1702 left no less than £40 for the Mislet school, the Trustees being local men including our friend John Braithwaite, now a yeoman, of Mislet.

But Thomas would be needing some simple schooling many years before that – in about 1655 say – and I cannot find evidence that this Quaker school at Mislet was in operation so early – though it may have been. However, at the two major towns nearby – Windermere and Kendal – there were ample facilities.

Windermere had built a school near Bowness, in 1633, helped by money from the hamlets of Applethwaite and of Undermilnebeck; this was a free school, only two miles from his home at Broadgate, but there is no evidence that Thomas did or did not attend it.

At Kendal, where he was to serve his apprenticeship, there had been a free grammar school since 1525 – free in the sense that, for a small entrance fee, a boy over eight would get free tuition in the classics. However, those requiring English, reading, writing, 'common arithmetic', geography or history had to pay an extra quarterly fee; for mathematics and the higher branches of knowledge the fee was rather greater. The only existing universities – Oxford and Cambridge – offered scholarships to boys of Kendal Grammar School. Some Salkelds did attend these universities, as their registers show – but not Thomas (VII).

And yet his will, as we shall see, was signed, when he was 48 years old, in a literate hand; perhaps his strong Quaker background ensured that Thomas was given – and pressed by his Quaker mother to take – some elementary schooling during his apprenticeship at Kendal.

His cousin Richard had married before reaching the age of 25 and it is possible that Thomas lived with Richard in Kendal during his apprenticeship or, if living-in with his master was demanded, Thomas would often see his cousin. But Richard was no scholar – he signed papers with his 'mark' – so Thomas was not likely to get much 'schooling' from that source. He might even pick up some less desirable habits, for Richard had been 'in trouble', concerning a certain Barbara Benson. The record book of the *Kendal Mens' Monthly Magazine*[74] for the period 1670 to 1724 contains an entry on 16 February 1670 that a Richard Sockold 'acknowledges an error' and so does Barbara,

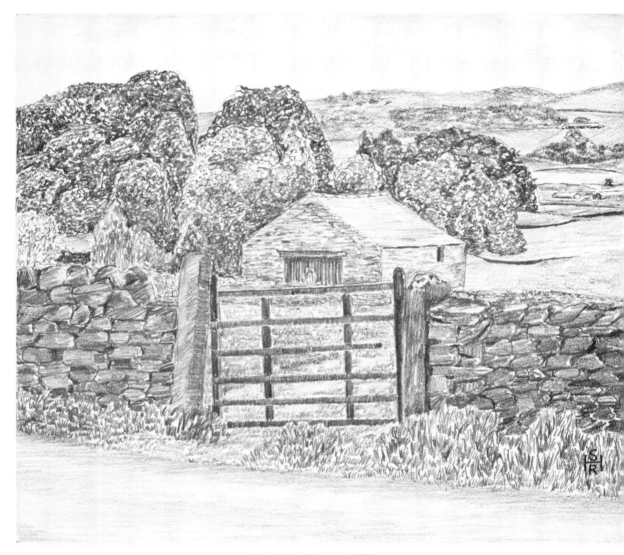

15.   School-house, Mislet.

who describes herself as unmarried. As a result, and with Quaker approval, these two were married on the following 6 August, the day also of the baptism of their first child (another Thomas!). Two years later they had a second son George, and later again twin boys. These are the four grandchildren to whom Ann the wife of old Thomas (VI) of Winster left, it will be remembered, the sum of 5s. to be divided among them; their ages would be 12, 10, and the twins, rising eight. They were a healthy lot, the first of the four to die being at least fifty-two. We must leave them with our good wishes, and return to Thomas (VII) the Joiner.

That Thomas was a joiner is clear from his own will; that he was of Kendal is equally clear from a later marriage entry. He would therefore be indentured by those Kendal J.P.s who were responsible for this activity. He would have to spend at least seven years learning his craft – some contend that the minimum *age* for completing apprenticeships was at that time no less than twenty-four. Be that as it may, he would have a few years, before he married and 'settled down', as a journeyman joiner in Kendal, earning his living as best he could. As a bachelor and care-free uncle, doubtless he would visit mother Isabell at Broadgate, only some eight miles away, to learn of her latest Quaker escapades.

Much was going on in the great world outside Kendal at this time. Perhaps the crowning of King Charles II brought the apprentices a day's holiday. Certainly the terrible Plague in London would remind the citizens of Kendal of their own plague in 1622 aown alone over a thousand were struck down in the two years. Then the stories coming through of a Great Fire in London would do little to make these town-dwellers sleep better of a night (in fact, the 'trained hands' were turned out).

Less spectacular but perhaps more important for Kendal, was the prohibition in 1660 of the export of wool – a new law which was to damage Kendal's thriving wool trade for many years to come. Other legislation – the first Turnpike Act for improving the terrible roads, a new Hearth Tax – and, specially meaningful for Thomas and his Friends, the Conventical Act in 1664 forbidding religious meetings other than those held under the auspices of the Church of England; and then the Test Act excluding all non-conformists from holding public office.

Fortunately, gathering clouds such as these are easy for youngsters to disregard and it is likely that young Thomas was more concerned about restrictions on his liberty such as the Kendal magistrates might impose, and about the level of his pocket money. As to liberty, rules in Kendal were strict. For example, in April 1657, when Thomas was aged 11, games such as 'Kattstick' and 'Bulyett' were specifically forbidden in the streets to any over 12 years of age, on penalty of a fine of 12d. per offence, to be levied on their goods; as youngsters rarely had goods, an alternative punishment (of being imprisoned for two hours) was available!

As to earnings, the Kendal Churchwardens Accounts for 1659 (when Thomas was 13) show that they paid a Thomas Birkett, 'joyner', the sum of 'vi shillings' for 'six days work about the new pews before the pulpit'. If an experienced tradesman was earning but a shilling a day, an apprentice such as Thomas would not have many pennies in his pocket.

At Kendal, all the carpenters and all the joiners lived and had their workshops in the street called Stramongate, inhabited also by blacksmiths, saddlers, dyers and weavers. So if cousin Richard were indeed a weaver, the two lads would be working near each other. This street had in it – as today – a variety of trade shops, and some gentlemen's houses with three to six hearths apiece.

Joiners and Carpenters

As a joiner, Thomas would soon be an expert in the art of framing and panelling, to produce furniture which did not split nor warp. Articles constructed in this way were called joined or jointed furniture. They were lighter and easier to move than those made by the heavy plank construction used by carpenters.[75]

Throughout the Middle Ages the *carpenter* was the most important of the craftsmen working in wood. He spent most of his time making the timber frames of medieval houses, as well as farm buildings and implements. . . . The earliest wood used was not sawn but was split by the carpenters with iron and wooden wedges and trimmed with an adze.

Carpenters joined the pieces of furniture they made with hand-wrought nails or wooden pegs. No glue was used; indeed its use was forbidden by the carpenters' Guilds which were in existence from the 12th century onwards . . . They were able to make mortise and tenon joints but only on a massive scale in structural work.

Most of the few articles of furniture required in medieval homes until the 15th century had been made by carpenters. The drawback to the furniture they produced was that it was heavy and inclined to split across the grain, and warp. The wood could not move, as it could under the later panel and frame construction of the joiner, introduced in the 15th century. The planks were held rigidly in position by the nails and pegs.

The joiners eventually took over furniture making, although as late as the 18th century country carpenters were still making chests and boxes using plank construction.

Life in Kendal

As now, Kendal was the meeting place of the 'roads' and tracks from the north, east, south and west and so was an important centre for travellers. In 1686 the town had 279 beds for guests and 439 stable places for horses – twice as many as Penrith. Only Carlisle with its 413 beds and 522 stables could compare.

Most of the big houses, and two-thirds of the innkeepers, were in nearby Strick-landgate: there were big houses too, in Highgate, the main street. In all, Kendal's resident population at this time was about two thousand, but this was much swollen on Saturdays by visitors to the fair or market – no doubt also the source of many of young Thomas's modest purchases. When he was 15, there was such a hard frost that from November to the following March he could skate over the lake at Windermere.

In some ways, Thomas was lucky; he was serving his apprenticeship within the period of Kendal's richest years in the wool trade. In June he could see the yeoman farmers sending their wool clip, by packman, to the central warehouses where the fellmongers disentangled the coarse fleeces and the sorters split them into qualities – neck wool for example being of higher quality than rump wool. Then the packman would take the sorted wool to various homes where the mothers carded the fibre and the daughters spun it into yarn. This was collected and sent to the homes of the weavers who had looms capable of making cloth a yard wide. The subsequent processes have been described elsewhere; they resulted in a woven cloth which often found its way back to Kendal for dyeing. Thus the farm girls – the 'spinsters' – would get to know the young weavers.

Young Thomas, living in Kendal, had no difficulty in meeting a girl called Ann, from a farm in Dentdale some fifteen miles eastward. Whether cousin Richard the Weaver did the introductions, or they just met at the Kendal market, matters not. They did meet; the year was 1672; Thomas was now 26, she was three years older. He was a Quaker, she was not – nor were her family. So the first thing to be achieved was her acceptance by the Friends – a very formal procedure, conducted by them with much investigation and care.

The local Quaker centre for this was at Brigflatts, a mile south-west of Sedbergh. Here a Quaker Meeting Place had been set up after the historic day in 1652 when George Fox, founder of the movement, had addressed a large gathering on Firbank Fell. Despite the incessant fining of members for refusing to pay tithes or to attend church services, it had flourished.

At first, the Meeting Place had beneath its roof neither floor nor ceiling, and two Friends were appointed each year to stuff the holes in the building with moss to keep out the rain and the snow. The walls were bare, but there was a large fireplace at the west end. At the foot of the stairs leading to a later gallery was a space for dogs, and the horses were accommodated after 1670 in stables which cost £33 to build; they had a mounting block at each end, the larger being six feet by four feet to give room for a pillion rider to dismount.

This was the building to which, on 25 June in the year 1672, Thomas Salkeld the joiner brought his bride Ann Haygarth, for their (illegal) marriage under Quaker 'laws'. Today, the Brigflatts Meeting House is, of course, completed, and in an excellent state of repair, with its own caretaker and many thousands of visitors. In 1672, the entrance porch did not exist – it was completed in 1675 – though it is unlikely that Thomas and his bride worried too much about that.

When Thomas's mother was under discussion, we had considerable difficulty in identifying her origin; with Thomas and his wife there is no such problem, for both left detailed wills. Her full name as a maiden was Ann Haygarth, and she was born at her parents' home farm, known as Broadfield House, some two miles east of the village of Dent (map reference 740865). Just as, at this period, the parish registers were completely oblivious to the existence of Thomas Salkeld because he was a Quaker, so the Dent parish register is full of details of the Haygarth family, including Ann, because up to her marriage in 1672, and beyond, they were not.

The Dent register shows that Ann was baptised on 14 May 1643, and was probably the third child of John Haygarth of Broadfield House. Her mother was possibly Siselle Jackson who had married John on 23 November 1637. (Jackson, curiously enough, was a rare surname in Dentdale, but common enough in nearby Sedbergh from whence possibly Siselle came.) Their first child John was baptised on 9 January 1638-9, which lines up with their marriage date; but young John died as a two-month-old infant. Their second child Richard, baptised on 26 September 1641, died five years later. Ann was probably the third child and Jane, baptised 2 October 1644, was the fourth and last surviving – a fifth was buried, apparently unchristened, on 29 October 1646. Their father John Haygarth did not live very much longer, being buried in Dent on 18 December 1651, when Ann was but eight years old. There is no record of her mother's death – it might of course have been in childbirth in October 1646. That same year, on 24 November, died old Matthew Haygarth who had farmed Broadfield since about the turn of the century.

John's early death – at age about 49, leaving no grown son – posed the usual problem of providing managership of the farm until Ann could take over or marry. To do this would be the task of Thomas Haygarth and his wife Isabel, who had worked alongside John at Broadfield for many years and who had several young sons for the future; this Thomas lived on until 6 January 1698, being perhaps eighty years old at his death.

16. Quaker Meeting House, Brigflatts.

17. Accommodation for Broadfield.

18. Broadfield House.

The Haygarths of Dentdale owned more than just Broadfield House; in addition, they owned a nearby farm described as 'Blandsgill House situate in Kirkthwaite in Dent in the County of York' and 'several other closes and parcels of land with their respective appurtenances commonly called and known by the name of the 'ffaws and High Croft'. Until Ann needed them these properties appear to have been left in trust for her, the trustees being 'John Haygarth of Hobsons in Kirkthwaite in Dent aforesaid yeoman' (probably an uncle) and 'Myles Hodgson of Overgallows . . . husbandman'. In her will of 25 October 1673 – a legally verbose document – Ann ensures that from her death they shall all pass to her husband Thomas Salkeld, joiner, and his heirs and assigns 'for their only use and behoofe' for ever.

In short, in marrying Ann, Thomas Salkeld was 'on to a good thing'; he could now pack up his joiner's bag of tools and lead what amounted to the life of a yeoman farmer, in what he describes in his will as 'the mansion house of Blandsgill'. As to consequential farming problems, was not his wife the daughter of a yeoman farmer and therefore well trained in the house end of the work? And for external assistance, had he not the excellent advice of the Haygarth family, practically next door?

19.   Blandsgill farmhouse.

So it was, after their marriage at the Quaker Meeting House at Brigflatte on 25 June 1672, that Thomas and his bride rode pillion to Blandsgill House, to start their married life.

No doubt the nearby Broadfield House was also playing a prominent part in the festivities, having been the home of the bride for the past 30 years. The rest of the clan Haygarth, spread down the Dent valley for several miles, was not likely to be unrepresented. Nor surely could Thomas's mother Isabell, of Broadgate near Windermere – despite her Quaker disapproval of alcohol – miss her only son's wedding? One would also be surprised if cousin Richard and his wife Barbara – with or without a 'little error' – had not come over from Kendal. Would the Vicar of Dent, who had baptised Ann and buried her infant brothers, be invited? Not if the decision were to be left to mother Isabell, Quaker to the last. But it probably was not left to her – the conventional Haygarth *church*folk would have strong views, too.

Chapter Nine

Married Life at Blandsgill

Marriage to Ann

To Thomas (VII), the contrast between life as a bachelor journeyman-joiner in Stramongate, Kendal, with its proliferation of noisy, cramped, overcrowded and smelly dwellings, and being suddenly translated at age 26 to become the married lord of the country 'mansion' of Blandsgill, with its miles of rolling fells and traditional methods of living and farming in the dales, must have been great. A look at a large-scale map of Dentdale will show how the narrow-streeted village of Dent, receiving traffic from four roads, lies in a broad valley down which flows the River Dee. On walking up river the valley narrows to Stonehouse, leaving on either side great swathes of open fell and hillside from which many streams run down to the river and to bridges across to take the closely accompanying road.

The farm buildings stand well back from the river, looking down on it and looking across the valley at each other; each has its little stream, arising from a nearby spring. The fine black lines on the large-scale maps are the stone walls which provide for each farm the essential 'closes' or low frontal fields for wintering stock, larger rear fields for growing cattlefood and household corn, and behind all, a slice of mountainside for grazing sheep and cattle. These stone enclosures may however not be older than about 1850, when land enclosure started in these parts, and the farmhouses and their outbuildings are today much modernised, though their outlines on the ground are probably much the same as in Thomas (VII)'s time.

As to people in the valley, we know from the wills of Thomas and his wife the names of their closest friends, whether relatives, trustees, witnesses, beneficiaries, debtors or creditors; those who were not Quakers were sufficiently well known in the church of Dent for the register to be able to tell us exactly where each lived in the 40 years which were to elapse between Thomas's marriage in 1672, and the sale of Blandsgill finally, in 1712.

Though Thomas called Blandsgill his 'mansion', it is today a stone-built house, map reference 741866, on the 725 ft. contour line, and facing south-east, some two hundred yards from the River Dee; in between are its considerable outbuildings which provided shelter for his beasts and very probably were also lived in by some of his family and helpers. On the ground floor of the 'mansion' was the 'forehouse' furnished (as we know from the wills) with cupboard, table, dresser, chairs, forms and stools, and a parlour apparently equipped with bedroom things. Above these was an upper room also furnished for sleeping, as was the separate loft which had a chest, a press, a bed and a spinning wheel. Water came from two springs on ·he 1,200 ft. level, feeding into a gill which passed the house and emptied into the river below. Fuel was turf, wood was scarce and the poor quality coal had to be brought from the Sedbergh fells by pack horse or sledge. Below the house was a five-acre meadow; behind the house a three-acre one, and behind that meadows of eight and another of nine acres, giving on to the

20.   Outbuildings, Blandsgill.

fell behind, where some seventy acres of rough grazing brought the total land of Blandsgill to a little short of a hundred acres.

Nearby, at Broadfield, was a considerably larger farmhouse, the home of Ann's parents the Haygarths, for the 29 years she had been alive; her father John having died when she was only eight years old, his place had been taken by her uncle Thomas and his wife Isabel (Holme), who had sons Matthew, aged 33 on Ann's wedding day, Richard (30) and William (26). William with his wife Elizabeth was later to move out to Crosshouse Farm (O.D. 727866) three-quarters of a mile nearer to Dent village. Ann's other uncle John lived a mile and a half in the opposite direction, at Hobsons (O.D. 760867). Between Broadfield and Blandsgill was a quite small farm, believed to have been called Perle, and consisting of little more than a barn with cattle below and a bedroom with a fireplace above; here lived one of the very large Fawcett family, Edward by name, destined to act as an appraiser of the Salkeld's property. But the Haygarths were a much bigger family in the Dent valley than that. At various times in this period we find John at Myregarth (728838), Thomas at Hackerill (743862), George at Westhouse (725858), another Thomas, at Kirkthwaite (now called Cowgill), William at Crosshouse (727866), John and his wife Jane at Fletchers (763867) and Lillegarth (765866), George and John his son at Cow Dub (767864), and John and his son-in-law Hodgson at Green Rigg (725868). Today, the only Haygarths listed in the Dent telephone directory as farmers are at Cowgill and at Flintergill; no doubt many of the above farms are still working, though in other hands.

After the Haygarths, perhaps the most important of Thomas Salkeld's friends were to be the three Mason brothers, Richard, Anthony and John, of whom Richard ranks as 'top' because in Thomas's will he was appointed a joint trustee and overseer, and was also a joint appraiser for the inventory. This Richard Mason, a Quaker, lived at Broadmire (745869) only a thousand yards to the north-east of Blandsgill, and about the same distance from Anthony's home at Mirehouse (754873). Though Thomas wouldn't know it, the Masons were to become increasingly important in the Dale, while the Haygarths were contracting in numbers, having in the period 1611 to 1669 only about half the baptisms per marriage of the Masons. [Today, the Cumbria telephone directory lists some 250 Masons, but only 17 Haygarths – and 29 Salkelds!]

Details of other friends and associates of Thomas and his wife Ann will become evident as our story develops. In those bleak hills and dales, far from shops (there *were* by now shops in Dent and in Kendal, and of course a Tuesday market in Dent) and with transport depending upon the health of one's horse, it would be hard to overestimate the importance of staunch and experienced friends and relatives, to one in Thomas's position. The ever-present perils of sickness, and of shortage of food, and the fear of foul weather for one's flock and beasts, let alone the loneliness of these great valleys, are essential components of our story. And although it brought further threats against mind and person, the knowledge that as a Quaker one was a member of a society of real friends would be most comforting whenever, as happened to Thomas and Ann, things began to go wrong.

Dent

Dent today is a pretty, cobbled village, with a handful of shops, an old church (St Andrew), a school and a small glass industry. Perhaps three- to four-hundred inhabitants, it is hard to realise that at one time it was larger than nearby Sedbergh.

Fortunately, the clerk who every Sunday recorded the week's baptisms, marriages and burials, decided in the years 1615 to about 1655 to add to the entry of names, a note of the occupation also.

There were several millers; there must have been other butchers, but the only one identified died in 1618. Tradesmen included five blacksmiths and four carpenters.

Shopkeepers included a glover, a hosier, a shoemaker, a shopkeeper and a hatter. There were also at least five tailors including George Mason, living in 1651. As for publicans, the only ones we know the names of are Edward Sidgwicke (living 1616), and of course our trusty friend and innkeeper James Hodgson who features in Thomas Salkeld's will.

The inhabitants of Dent and its dales were well known for their addiction to the gentle art of knitting, which was taught in special schools and practised day and night not only by the female inhabitants, but equally, it is stressed, by the men as they strode along. This would be a valuable extra source of revenue, once the products (generally socks and stockings) had been sold, and there was a big market for them every week at Kendal. In his 30-year sojourn at Blandsgill, ancestor Thomas (VII) Salkeld would have joined his friends in 'knitting evenings' over their peat fires, as the winds and snow blew round their houses, and the sheep, who had produced the essential raw material the previous June, huddled for shelter on the fells.

But with a few exceptions, those Dentdale families who produced the most children for baptism over the years 1611 to 1712 – that is, the 'Top Twenty' families – included the Linseys, the Hodgsons, the Willans (who are also in Deepdale), the Masons, the Capstacks, Haygarths, Sidgwicks, Burtons and Thistlethwaites.These were also the families with whom the Salkelds in their thirty-odd years' occupation of Blandsgill had most associations.

In Dentdale in this 100-year period are recorded 3,552 baptisms, excluding those for the years 1655 to 1659 for which the records are missing, as too they are for other odd years.

Of these 3,552 baptisms, some 427 can be identified as 'casuals', that is, single unexpected entries or entries with very infrequent repeats, or with a tiny total in random periods. If these 'casuals' are eliminated, 3,125 baptisms are left and these may reasonably be ascribed to genuine residents of Dentdale, and of other nearby dales, using Dent church; using, that is, the church throughout most of their lifetimes, although of course some will move in time, and so their children will be baptised elsewhere.

The number of the individual families who made up this 3,552 total, was only 148, and of these no less than 83 were 'casuals', leaving only 65 surnames as responsible for the 3,125 'regular' entries; 75 per cent. of these entries were from 20 families only, over the 101-year period. I have called these the 'Top Twenty' families, and their names are shown, in order of virility, in the attached table, in which the 101-year period has been sub-divided into more-or-less 15-year intervals.

It will be seen that the Mason family are consistently the leaders, and with the Hodgsons and the Burtons added, made up 25 per cent. of the total baptisms. The Haygarths are notably less virile and the Salkelds – like other Quakers – are completely absent.

These baptisms of course arise from inter-marriages, which had a profound effect on every aspect of dale life, in such an isolated community. For example, the Dent marriage

21.   Dent church and village.

registers show that in the short period of 1611 to 1669 (50 effective years), no less than 34 per cent. of the marriages were between members of these 'Top Twenty' families and a further 47 per cent. of the men, and 53 per cent. of the women, who married from 'Top Twenty' families, did so to an 'outsider', leaving only 18 per cent. of the weddings as having between completely 'Top Twenty' free families.

A detailed chart of all these marriages shows for example that the Haygarth girls ('Top Twenty') married Capstacks, Hodgsons, their own kin, Masons and Sidgwicks; the Haygarth men married Burtons, Craggs, their own kin, the Masons (no less than four times), Sidgwicks, Thistlethwaites, Willans and Wittons, from within the 'Top Twenty', as well as marrying outside it.

As for the Salkelds, Thomas (VII) married into the Capstacke and Haygarth families while in Dentdale, and though we know that some of his children married elsewhere, at least one (young Grace) and perhaps another (young Thomas) married into Dentdale families.

NUMBERS OF BAPTISMS, BY MAIN FAMILIES,
IN THE PERIOD 1611 to 1712, AT DENT

Rank	Surname	Years							Total	Cumulative percentage of
		1611 to 1624	1625 to 1639	1640 to 1653	1660 to 1675	1676 to 1690	1691 to 1705	(1706 to 1712)		
1	Mason	47	72	51	35	38	42	15	300	9.6
2	Hodgson	64	57	28	38	23	28	12	250	17.6
3	Burton	30	34	28	59	34	39	10	234	25.1
4	Capstacke	29	34	34	29	33	42	27	228	32.4
5	Thistlethwaite	29	35	14	24	46	30	6	184	38.3
6	Sidgwick	31	40	26	25	24	28	5	179	44.0
7	Willan	28	34	31	15	24	23	11	166	49.4
8	Linsey	24	20	15	5	15	6	9	94	52.3
9	Cragg	27	16	20	13	6	7	3	92	55.3
10	Haygarth	17	11	18	10	12	7	1	76	57.7
11	Pettie	7	8	13	14	4	9	4	59	59.6
12	Middleton	7	6	9	14	12	4	6	58	61.4
13	Trotter	15	14	13	5	1	6	2	56	63.2
14	Smorthwaite	15	7	6	5	11	8	4	56	65.0
15	Tennant	11	7	11	10	2	8	1	50	66.7
16	Sill	14	3	11	2	12	6	2	50	68.2
17	Witton	10	14	12	5	7	1	0	49	69.9
18	Greenwood	11	10	8	4	6	4	4	47	71.2
19	Fawcett	4	5	4	11	10	7	6	47	72.7
20	Greenbank	2	10	4	3	11	10	5	45	74.2
TOTALS		422	437	356	326	331	315	(133)	2320	74.2

'THE SALKELD CIRCLE' – DENTDALE

1. Birchentree Farm – Location O.S. 643862

Of special interest as the home of the Garthwaites, who later (in 1712) bought Thomas Salkeld's home, Blandsgill; the two buildings face each other across the Dee valley. Thomas Garthwaite, the purchaser of Blandsgill, was born 20 May 1684 and so was only 28 when he made the move; he then had a baby girl Elinor, and a boy Philip was on the way. His father's name was Philip, and his grandfather's was Thomas, a good example of eldest children being named after their grandparents. Young Thomas Garthwaite had four younger brothers, and a youngest sister (b. September 1710), so when he started his own family he had to seek fresh accommodation – hence the purchase of Blandsgill.

2. *Broadmire* 746849

Before Thomas Salkeld came to Dentdale, this house was occupied by James Hutton (in 1629) and later by James Burton (1636 and 1637) but it was then acquired by Richard Mason, a husbandman and a prominent Quaker whom Thomas Salkeld was to appoint a co-trustee under his will of 1694; Richard also helped Francis Lund to do the appraisal of Thomas Salkeld's things, in 1700 and, when Grace Salkeld died some two years later, she owed him for a bond of £6 6s. 0d., plus about 18s. 0d. cash.

3. *Cowgill* 756872

This area was originally called Kirkthwaite (as in Thomas Salkeld's will of 1694) but under the sponsorship of the famous Adam Sedgwick an Act of Parliament restored it to its original name of Cowgill. It was for long years the home of the Mason family; but which buildings housed which Mason it is not possible to tell from the Dent parish register.

4. *Clint* 7388859

Today there are two farms at Clint – West Clint, in a modest state of repair – and East Clint, which was I believe the home of my ancestor Grace Capstacke, second wife of Thomas (VII) Salkeld of Blandsgill. The owner, in the years 1648, 1651, 1665 was undoubtedly John Capstacke, according to the Dent parish register; a Grace was baptised at Dent on 17 December 1662 to a John Capstacke, and her birthdate fits in with the other Clint children.

I visited it in June 1978 and was shown over by Mrs. R. Timpson. It is a most attractive old farmhouse, looking across the valley to Broadfield and Blandsgill, with the date 1511 on what is now a hearth stone but may have been a lintel stone at some other time. On a wooden spice cupboard are the initials M^{B}E and the date 1727. One can so easily picture the widower Thomas Salkeld climbing up the hill path to the front door, where a young girl of 18, called Grace, watched him coming into her life. Had she said 'No', this book could not have been written, 300 years later!

5. *Green Rigg* 725868

This farm is not mentioned in the Dent church register but is in the will of John Haygarth, dated 11 March 1708, wherein he leaves it to his 'son-in-law's eldest daughter Agnes Hodgson'. It lies adjacent to High Chapel farm, and is of special interest as an example of the inter-marriage of Hodgson and Haygarth; it may be a clue to the mystery of how Thomas Salkeld had a 'relation' James Hodgson, as described in the will of 1694, for of course his first wife was a Haygarth.

6. *Haber Gill* 764868

This was the home of William Thistlethwaite, a leading Quaker whose signature testifies to his witnessing Ann Haygarth's will in October 1673; the home also of Richard

22.   Clint farmhouse.

Thistlethwaite in 1685. The following is taken from the Quaker booklet 'The birthplace of Quakerism' by Elfrida Vipont Foulds:[76]

> Beyond Dent are other houses where meetings were sometimes held; High Chapel [see above] to the north, and further on beyond Leayat, Stonehouse the home of the Masons who were amongst the first in the Dale to be convinced. It was at Stonehouse that George Fox's first meeting was held when he visited the Dale on his way to Sedbergh. Further on is Habergill, the home of William Thistlethwaite, whose initials are carved on the porch date 1700.

7. *High Croft* 730865

This small farm on the Dent side of Blandsgill is first mentioned in the Dent register as the home of William Hodgson whose daughter (no name given) was baptised on 17 January 1634; her mother may have been Diana Coate who married William Hodgson on 22 July 1632. The property is mentioned in Ann Haygarth's will of 24 October 1673 when she leaves it, with her other property of Blandsgill and the 'ffaws', to her husband Thomas Salkeld. In 1694, the year of Thomas's own will, there is mention of Richard Thistlethwaite of High Croft having a daughter Ann (or could be Agnes) baptised from that address, presumably a tenant of the Salkelds, for it is again mentioned in the deeds of sale of Blandsgill in 1712, and so presumably had been in Salkeld hands throughout that period.

8. Hobsons 760867

This farm, in the Cowgill area, is mentioned in Ann Haygarth's will as the home of John Haygarth, yeoman, and holder of the trust until her marriage. He was living there in 1638, 1647 and on 22 February when his wife was buried in 1648-9, but must not be confused with the John Haygarth who was having children at much the same period, at Broadfield.

9. Mirehouse 753874

This farm, in the Cowgill area, was the home of Anthony Mason, one of the appraisers of Grace Salkeld's inventory of 1702; in earlier years it had been home to Christopher Mason (1641), John Burton (1648) and Richard Hodgson (1637-41).

10. Tubhole 732860

This picturesque name was given to the farm a mile from Blandsgill but on the south side of the River Dee, which for many years was the home of various members of the Capstacke family – in addition to Clint. George lived there from 1644 to 1660; earlier, John and his wife Grace had lived together there in the years before 1629, when Grace was buried.

11. Westhouse farm 725858

A little to the west of Tubhole, this farm is recorded as the home of many more Masons, from George and John in 1625, to other Georges up to 1694, and a John in 1700. Haygarths were also there.

Chapter Ten

A Second Marriage at Blandsgill

When she married Thomas (VII) Salkeld, Ann Haygarth was just 29 years old – some three years older than he was. Fifteen months later, in that upstairs room at Blandsgill, their first child Francis (II) was born. He was baptised on 17 September 1673 as a Quaker child, at the Quaker Meeting House at Brigflatts, where his parents had married. It is interesting to note that he was given the Christian name of his grandfather, Francis (I) Salkeld (of Broadgate, then 27 years dead). But there were signs of trouble when, on 25 October, five weeks after the birth 'being weak in body', Ann made her will. Written obviously by a lawyer, full of rambling sentences and much repetition, it left everything to her husband whom she made her sole executor.

In the next few months however, Ann recovered; in March 1677 she presented Thomas with their second child John, who was baptised on 18 March of that year, being given the same Christian name as had his maternal grandfather Haygarth. But this time Ann did not recover from the birth, and her funeral took place 10 days after the baptism; she was buried at Brigflatts, by Quaker practice; there is of course no record of this in the Dent Church of England register.

Thomas now had to cope with an infant and a three-and-a-half year old boy, as well as his 100 acres. Help would be forthcoming from Ann's many relatives, and one imagines that perhaps her only sister Jane, then 33 years old, might, if still unmarried, and living possibly next door at Broadfield, be asked by Thomas to help. There is no record of his mother Isabell taking a hand, though quite possibly she did.

But Thomas was still quite a young man – only 31 on Ann's death – and it is not surprising that he decided to remarry. Her name was Grace, but there is no formal record of her surname. (Arguments for the various possibilities have been relegated to the following pages entitled 'Who was Grace?'.) Her surname was the unusual one of Capstack (the present spelling is 'Capstick') and she lived on the farm called 'Clint', immediately opposite Blandsgill, but across the valley. She may or may not have already been a Quaker, but as there is no record either at Dent or at Brigflatts of their marriage, we must be guided by the undoubted record in the Quaker registers of the birth of her first child Ann, baptised on 2 May 1682. One might therefore assume that Thomas and Grace married in 1680 or 1681, perhaps rather more than three years after Ann's death. I find it moving that Grace's first child was given the same name as had Thomas's first wife – Ann. Little Ann was not born at Blandsgill, but at Broadgate, the home of Thomas's mother Isabell. That this is so is very clearly shown in the Quaker Records held in the Friends' Meeting House in the Euston Road in London; without this tiny piece of information one would have assumed that the birth of Ann took place at Blandsgill, as indeed did that of all the other children born to Grace. The identification of Thomas (VII)'s mother and father – the latter from the Windermere registers – would not then have been possible, and this pedigree would have ended at Thomas, the joiner of Dent.

Who was Grace Salkeld?

We know that Grace was the Christian name of the second wife of Thomas (VII) Salkeld of Blandsgill, Dentdale, because his will of September 1694 says so. They must have been married in 1680 or 1681, because the Quaker records say that her first child Ann was born at Broadgate on 2 May 1682. She went on to have other children (at Dent) and her husband Thomas died in 1700; she was buried on 25 January 1701-2. As the mother of William (I) (baptised 8 December 1683) our direct Salkeld ancestor, one would like to know a little more about her.

On the assumption that Grace came from Dent or from nearby Sedbergh, their parish registers have been searched. Grace was not a very common name, and it is found that the only Graces to survive, or who did not marry others were, in our period: (1) Grace, daughter of Richard Smorthwaite, baptised Dent, 11 November 1632; (2) An un-named child, born to a John Capstacke of Clint, baptised 16 February 1648; (3) Grace, daughter of John Capstake, baptised 17 December 1662.

On dates, (1) can be eliminated as she would have been 50 years old at the birth of Ann Salkeld at Broadgate; by the same token, (2) would have been 44 years old at the birth of her last Salkeld child. This leaves only (3), who would have been $19\frac{1}{2}$ at the Broadgate birth, and only 39 at her own death. That her father, according to the Dent register, was a John Capstacke, and a John Capstacke *of Clint* had been having other children baptised at intervals both before and after the baptism of (3), suggests also that she was of the same stock, and born at Clint; but because the register does not in her case add the words 'of Clint', this must be regarded as a possibility, not a certainty. Similarly, that in later years her youngest daughter Grace Salkeld, was to marry on 1 May 1711 a smith called John Capstacke, is interesting but no more.

As to her parents, the dates of the baptisms of the various children shown in the register as of John and of Clint, indicate that they would have been married between 1646 and 1647, which is one of the periods for which Dent registers (sheets 90 and 91) are missing. Later, the registers show the burial, on 27 February 1697, of Grace Capstacke of Clint, a widow, and of John Capstacke of Clint, on 30 July 1694; on all scores, these two qualify as meeting the tests of parenthood of the Clint children.

At Broadgate the birth went well, and Grace with her infant Ann returned to Blandsgill; at the end of the following year she had her next child and eldest son William (I), baptised by the Quakers on 8 December 1683; William is a direct ancestor and his career, mostly in Suffolk, will be investigated in more detail in a later chapter.

Thomas made his will in 1694, six years before his death, and in it he names two more children – Isabell, a compliment to his own mother, and Grace, a compliment to his wife; but before their birth Grace presented him with another son, Thomas (VIII), baptised in 1691 as a Quaker. So the last two children must have been born between 1691 and the date of Thomas's will, although the Quaker records are silent on this. Unhappily little Isabell died in December 1701, at the tender age of eight, but little Grace grew up and in due course married a smith of Dent, with the interesting name of John Capstacke! Their marriage was on 1 May 1711 and their first child, James, was baptised in Dent church (so no longer a Quaker) on 16 March 1712. In leaving the Quakers perhaps young Grace was following the lead of her brother Thomas (VIII) who had started life as a Quaker, but is recorded in the Dent register as presenting himself in 1709 (at age 17) for baptism into the Church of England. By then, of course, their Quaker mother and their Quaker father had died.

We must now retrace our steps a little, to say more about father Thomas (VII) and what happened to him after his first wife Ann died – apart, that is, from marrying Grace and having more children. For example, did he follow his trade as a joiner? I think if he did, it was very rarely – for his inventory includes only 'small joiner tools . . . value 1s. 6d.' Allowing for the quite different values of money, there are plenty of records of other practising joiners having tools worth a pound or more. What transport had he? His inventory shows that in November 1700 there was at Blandsgill but 'one brown mare . . . £1 1s. 6d.' – a poor mount compared with his grandfather Richard (VI)'s horse at Winster, for instance. Thomas did have a bridle and saddle for it – shown separately with his 'apparell'. No doubt he would use them on the Tuesday market day to trot into Dent and visit his 'well beloved friend and relation' James Hodghson, 'Innholder' (so described in Thomas's will). He made this James Hodghson his joint trustee and overseer (with Richard Mason). It is an interesting conundrum, that Thomas the Quaker joiner should have a beloved friend and relation who was an innholder. Certainly Quakers do not approve of the use of spirituous liquors, and there is no doubt that Thomas was a convinced Quaker. In those days the word 'innholder' did not necessarily imply one who sold liquor, but rather one who entertained *travellers* in the inn (like an hotel or lodging house) [Chambers *Encyclopaedia* (1950) 7, p. 587], in which capacity there could not be any objection to Thomas paying his friend James a visit. But this does not explain how James was a 'relation' of Thomas's. I have examined some of the possibilities in the pages entitled 'James Hodghson, relation', for it is this sort of clue that confirms or otherwise the correctness of our story.

When Thomas made his will, on 7 September 1694, his eldest son (Ann's child) was within 10 days of becoming 21, which I think explains why he (Francis II) is not listed with the six 'younger children' at the foot of the first sheet; Thomas is clearly very concerned that these six shall not suffer by his death as regards education; he obviously regards the eldest boy Francis as sufficiently educated, and he is charging his trustees to take the same view. But when Grace dies, he wants things to alter – Francis is to have first refusal of the 100-acre estate, which must be put up for sale; each child including Francis to have an equal share of the proceeds. In the event, the property was not sold immediately on Grace's death (which occurred eight years after this will was written). Why this was we will explore later. I have included his will, and the short inventory of his goods and chattels made on 28 November 1700 by two of the Masons and Matthew Haygarth (probably the eldest son of Ann's Uncle Thomas of Broadfield) and another old friend Ffrancis Lund; the modest total value of the inventory – £19 10s. 8d. – is swamped by the item £33 0s. 0d. written underneath that total, and marked 'Debitary' which I take to mean a sum owing by, rather than a sum owed to, Thomas (VII). When we see the inventory of his wife Grace, made 18 months later and by quite different appraisers, we shall note that the debts had risen to over £40, against an inventory of a little less value than Thomas's.

Through this will we get another peep inside a home of our ancestors, to see what rooms it had; as already said, there was a fore-house, furnished rather like that at Rosgill, though much less grand in style; a parlour – used for sleeping also; an upper room, also for sleeping, and a loft with spinning wheel and wool and some more beds, and – though not mentioned other than by what it contained – a kitchen, and outhouses for the cattle which in total were rather more valuable than were the sheep. Of special interest in Thomas's inventory is the item '1 Bible with other small books' (not mentioned in Grace's list), because books were rarely met with in homes at yeoman and lower level. No doubt many of his literate Quaker friends were responsible, and we note also that Thomas signed his will with his full surname.

Rather more than a year before Ann's death something very dramatic occurred. Thomas and two of his friends were sent to prison by the Ecclesiastical Court for failing to pay, to the vicar of St Andrews, Sedbergh – one Leonard Barton – the 1½d. per year demanded as an Easter Offering. This was on 8 February 1676, the writ being one of *Excommunicato Capiende*; the 'friends' who went to prison with him were Thomas Wilkins and Francis Lund – already mentioned as later to be one of the appraisers of Thomas's estate. Francis Lund had married Mabel Hodgson of Sedbergh on 29 May 1673 – three years before this committal – and had quite a family of youngsters baptised at Dent, although a Quaker himself. There is no record of how long they were in gaol, but the vicar, who for some years had had quite a 'hate' on about Quakers, died shortly afterwards.

Francis Lund later joined Thomas in a 'round-robin', signed by 33 Dent Quakers on 6 June 1681, pleading for their own Dent Monthly Meeting, instead of being subservient to the Sedbergh Meeting, to which the appeal was addressed. At first Sedbergh said 'No', referring the matter to the more senior Quarterly Meeting, on the grounds that they doubted whether Dent was to be trusted to maintain the required levels of 'Quakery'. But it is apparent that in due course the request was granted, for years later (in 1706) there was a monthly meeting held at Dent – at the Loneing, a now lost Meeting place and Quaker burial ground, where, by then, Thomas and his second son John lay buried. I copied the list of Dent Quaker signatories (see note '33 Quakers of Dent') and the reader will note some familiar names both on it, and missing from it; the list of ladies follows after that of the men, but many of the surnames in each list correspond – for example, Francis and his wife Mabel Lund. Obviously Ann Salkeld did not sign it (being dead). Thomas did, but there are no Haygarth signatures. And, in view of my belief that Grace the second wife of Thomas was a Capstacke before her marriage, it is interesting to see that a James and a Mary Capstacke signed the list; not her parents, but possibly an uncle and an aunt by marriage. Because of the absence of Grace's signature, it may be that by this date – 6 June 1681 – she had not yet become a Quaker, and even possible that she had not yet married Thomas, although their first child was born on 2 May of the following year, at Broadgate, as we know.

Thomas died just six years after making his will, and in it are none of the usual references to 'being sick and weak in body' etc. – probably because, as suggested earlier, he was making it with his eldest son's approach to majority in mind. Thomas was buried on 25 September 1700, in the Loneing, and his inventory was completed a month later. Grace then took over, under the guidance and advice of the joint trustees, Richard Mason of Broadmire and Thomas's 'beloved friend and relation, James Hodghson, the Innkeeper of Dent'.

James Hodghson, 'Relation'

We can safely assume that, at the date of Thomas's will, to be 'eligible' as a trustee James must have been at least twenty-five years old, and as Thomas himself was only

48 he would be unlikely to choose, as one who was to take responsibility for a considerable family, someone older than his dying self – so we can say that James would be under fifty; he was therefore born within the period 1640 to 1670. A search of the Quaker Records in London shows no James Hodghson buried as a Quaker in the Westmorland burial register for the whole period 1567 to 1755.

Of the James Hodghsons baptised at Dent between 1640 and 1670, there are only two, one of whom is buried two months later. The other, baptised 11 December 1655, is the son of Willyam Hodghson of Haycote. This birthdate would make James 39 when Thomas appointed him his joint trustee, Thomas himself then being forty-eight. When Thomas Salkeld made his will, in September 1694, this trustee already had two little boys of his own; their names were William and Nicholas. I have searched the archives at Preston for a will or inventory to confirm this, but none can be found.

This does nothing to explain just how James is a 'relation' of our Thomas Salkeld the joiner of Dent. An obvious answer would be that Thomas's own mother was an Isabell Hodghson before her marriage, and the daughter of Willyam of Haycote. This very convenient solution unfortunately cannot be supported by facts, for the only William Hodghson who had a daughter Isabell in this period, in Dentdale, did so in October 1627, some twenty-eight years before the baptism of James. We know that Thomas's own mother lived 26 miles away from Dentdale, at Broadgate in Hugill near Windermere, and that he took his second wife Grace to have her first child there – and in short, that his mother was a Braithwaite; so that does not explain how James Hodghson was a 'relation' of Thomas's.

So I have not yet been able to answer the question 'how does James Hodghson become a "relation" of Thomas Salkeld?'.

Thirty-Three Quakers of Dent

In June 1978 Mr. David Butler, Secretary of the Kendal Society of Friends, kindly let me see the minute book of the Sedbergh Men's Monthly Meeting[74] which covered the years 1676 to 1713; the Meetings had been held at Anthony Robinson's house at Brigflatts, or at James Thompson's at Hallbanke.

These showed that 'in the 6th month of 1681' a 'round-robin' had been signed by 33 of the Dent Quakers, addressed to the Sedbergh Monthly Meeting, requesting that Dent be allowed to hold its own Meetings – a request not initially approved but later agreed. It is interesting to record the names of the Dent Quakers who signed the 'round-robin', as part of our study of Thomas Salkeld's circle there.

The handwriting throughout appears to be all one person's, as was the common practice in keeping minutes. The list, exactly in the layout given, is:

James Greenwood	Thomas Salkeld	Mabel Lund
Jno Hugginson	Rich Simpson	Mabel Simpson
Ric Harrison	Tho Simpson	Mary Capstacke
John Hugill	Gilbert Lund	Dorothy Winster
John Mason	Alex Hebblethwaite	Doro Hodshon
Francis Lund	George Mason	Elizabeth Wilkinson
Robert Lund	Tho Atkinson	Emma Dorrosin
James Capstacke	Chas Coupland	Mary Hugginson
William Mason	Elizabeth Greenwood	Isabel Simpson
James Burton	Margaret Hugginson	Isabel Hodgson
John Burton	Mabel Harrison	Mabel Atkinson

It will be noticed that the women's names follow the men's, but that, if they are regrouped into families, there are four Lunds and four Simpsons, three Masons and three Hugginsons, two each of Greenwoods, Harrisons, Capstackes, Burtons, Atkinsons and Hodgsons, and seven single names. Notable absentees are the Haygarths, and the John Capstackes of Clint, and their daughter Grace, second wife of Thomas Salkeld – whose own name heads the second column of men's names, however.

Later, there was a Quaker Meeting House established at Lea Yeat (gate) just off the main road (at O.D. 761869), and is so marked on the large-scale maps. Lea Yeat is also mentioned as the address of the Sidgwick family in 1648, and of the Burton family in 1682 – two of whom signed the 'round-robin'.

(For the avoidance of doubt, it perhaps should be pointed out here that John the second son of Thomas Salkeld was buried in the Loneing on 22 October 1697, and so cannot be the John referred to in another of these Sedbergh minutes [26 February 1698] giving him the Meeting's authority to preach abroad including Ireland. That Meeting was also held at Anthony Robinson's house at Brigflatts, but 17 years after the 'round-robin' minute.)

A Key Will

WILL OF THOMAS SALKELD OF DENT NEAR SEDBERGH, WEST YORKSHIRE (1694)
(Obtained not from Carlisle but from *Preston* Record Office). He died 25 September 1700.

In the name of God amen the Seventh day of September in the Sixth year of the reign of our most gracious Sovereign Lord and Lady William and Mary by the Grace of God, of England, Scotland, France and Ireland, King and Queen, Defenders of the Faith Anno Dom., 1694, I, Thomas Salkeld of Blandsgill in Kirthwaite in Dent in the County of York, joiner, calling to mind the uncertainty of this mortal and transitory life and that all flesh must return to dust when it shall please Almighty God: and being fully mindful of the settling and disposing of all such my Estate both real and personal which it hath pleased Almighty God far above demerit to bestow upon me, I do therefore hereby make, ordain and declare this my last Will and Testament in manner and form following, revoking and by these presents disanulling, all former and other Will and Wills, Testament and Testaments whatsoever heretofore by me published or declared either by word or writing. And first and principally I commit my soul to the mercy of Almighty God hoping through the merit, death and passion of my Saviour Jesus Christ to have full and free pardon and forgiveness of all my sins and to merit eternal life. My body I commit to the earth to be decently buried at the discretion of Grace my kind and loving wife whom I do hereby nominate and appoint, ordain and make sole Executrix of this my last Will and Testament. And I do likewise hereby nominate and appoint ordain and make my trusty and well beloved friend and relation James Hodghson of the town of Dent in the County of York aforesaid, Innholder, and Richard Mason of Broadmire [746849] in Kirthwaite in Dent aforesaid in the County of York aforesaid, Husbandman, Trustees and Overseers of this my last Will and Testament, hoping that they my said Trustees and Relations will see to the due performance and Execution of this my last Will and Testament as my faith and trust is in them. And as touching the disposition of such Personal and Real Estate wherewithal it hath pleased Almighty God to bestow upon me, I do hereby give, bequeath and devise the same as followeth: first, I do hereby give, bequeath and devise – All my said personal Estate, goods and chattels and Cattle and implements of household whatsoever, moveables and immoveables to Grace my said wife and her assigns – Nevertheless to and for such use and uses intents and purposes as are hereinafter expressed. That is to say that the said Grace my said wife shall with and out of my said personal Estate in such manner as she shall think fit, pay my funeral expenses and all my just debts, and shall therewithall and thereout educate my younger children John, William (I), Thomas, Anne,

Isabel and Grace Salkeld and others of my younger children which hereafter may be borne till they shall severally and successively attain the age of twenty one years or be married. Then the remainder of my said personal Estate I give, devise and bequeath to the said Grace my said wife, her Executors, Administrators, and Assigns forever, if she continues to live singly and die in pure widowhood. But if the said Grace my wife shall fortune to marry again or miscarry, that then, and in such case and immediately from and after such her marriage or miscarriage I give and devise the remainder of my said personal Estate to my said younger children, their heirs and assigns for ever and the moneys arising thereby and therefrom to be by them, my said Trustees and Overseers and their heirs and the surviving of his and their heirs, equally divided amongst them my said younger children, and put to interest for the respective uses of them, their heirs and assigns forever. And if the said Grace my said wife to whom I hereby grant the tuition of all my children shall fortune to die before they or any of them my said children shall be of lawful age to select and choose their own Guardians, that then my said Trustees and Overseers, their Executors and assigns shall have the Tuition of my said younger children till they shall be of lawful age to select and choose their own Guardians. And whereas I the said Thomas Salkeld am possessed in fee simple or some other good Estate or inheritance of and in one messuage and Tenement with the appurtenances called and known by the name of Blandsgill House situate in Kirthwaite in Kent aforesaid in the County of York aforesaid and also of and in several other closes and parcels of land with their respective appurtenances commonly called and known by the name of the ffawes and High Croft, which said messuage and Tenement and closes aforesaid with their respective appurtenances were late the only and proper inheritance of Anne Haigarth my late wife deceased when a singlewoman which said Anne my late wife deceased when under coverture pursuant to a certain deed of feofment and contract made by her before our marriage bearing date the fifth day of August in the twenty fourth year of the Reign of our late Sovereign Lord Charles the second and Anno Dom. 1672. And by her last will and Testament made with my consent pursuant to the said deed bearing date the third day of October in the Twenty fifth year of the Reign of our late said Sovereign, Charles the second and Anno Dom. 1673, did give, grant, devise and bequeath the said messuage and Tenement and closes aforesaid with their respective appurtenances to me the said Thomas Salkeld my heirs and assigns for over as by the same Deed and Will, recorded, may more at large appear. Now it is my will and mind and so hereby declared to be and I do hereby give, grant, devise and bequeath the said messuage and Tenement called Blandsgill House aforesaid with all houses and edifices thereon standing and all the rights, privileges, hereditaments and appurtenances whatsoever thereunto belonging or therewithal at any time heretofore usually enjoyed with the same, together also with the closes, inclosures or parcels of land aforesaid called the ffawes and High Croft with their respective appurtenances, unto them the said James Hodghson and Richard Mason (my said Trustee and Overseers), their heirs and assigns for ever. Nevertheless upon such special Trusts and confidences and under and upon such limitations, intents and uses as are hereinafter expressed, and declared, and to and for no other use or uses, intent or purpose whatsoever. That is to say that they the said James Hodghson and Richard Mason and their heirs and the survivors of his and their heirs shall suffer and grant the said keld my said wife to live in the mansion house at Blandsgill aforesaid and to receive and take the whole profits of the messuage and Tenements and closes aforesaid during such time as she continueth to live single and in pure widowhood and no longer, which said profits of the messuage and closes aforesaid shall by her the said Grace my said wife be converted towards the maintenance of herself and education of my younger children in their minorities. And the surplussage if any be after such maintenance and education, shall be yearly at the discretion of my said Trustees, equally divided amongst these my said younger children and put to interest for their respective uses. And it is my will and mind that immediately from and after the death and decease or marriage again or miscarriage of the said Grace my said wife which shall first happen, that then the said James Hodghson and Richard Mason and their heirs or the survivors of his and their heirs, shall sell and convey the said messuages and Tenements called Blandsgill House with the appurtenances and the closes and parcels of land called the ffawes and High Croft aforesaid with their respective appurtenances to such person or persons as shall be disposed to buy the same and the moneys which shall arise by the sale and conveyance thereof shall by them my said Trustees and Overseers and their heirs and the survivors of his and their heirs be equally divided amongst all my children the living, share and share alike, beginning with Francis my eldest son and so to

John, William (I), Thomas, Anne, Isabell and Grace Salkeld and an equal share and proportion to children hereafter to be born on the body of the said Grace my said wife. And that my said Trustees and Overseers shall after such division put forth my said children's respective parts and portions of the said moneys to interest to and for the only and respective use and uses of them my said children, their heirs, Executors, and Assigns for ever and to and for no other use, intent or purpose whatsoever. And it is my will and mind that Francis Salkeld my eldest son shall have the first refusal of or nay say in the purchasing the messuage and Tenements aforesaid and the closes aforesaid. And I do hereby give and bequeath unto my said Trustees and to each of them the sum of Ten shillings of lawful English money to be paid them within one month after the probate of this my last Will and Testament. In witness whereof I have hereunto set my hand and published and declared this my last Will and Testament.

The above was followed by:

September the 7 1694 then
Sealed and signed published and declared by the within named
Thomas Salkeld to be his last will and testament in the presence of Nicholas Crowdson, his mark
William Garnet
George Yeates
– Foster

but the will was signed by Thomas Salkeld.

Inventory of Thomas (VII) (28 November 1700)

A true and perfect Inventory of all the goods Rights and Chattells belonging to Thomas (VII) Salkeld of Blandsgill in Kirthwayte in Dent in the County of Yorke, deceased, made and Apprized by John Mason, Richard Mason, Mathew Haygarth, Ffancis Lund the 28 day of November 1700.

	£	s	d
Money in his own custody and apparell with bridle and saddle	2.	5.	0
In the forehouse, cupboard & table & Dresser, with chairs, formes, stooles and cushions	1.	7.	2
Brass Pewter Earthen vessels & other things, with barell and all the rest of wooden vessell		10.	4
Dresser		5.	2
In the Parlour, Chest with some small boxes and 3 Bedstocks, Buffett and 1 Almry		10.	4
In the Upper room 2 Bedstocks, Chest with Bedding		10.	8
In the Loft, Chest with some more Bedding in the Parlour		14.	6
Wheel and Cards with a small parcel of wool and Press		6.	9
Meale Butter Cheese and Beef		8.	6
Girdle Brandreth Rackencrook & Tongs with other small iron stuff		2.	2
Posts and Hay	2.	10.	0
Carts Wheels Harrow Plough Cranes with other Husbandry gear		19.	0
Some small joiner tools		1.	6
In Beasts	4.	6.	8
1 Brown Mare	1.	1.	6
Sheep	3.	0.	4
1 Bible with other small books		2.	1
Some small groceries		9.	0
	£19.	10.	8
	£33.	0.	0

John Mason
Richard Mason
Math Haygarth appraisers
Ffancis Lund

Chapter Eleven

Last Days at Blandsgill

Shortly before Thomas (VII)'s death, their second son John died, and was buried at the Loneing, Dent, on 22 October 1697. In many parts of Cumbria this particular year saw great devastation due, it is said, to the Plague, and probably also to famine, but we do not know whether these were in any way responsible for John's early death at the age of 20 – certainly there is no evidence that Blandsgill was short of essential foods at that time; but it may have been.

Thomas's death in September 1700 left his wife Grace with an eldest (step-son) Francis (II), aged then 27, an eldest daughter Anne then 18, her (own eldest) son William (I) (rising 17), young Thomas (VIII) aged nine, and two little girls, Isabel aged perhaps six, and little Grace; all at that stage in their lives were Quakers. Whereas their father Thomas had envisaged that Francis would take charge of the 'estate' and support Grace and the children from it, we have to remember that as a going concern the farm was in considerable debt to local friends, though the freehold was their own. It would be a struggle to carry on.

At the Restoration, King Charles II had granted the manor of Dent with all its rights to Sir Allen Apsley, who had faithfully attended the king in his exile. In 1670 Sir Allen sold the manor to Richard Trotter of High Hall, and others, in trust for the tenants in general, and the land now became freehold. The letters of Administration granted to Ann Salkeld on her mother Grace's death were signed by no less a notary public than this Richard Trotter, and by a second notary public John Capstack. Thomas's will of 1694 shows that the original inheritor of these estates had been Ann Haygarth, who in her own will had them made over to her husband Thomas, so that on Grace's death there was a substantial capital sum tied up which under his will could only be released by the sale of the property. If Francis the eldest son then wished to exercise his rights under the will to buy Blandsgill back, he would presumably have to do this by raising some sort of mortgage amongst his friends. Some of these friends, as is clear from Grace's inventory of 1702, had already put up capital; £10 from Thomas Inman, about £7 from the Masons, and smaller sums from another six of them; a small total certainly compared with the market value of Blandsgill including the other small properties mentioned in Thomas's will (and no doubt leased and paying the Salkelds a small rent). In the event, Blandsgill was sold to a Thomas Garthwaite, of Birchentree farm, opposite and across the River Dee, but that was not for another 10 years.

I think it likely that Francis did what he could to support the family, but soon after Grace's death he decided to marry – a Quaker marriage, on 12 March 1703. His bride was Judith, eldest daughter of William Satterthwaite, an ironmonger of Coulthouse in Lancashire. I suppose there was just not room enough for them all at Blandsgill, for shortly after the wedding Francis and Judith moved from Dent right away to the east coast of Yorkshire – to Whitby – where the Quaker records (in London) say that he served for over fifty years as local Quaker secretary, and died there. Francis was buried on 3 August 1754, so to do all this he must have moved to Whitby in about 1703 – his wedding year. He had at least five children, only two of whom, Mary (b. 13 May 1704) and Ann (b. 21 June 1709), appear to have reached their twenties, although William (b. 26 October 1707) lived long enough to be apprenticed, for £50, in 1723, to an apothecary Zach Routh of St Saviours, Southwark; he died in London, in March 1728, and was buried on 14 March (Quaker Records). The letters of Administration granted to young Anne Salkeld – mentioned previously – make her, and not her elder brother Francis, the administrator, though he signs as well. Being away in Whitby, one can understand why he left this job to his sister.

Whether they could not find a satisfactory buyer, or because they wanted with the help of friends or relatives to 'have a go' themselves, the fact remains that, contrary to their father's will, the children did not sell the property until 1712 – 10 years after their mother's death. Although the physically nearest 'in-laws' were then the Haygarths at Broadfield, both of the children of the late Ann Salkeld had now left the scene to young Anne, the eldest grand-daughter of the late John Capstack of Clint farm. Emotionally perhaps young Anne might, though her own grandparents were now dead, still have looked to Clint farm, across the River Dee, for help. By her side was her brother William (I) (our ancestor who did not marry until 4 April 1707). I do not know whether William stayed for a few years after his mother's death, at Blandsgill, but it is certain that his bride was Elizabeth Riggs, daughter of Edward Riggs, a baker and a Quaker, of far-away Woodbridge in Suffolk, so maybe he packed up his things and moved to Suffolk before his wedding day in April 1707. We are sure that Anne's remaining brother Thomas (VIII) stayed on in Dent, because in 1709, at the age of 17, he applied to the Vicar to be baptised into the Church of England; and that this was done is shown in the parish register. Presumably the lad was living still at Blandsgill, therefore, in 1709. Perhaps his 'intended' had decided not to become a Quaker, and had persuaded Thomas to enter the Church of England.

These documents, signed by young Anne and her brother Francis, show that both wrote a good firm hand, no doubt due to their attendance at Dent Grammar School. This school dated from the first year of the reign of James I (1603), who had conferred on it a charter after it had been built and endowed by the dalesmen.

What happened to young Anne Salkeld, after discharging her duties as Administrator of her mother Grace's estate? I have found a Quaker record of the marriage of Anne Salkeld of Dent, daughter of Thomas, deceased, born, as she was, in the year 1682; on 2 November 1716 she married a Joseph Linskill, *at Whitby*, but I have no further information of them. Her name does not appear in the sale document of Blandsgill dated 11 March 1712, registered on the 24 March 'at ten in the forenoon', as follows:

Indentures of Lease and Release the Lease bearing date the Eleventh and the Release the Twelfth day of March Anno Dom 1712 made between Francis Salkeld of the town of Whitby in the County of Yorkshire schoolmaster on the one part and Thomas Garthwaite of Birchintree in Kirthwaite in Dent in the said County of York yeoman on the other part whereby the said Francis Salkeld doth absolutely grant release and confirm unto the said Thomas Garthwaite his heirs and assigns for ever all that his messuage and tenement with appurtenances [sic] called Blandsgill house situate and lying and being in Kirthwaite in the said Dent in the said County of York and also two severall closes there called ffawes and Highcroft together with all and singular houses edifices buildings barns stables orchards gardens meadows closes pastures feedings hereditaments priviledges and

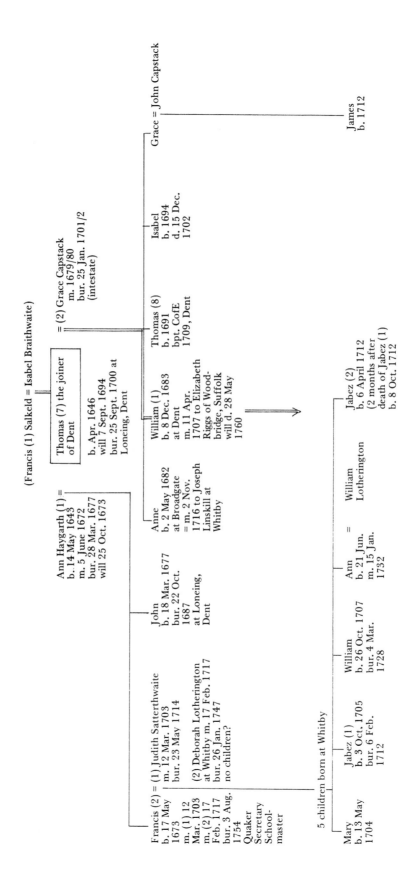

(Francis (1) Salkeld = Isabel Braithwaite)

Thomas (7) the joiner
of Dent

b. Apr. 1646
will 7 Sept. 1694
bur. 25 Sept. 1700 at
Loneing, Dent

= (2) Grace Capstack
m. 1679/80
bur. 25 Jan. 1701/2
(intestate)

Ann Haygarth (1) =
b. 14 May 1643
m. 5 June 1672
bur. 28 Mar. 1677
will 25 Oct. 1673

Grace = John Capstack

James
b. 1712

Isabel
b. 1694
d. 15 Dec.
1702

Thomas (8)
b. 1691
bpt. CofE
1709, Dent

William (1)
b. 8 Dec. 1683
at Dent
m. 11 Apr.
1707 to Elizabeth
Riggs of Wood-
bridge, Suffolk
will d. 28 May
1760

Anne
b. 2 May 1682
at Broadgate
= m. 2 Nov.
1716 to Joseph
Linskill at
Whitby

John
b. 18 Mar. 1677
bur. 22 Oct.
1687
at Loneing,
Dent

Francis (2) = (1) Judith Satterthwaite
b. 17 May   m. 12 Mar. 1703
1673   bur. 23 May 1714
m. (1) 12
Mar. 1703   (2) Deborah Lotherington
m. (2) 17   at Whitby m. 17 Feb. 1717
Feb. 1717   bur. 26 Jan. 1747
bur. 3 Aug.   no children?
1754
Quaker
Secretary
School-
master

5 children born at Whitby

Jabez (2)
b. 6 April 1712
(2 months after
death of Jabez (1)
b. 8 Oct. 1712

Ann   =   William
b. 21 Jun.   Lotherington
m. 15 Jan.
1732

William
b. 26 Oct. 1707
bur. 4 Mar.
1728

Jabez (1)
b. 3 Oct. 1705
bur. 6 Feb.
1712

Mary
b. 13 May
1704

appurtenances whatsoever thereunto belonging which said Indentures are witnessed by Thomas Currer of Sedbergh in the said County of York Attorney at law Henry Holm of the said Sedbergh yeoman and Richard Tennant of the said Dent yeoman sealed and signed in the presence of us Thos. Currer Richard Tennant (jurat) Ffrancis Salkeld.

A further search of Supplementary Records at the Friends' Meeting House, Euston Road in March 1980 revealed that[72,73] Anne's brother Francis, having had a daughter Mary born 13 May 1704, and a son Jabez (I) on 3 October 1705, lost that boy on 6 February 1712 but named his *fifth* child, born 6 April 1712, Jabez, though only two months later, and this infant then died and was buried 8 October 1712. Between these two Jabez there was William born 26 October 1707 who died aged 21 on 14 March 1728, and 'young' Ann born 21 June 1709 who later married William Lotherington on 15 January 1732. But their mother Judith died and was buried on 23 May 1714.

After Judith's death, her husband Francis remarried, his second wife being Deborah Lotherington, on 17 February 1717 and she died 26 January 1747. No record of any children of the second marriage survives, but it does look as though young Ann's husband (Lotherington) might have been related to Francis' second wife Lotherington.

Hence no *male* Salkelds seem to have survived in Whitby after 1728.

[Inventory – Grace Salkeld]
[dated 30 March 1702]

A True and perfect Inventory of all and Singular the Goods, Chattels Household Stuff Husbandry Gear and Rights whatsoever which were or did belong unto Grace Salkeld widow late of Blandsgill in Kirthwaite (now 'Cowgill') in Dent in the County of York, deceased, made and apprized the 30 March 1702 by *Anthony Mason* of Miershouse (Mirehouse 753873), Nicholas Crowdson of Bark, *William Thisthethwaite of Havergill* (Haber Gill House 765868) and Edward Fawcett of Perle-hill all in Dent aforesaid.

Two Saddles & Pillion & a Bridle	0.	3.	0
Brass and Pewter	1.	0.	8
Earthen Pots, Cups and Glasses		2.	0
Wood Vessells		6.	8
Chairs and Stools and Forms		8.	0
Tables		6.	8
Chests & Boxes		11.	0
A Wheel Hose Press, Basketts & other odd things		5.	0
A Presser & two old Omeries		13.	4
One little Cupboard		6.	8
Boords Glass Case and other odd things		2.	6
Girdle brandritts and other iron things		8.	0
Bedstocks		6.	6
Bedding	1.	2.	6
Milk basins and cushions		3.	0
A Lantern Saw and other odd things		2.	3
Sacks Bags and Sieves		3.	0
Plow and Plow gear		6.	8
Cartwheels and Cargear		10.	2
Two Barrows 2 Pitchforks and other odd things		3.	0
Ladders Bands and other odd things		1.	4
Hay		3.	6
Black cattell (? for Scotland)	7.	0.	0
A Mare	3.	0.	0
	17.	15.	5

Noverint universi per presentes Nos Annam Salkeld Spinster...
...Francis Salkeld...

The Condition of this Obligation is such that if the above bounden Ann Salkeld Administratrix of all and singular y goods chattells and credits of Grace Salkeld her Lat: Mother late of Dent deceased doe make or cause to be made a true and perfect Inventory of all and singular the goods chattells and credits of the said deceased which have or shall come to the hands possession or knowledge of her the said Administratrix or into the hands and possession of any person or persons for her and the same soe made doe exhibit or cause to be exhibited into the Registry of the said Administracon kept at Kendal at or before the Thirty day of August next ensuing And the same goods chattells and credits and all other the goods chattells credits of the said deceased at the time of her death which at any time after shall come to the hands or possession of the said Administratrix or into the hands or possession of any other person or persons for her doe well and truly Administer according to Law or further doe make or cause to be made a true and Just accompt of her sd Administracon at or before the Thirty day of March next ensuing and all the rest and residue of the said goods chattells and credits wch shall bee found remaining upon the said Administracon accompt the same being first examined and allowed of by the Judge or Judges for the time being of the said Court shall deliver and pay unto such person or persons respectively as the said Judge or Judges by his or their order or sentence pursuant to the true intent and meaning of a late Act of Parliament made in the two and twentieth and three and twentieth years of y reigne of our late Soveraigne Lord King Charles the Second Intituled ane Act for y better settling of Intestates Estate) shall limitt and appoint And if it shall hereafter appeare that any last will and Testament was made by the said deceased and the Executor or Executors therein named doe exhibit the same into the said Court makeing request to have it allowed and approved accordingly if the said Administratrix above bounden being thereunto required doe render and deliver the sd lrae of Acton (approbation of such testament being first had and made) in the said Court Then this Obligacon to be void and of none effect or else to remaine in full force and vertue

Sealed and delivered
in the presence of

Rich: Trotter
no: ij Subri
Jo: Tunstack
no: ij Subci

Anne Salkeld

Francis Lund

Francis Salkeld

Apprizors	*William Thistlethwaite*			
	Anthony Mason			
	Edward Fawcett			
	Nicholas Crowdson			
Debts owing by Grace Salkeld deceased		10.	10.	0
Upon Bond to Thomas Inman				
Upon Bond to *Richard Mason*		6.	6.	0
Upon Bond to John Brown		6.	6.	0
Book Debts to Bryer		4.	6.	4
To Godsayle		3.	0.	$6\frac{1}{4}$
To Hutton		2.	18.	0
To Inman		3.	2.	$2\frac{1}{2}$
To Thomas Dawson		1.	2.	0
To Richard Baynes (tho' he hath nothing to shew for it)		2.	0.	0
To *Richard Mason* about			18.	0
		40.	9.	$0\frac{3}{4}$

The obligation to execute the provisions of the administrator rest with
  Ann Salkeld (Grace's daughter)
  Francis Lund (not known)
  Francis Salkeld (Thomas Salkeld's eldest son by his previous wife.)

Information on the names in italics is from the booklet *The birthplace of Quakerism. A handbook for the 1652 Country* by Elfrida Vipont Foulds, from Friends House, Euston Road, London NW1, which mentions them as eminent Quakers – 'Stonehouse the home of the Masons, who were amongst the first in the Dale to be convinced . . . it was at Stonehouse that George Fox's first meeting was held . . . further on is Harbergill the home of William Thistlethwaite whose initials are carved over the porch, with the date 1700' – (just two years before they made Grace's inventory!).

Chapter Twelve

Woodbridge

Woodbridge is a small inland port, some ten miles up the River Deben from the sea, and about seven miles east of Ipswich. During the reign of Elizabeth I it prospered; local industries such as weaving, sailcloth manufacture, ropemaking and the manufacture of salt were outshone by the wool trade; port facilities were expanded and the excellent supply of oak from nearby woods stimulated both the timber trade to London, and the building of boats at Woodbridge; a Custom House was built in 1589 and between 1625 and 1638 11 large merchant vessels were constructed. Shipping however became increasingly hazardous and expensive, due both to the growth of piracy, and the insatiable demands of the Treasury for ship money which at one time (in 1627) the residents simply refused to pay.[77]

From 1630 to the end of the century some fifteen men-of-war were launched at Woodbridge, every piece of wood being hand-sawn, and so demands for labour were high; but by the end of the century the only shipyard left was at Lime Kiln yard, between the river and the main road known as the Thoroughfare, the timber being stored at the top end of the yard and the ships being built where the Limekiln Road houses now stand. The Woodbridge yards have built ships to defeat the Dutch off Southwold in 1656, to provide many tons of Suffolk cheese for the Army in Scotland, and, although the dock which had seen the construction of the 663-ton *Kingfisher* in 1730, silted up, and was eventually filled in, to continue to build ships for the coastal trade; in 1865, 699 commercial vessels sailed up the Deben to Woodbridge with 37,200 tons of coal, corn, flour and malt arriving or to be cleared for London.

It is against this background that the foundation, in 1662, of Woodbridge Free School is to be viewed, one of the sources of capital and income being an endowment by Dorothy Seckford (wife of a wealthy lawyer) and others. This may have been the school at which our ancestor William (I) was a one-time master, in the period of his life in Woodbridge which started with his wedding in 1707 and ended with his death in 1760. Only 14 years after his death the local churchwardens were advertising – again – for staff for the school, the following appearing on 3 January 1774:

> A master of the Free Grammar School at Woodbridge in Suffolk the mastership of which is now vacant:
> The appointment to the Master is an annual stipend of upwards of thirty pounds a year together with a large house and garden very commodious for the reception of boarders and other advantages, for which the Master is required to instruct ten boys gratis in writing and Arithmetic and in the Learned Languages if required by the parents.
> Woodbridge is a flourishing trading town and particularly well situated for the reaising of a large boarding school. Any gentleman well qualified and properly recommended who shall be desirous of offering himself as a candidate is desired to make immediate application to the churchwardens of Woodbridge of which further Particulars relative to the School may be had. A master will be chosen in a few weeks. Leon Julian and James Hammond Churchwardens.

It is unlikely that earlier occupants of the position had any substantially better conditions than those described above.

Following the war with France, in 1803, extensive barracks were built at the top of Drybridge Hill, covering 50 acres and linked in with the Martello tower near Bawdsey. It housed 5,000 soldiers including 700 cavalry and their horses, and by 1811 there were also some 650 camp-followers. For the officers and their families houses of good quality were built or adapted along Cumberland Street – so called after the Prince Regent's ducal brother who commanded troops here for a while. When the soldiers departed in 1815 the barracks were pulled down, with great rejoicing, but the improved houses in Cumberland Street and on Market Hill remain. In 1820 post-war vagrants invaded the town but did little damage to the better properties which include, in Cumberland Street, Cumberland House. Opposite the *King's Head* is a late Tudor house with a 19th-century red brick front – Woodbridge School was housed here from 1662 to 1864 when the buildings became a library. As for the famous old Tide Mill, whose hours of work were of course determined by the tides – 'Oft in the past the still of the night was broken by the sounds and vibrations of the busy working mill'. See C. A. and M. A. Weaver, *Woodbridge, a short history and guide*, published by the authors at Woodbridge in 1976.[80]

The Salkelds of Woodbridge

Anyone searching Suffolk records for details of Salkelds, will come across a quite large collection in the area of Walsham-le-Willows (mostly having Biblical Christian names such as John, Samuel, Rebecca), from about 1650, and spilling over into the early 1700s. These are not close relations, springing I believe from a John born in 1622 at Hensingham in the Cumberland parish of St Bees. As a separate task it would be interesting to establish their pedigree with much more precision, particularly as this John Salkeld, one time Fellow of Queens' College, Cambridge, did great work in founding, and being the first pastor of, the church of the Presbyterians at Walsham where he died in December 1699 at the age of seventy-seven. Walsham, near Bury-St-Edmunds, is some thirty-five miles as the crow flies from Woodbridge, and formed therefore its own close Salkeld community which may, or may well not, have had contact with our particular branch, which was 'founded' by the arrival at Woodbridge of William (I) Salkeld, from Blandsgill in Dentdale, in or a little before 1707, then a lad of about twenty-three years of age.

Why did he come? The plain answer is, I do not know. Certainly he had to follow his star sooner or later, for Blandsgill had to be sold under his late father's will of 1694 and if anyone was to have it within the family that anyone was the eldest brother Francis. There were five of the original children to share, and debts to be paid. True, young William who had been born in December 1683 had been left a legacy by a spinster, 'a near relation', who died in nearby Broadgate in Hugil in August 1688, when William would be only five years old; true, too, that her will says she was possessed 'of very great personal estate'. But this was to be kept in trust until he was 21 – that is until 8 December 1704 – which would no doubt give William some useful household goods when in April 1707 he married Elizabeth Riggs at Woodbridge, but would not help him while still a teenager except through the good offices of Margaret Grave's executors who were her brother Miles Grave of Broadgate, yeoman, Thomas Salkeld, and Francis Lund, with her yeoman supervisors her brothers William and Thomas.

The fact that Thomas Salkeld and his five children found it necessary to file, as plaintiffs, a bill dated 16 November 1691, suggests that the control of Margaret's estate under her will was meeting difficulties; yet the Grave family of Broadgate were old friends of the Salkelds of Dent – see pages 84 to 86 – and like them were Quakers and suffered accordingly.

I am much obliged to Mr. Roy Hudleston for drawing my attention to this will of Margaret Grave's, which he found in Chancery Suit C5 183/52 during studies he was making in October 1985. It would sometime be of interest to look more closely into the Grave family, and their wills and inventories, as a possible source of Salkeld information in the 1600-1700 period.

Despite this legacy, I doubt whether there was much money in young William's pocket, as he started the quite long journey from Dent to Woodbridge – at least two hundred and fifty cross-country miles – and in the days before stage coaches ran in Cumbria; it had to be made on foot unless one had, or could borrow, a horse; certainly there was no lack of the spirit of adventure in his family – his brother Francis had a few years beforehand left home and made an eastwards crossing to Whitby, all of a hundred miles, and taking a wife with him. What then, was a journey of 250 miles, to Woodbridge? Quite a long way, and this time with no wife – yet. [Or perhaps he went out to Whitby, stayed with his brother there, and hitched a lift to Woodbridge on a coastal vessel out of Whitby?]

And why Woodbridge? The possible reason would be that it was at that time a very busy centre for the building of wooden boats of modest size, for the east coast trade in coal and farming produce, to London. His father had been a tradesman joiner, and it may be that, while living at Blandsgill, young William had turned his hand – by apprenticeship or otherwise – to that very trade. There were at least four carpenters earning their living in Dent in the years 1646-53, one of whose sons might gladly have taken young William on and taught him the trade. Pure speculation, of course, but there is no room for speculation on the fact that William, somehow and for some reason, did make the journey, and then got married and settled down in Woodbridge. Not however as a joiner or carpenter – but (like his eldest brother) as a schoolmaster! As a Quaker, he may have been helped to this position by Quaker Friends either in Dentdale, or in Suffolk; he would almost certainly have been taught at the flourishing grammar school at Dent (later good enough for the early schooldays of the famous Professor Adam Sedgwick); perhaps his own master had inspired young William to enter the teaching profession as a better prospect than trying to scratch a living on the fells around Blandsgill.

That he married on 11 April 1707 is clear from the Quaker records of the Woodbridge Meeting House, under that date:

> William Salkeld of Woodbridge, schoolmaster, son of Thomas [VII] Salkeld late of Dent in the County of Yorkshire, joiner, deceased; and Elizabeth Riggs daughter of Edward Riggs late of Woodbridge in the County of Suffolk, Baker, deceased, were married.

Relatives signing the Marriage Book were Sarah Riggs, Ann Salkeld, John Gouch and Rose Carter. Of these, Sarah Riggs was probably the sister of the bride, because we know from another Quaker entry that Edward her late father had on 5 November 1667 married Millison Farthing; so presumably the bride's mother, had she still been alive, would have signed the Book as Millison Riggs. Thus it appears that the bride had neither father nor mother to witness her marriage to William Salkeld, at Woodbridge, on that April day in 1707. It is very nice to see that Ann Salkeld was there (she had not yet married Joseph Linskill) – almost certainly I think the already-mentioned 25-year-old sister of the groom and the Administrator of their mother Grace's inventory. Perhaps it was a really well-attended wedding, with their elder brother Francis (and his wife Judith) over from Whitby (by boat?) with young Thomas (VIII) (then 16) and even little Grace (herself to be married in another four years – to live no doubt in Dent with her Capstacke in-laws).

The omens were good, the bride Elizabeth Riggs was to live for 50 more years and her groom for two years longer still; but they seem only to have had two children, Thomas (IX), baptised a Quaker, at Woodbridge, on 23 July 1710, and his younger brother (our ancestor) baptised William (II) on 20 February 1713 – again we see the convention that the eldest child is named after the grandparent.

Father William (I), the schoolmaster, prospered, and it is said (I cannot confirm this) eventually became 'mayor' of Woodbridge – sometime presumably in the period 1715 to 1750; Elizabeth his wife died in 1758 and was buried in the Quaker Burial ground at Woodbridge on 29 October. Her husband William followed her there, on 28 May 1760.

Thomas (IX), the elder of the sons of William and Elizabeth, was born at Woodbridge and baptised as a Quaker there, on 23 July 1710; he would perhaps attend his father's school, and at the age of 24 (on 26 January 1734) we know that he married Elizabeth Routh, of St Olave's, Suffolk (probably Greeting St Olave's, two miles north-east of Needham Market), not in Suffolk but at St Gregory's in Middlesex. Both these churches have now disappeared – the St Olave's in Suffolk was standing in 1532 (White's *Suffolk*, 1844, p. 232)[83] but 'it went to decay in the seventeenth century and no traces of it now remain' and the parish forms part of the two others which are served by St Mary's church at Greeting; whereas the original St Gregory's in Middlesex was burnt down in the Great Fire of London and its records are now (1979) in the possession of the church of St Martin, Ludgate Hill and contain the record

26 Jan. 1734 Thos. Salkeld of Woodbridge Suffolk married Elizabeth Routh of St Olave's Suffolk.

Why two Suffolk folk should marry in the City of London in 1734, in what was in fact then the church of 'Saint Gregory by Saint Paul' is far from obvious. A clue may perhaps be in the surname 'Routh', an uncommon name.

In the records of apprentices (Inland Revenue – PRO)[82] there is an entry in 1723 that William Salkeld the son of Francis Salkeld merchant of Yorkshire was indentured, for the sum of £50, to one 'Zach Routh', to be an apprentice apothecary. This is almost certainly the William born in October 1707 and baptised on 26 October at Whitby, the only surviving son of Francis (II) Salkeld and Judith Satterthwaite. Moreover, this Zach Routh is described as of St Saviour's, which is of course the cathedral church of Southwark and near to St Gregory by St Paul. We know that this young William was buried on 14 March 1728, and buried in London, at the age of twenty and a half. So although his career as an apothecary was a short one, he leaves us with the thought that his half-cousin's wife Elizabeth Routh may have been related to the Zach Routh to whom young William had earlier been apprenticed. Moreover, this London wedding raises the prospect that Thomas and Elizabeth may then have stayed there, and been seen in Woodbridge no more. I have not, at the time of writing, studied further the various records and registers which could confute or confirm this theory, because none of these Salkelds is a *direct* ancestor, though Thomas was the brother of one.

And as for London, we shall also find that that ancestor's wife, Hannah Gooding, briefly mentions in her will of 4 June 1798 one 'son-in-law' William Wilson, who married her daughter Hannah in 1773. As Hannah is left out of the will, she may be presumed to be dead by 1798, though in it William Wilson receives a small legacy; the point however is that Hannah married William Wilson at St Vedast's church in Foster Lane, London, thereby being the third of these Salkelds to desert Suffolk for the Metropolis. As we shall see, she was soon followed by Hannah (Gooding's) son Francis (III), who inherited a slice of the Suffolk properties, but enjoyed them from London.

There seems to be a curious clock-wise motion in the various migrations of these Salkelds over the years – a sort of 'never go back' philosophy, biased also to right-handed turns. Rosgill, to Pardshaw, to Winster, to Mislet, to Broadgate, to Dentdale, and then on to Whitby, or to Woodbridge, and now to London; but it did not stop there, as we shall see. Most of the time it leaves behind a few Salkelds, as though to blaze where the trail had been. But sometimes, as at Winster, it is a blaze of names only, not of people.

A Note on Woodbridge School

Information from Dr. Briscoe of 7 Seckford Street, Woodbridge (Wednesday, 27 June 1979).

Liber Admissionum
Seckford Grammar School, at Woodbridge, Suffolk

Printed Private Press of Frederick Arthur Crisp, 1900[84] (100 copies printed)

Produced with the assistance of Vincent Burrough Redstone.

Extract – Among 'pupils admitted' –

1758 Thomas Salkeld [X] of Woodbridge [b. 1749].

Pursuant to Notice given at Church on Sunday Jan.y 2 1774. A meeting was held at the Vestry and the following resolution Agreed to –

That the following six principal Inhabitants are appointed to join with the Minister and Church-wardens to elect a proper person to be Master of the Grammar School in this Town.

Jonathan Burwood Esq
Rev.d M.r Carthew
Mr John Page
Mr William Walford
Mr Nathanieirson
Woodbridge 3 Jan.y 1774

Among the signatures of 17 Inhabitants, in addition to the Minister and Church-wardens, was the name of Tho. Salkeld (aged 25!).

Lands at Hasketon

We must now turn to the younger son of William and Elizabeth, who was born in 1713 and baptised with the name William (II), as a Quaker, some two-and-a-half years after the birth of their first child Thomas (IX); the baptism was on 20 February 1713, at Woodbridge. The Friends Meeting House, in Turn Lane, had been built in 1678 to seat 300, so the little christening party would be lost in a corner of it; today, just 300 years later, it is a private house.

No doubt young William would, as a boy, attend the school, opposite the *King's Head*, at which his father taught. I have not yet been able to find out how he then earned his living – perhaps he too taught – until he had the good fortune to meet and marry, when he was 23 years of age, a girl from nearby Hasketon, who was the daughter of Joseph Gooding and his wife Sarah; the wedding was at St Mary the Virgin, Clopton (O.S. Sheet 156, 2252) on 22 September 1737, his bride being about twenty-one years old; I suspect that William then went to live with her parents at Hasketon. His will is about as uninteresting as it could be; he made it on 12 November 1773 when he was 60; it leaves everything to his wife Hannah, not a child being mentioned – though they had no less than six of whom two died in infancy. If his will is read alongside hers, it does give the very strong impression that she 'wore the trousers'. She also survived him by 26 years, and whereas he died in 1775 at the age of 62, she lived until 1801 and was buried on 4 April at the very decent age of eighty-five. And all this was I think because Hannah brought to her marriage prospects of a very considerable estate at Hasketon, about which something must now be said. I also suspect that Hannah knocked any lingering taste for Quakerism out of her husband; from now on there is no evidence of it in the Salkeld progeny, apart from her own unusual request to be buried in their private plot of land, since identified as that opposite Grange Farm, Hasketon. Outside Woodbridge is Hasketon, a hamlet two miles to the north-west, and off the main roads. John Bennet left lands and buildings there to his son, and then on to his grandchildren, who happened to be two girls named Sarah and Hannah; they were jointly admitted into possession by Hasketon Court Baron on 18 May 1764, on the death of their father. By that time Hannah was married to our ancestor William Salkeld and had had her last child, and her sister Sarah had married Thomas Gooding, presumably a cousin but certainly of her own kin; Sarah 'surrendered' her holdings to Hannah on 10 June 1783 (shortly after Hannah had become a widow), so there were 18 years left to Hannah to enjoy her wealth and her widowhood. Those of her children who were living in the year 1783 (when she had got full control of the Hasketon properties) were reduced to two – Thomas (X) (born 1749) who had married Elizabeth Guichenet in 1776, and Francis (III) 'of London'. Both her daughters Sarah and Hannah were dead – though the latter's husband William Wilson lived on – and dead too now was her son the infant Thomas. Her son William whose widow Hannah (née Cross) was living was not in Woodbridge but in Shrewsbury.

So the old lady, in her will of 4 June 1798, made when she was 82, left the lands (and buildings) at Hasketon entirely to her beloved son Thomas (X); she split up her possessions in Woodbridge proper, to give Thomas those in the 'Thorofare' (the main street) which were occupied by William Buckingham, and those in the same street, but in which *she* had been living, to her son Francis of London. Her son William (III), being dead, gets nothing, and his widow Hannah, being in Shrewsbury, gets treated as though she were dead also – which she wasn't. The five grandchildren the testator had from her dead son William, each inherited £400, and in addition the three girls each got a diamond ring and some household and wearing apparel.

Had William, our ancestor, not died in 1782 at the age of perhaps forty, but had survived his mother even by a few days (i.e. had not died until he was at least sixty, like his brothers Francis and Thomas) – one wonders how mother Hannah would then have disposed of her not inconsiderable wealth. I think Thomas would still have been

23. Grange Farm, Hasketon.

the most favourably treated, not least because he did elect to stay on in his mother's town of Woodbridge and make a real home for himself there (as we shall shortly see). But she would I think have been stricter in her bequests to the absent Francis, 'of London'.

THE WILL OF WILLIAM (II) SALKELD OF WOODBRIDGE,
12 November 1773

Original in Ipswich Record Office

This is the last will and testament of me William Salkeld of Woodbridge in the County of Suffolk Gentleman made the twelfth day of November in the year of our Lord one thousand seven hundred and seventy three in manner and form following that is to say

First I will order and direct that all my just debts and funeral charges and the charge of proving and attending the execution of this my will shall be fully paid and satisfied out of my personal estate and from and after payment of the said debts and other charges as aforesaid I give devise and bequeath all and every my messuages lands and tenements and hereditaments and all the residues and remainders of my personal estate goods chattels and effects whatsoever and wheresobe unto my loving wife Hannah Salkeld and to her heirs executors and administrators forever

And lastly I so nominate constitute and appoint my said wife Hannah Salkeld executor and my good friend Nathaniel Randall of Woodbridge aforesaid gentleman executor of this my will and I give to the said Nathaniel Randall out of gratitude and great esteem one guinea desiring he may be moreover reasonably paid and satisfied for his trouble journeys and expences in and about the the trust hereby in him reposed and I so revoke and make void all former and other wills by me heretofore made in witness whereof I the said William Salkeld have to this my last will and testament contained in one sheet of paper set my hand and seal the day and year of first written.

THE WILL OF HANNAH SALKELD [née GOODING], WIDOW
Wife of William (II) Salkeld. Will of 4 June 1798, proved April 1801.

All just debts etc. to be paid.

Item, I give devise limit and appoint unto my son Thomas (X) Salkeld all that my Messuage Tenement and farm with all and every the outhouses Edifices, Buildings Yards Gardens Orchards Lands and Hereditaments whatsoever to the same belonging or in any wise appertaining with their and every of their appurtenances situate and lying and being in Hasketon in the aforesaid County or in any other parish or place thereunto next or near adjoining now in the tenancy or occupation of James Smith his undertenants or assigns. To hold all and singular the said Messuage, Tenement and farm lands and hereditaments with their and every of their appurtenances unto my said son Thomas Salkeld and to his heirs and Assigns for (ever) or provided nevertheless and my Will further is that as in one of the fields belonging to my aforesaid Estate and lying next the Kings High Way leading from Woodbridge aforesaid to Grundisburgh a small piece of Ground now is and for many years last past had been enclosed with a Gate and whitethorn hedge and used as a burial place for my family. My desire therefore is that my Executors do directly inter my remains therein as near to my late affectionate husband as may be.

Then follows a bequest of £20 to the Minister and Churchwardens, for ever, for the upkeep of the gate, fence and ground of the burial ground. Also a bequest of 40s. to be paid as a reward to anyone who reports the land, fence, gate as falling into disrepair.

Item. I give and devise unto my aforesaid son Thomas Salkeld all that my messuage or Tenement with the Outhouses, Edifices, Buildings, yards, Gardens Land Hereditaments and premises with the appurtenances thereto belonging situate and being in the Thorofare in Woodbridge aforesaid and now in the occupation of William Buckingham his undertenants or assigns To hold all and singular the said last mentioned Messuage or Tenements Hereditaments and premises with the appurtenances unto my aforesaid son Thomas Salkeld and to his heirs and Assigns for ever.

Also I give and bequeath unto my aforesaid son Thomas Salkeld my Household Linen of every description as and for his sole property.

Also I give to my Grand daughter Hannah, eldest daughter of my said son Thomas, my Gold Watch with the chain and all the Trinkets appurtenant thereto.

And to my Grand daughter Elizabeth, the youngest daughter of my said son Thomas, my Gold Necklace to be delivered to them at the direction of their father.

Item. I give and devise unto my son Francis (III) Salkeld all that my Messuage or Tenement wherein I now dwell with the Outhouses Edifices Buildings Yards Gardens land Hereditaments and Appurtenances thereto belonging situate and being in the Thorofare in Woodbridge aforesaid, to hold all and singular the Buildings with the said Messuage or Tenement Land Hereditament and Appurtenances unto the said Francis Salkeld my son and to his heirs and Assigns for ever. And my will further is that my aforesaid son Francis shall be entitled to and I do give him the Coal Range in my Kitchen, the painting over the chimney piece in my little parlour, the Corner Cupboard therein, the two Corner Cupboards in the Hall and an Indian painting over the Chimney piece there, and all the dressers shelves stoves locks bolts and other fastenings affixed to the said last-mentioned premises. But it is not my intent and meaning to include or comprise in this bequest the Copper and Irons affixed in my Wash House.

Item. I give and bequeath unto my aforesaid son Francis Salkeld fifteen hundred pounds of lawful money of Great Britain to be paid to him six months next after my decease.

Item. I give and bequeath unto my Grand children following, namely, Harriet Salkeld, William Salkeld, Charlotte Salkeld, Maria Salkeld and Francis (IV) Salkeld, four hundred pounds apiece of lawful Money to be paid to them respectively out of my personal Estate within six months next after my decease or when and as they shall attain their several and respective age and ages of twenty one years. But in case any one or more of them my said last named Grand children shall happen to depart this life under age not leaving any Issue of his her or their Body or Bodies Then I give and bequeath the sum of Money hereinbefore given to such of them my said Grand children as shall so happen to die, unto and amongst the survivors or survivor of them my said Grand children equally to be divided amongst them share and share alike.

I also give unto my aforesaid last named Grand daughters (daughters of William III) Harriet Salkeld, Charlotte Salkeld and Maria Salkeld, one diamond ring each.

Item. I give and bequeath unto my faithfull servant Alice Banyard thirty guineas to be paid to her two months next after my decease.

Item. I give and bequeath unto my son-in-law William Wilson the sum of one hundred pounds in case he shall be living twelve months after my decease but not otherwise.

Item. I give and bequeath unto my aforesaid Grand daughters, the two daughters [Hannah and Elizabeth II] of my said son Thomas and the three daughters [Harriet, Charlotte, Mary] of my late son William, all my wearing apparel clothes and wearing Linen to be equally divided between them or such of them as shall be living at the time of my death by my Executors hereafter named, as near as may be share and share alike – and my will is and I do hereby order and direct my Executors hereinafter named as soon as conveniently may be after my decease to make or cause to be made a true and perfect Inventory and appraisement of all my Household furniture Goods Chattels and Effects and then forthwith make sale of the same for the best and most advantage that they can save in respect of such part thereof as I have disposed of by this my will and the money arising thereby I will shall fall into the Residue of my personal Estate and from and after payment of my said just debts and funeral and testamentary Expenses the Legacies hereinbefore set forth and the Legacy hereinafter mentioned I give and bequeath all the rest residue and remainder of my personal estate unto my aforesaid son Thomas Salkeld and my said son Francis Salkeld and to their executors and administrators for ever equally to be divided between them.

And I do nominate constitute and appoint my aforesaid son Thomas Salkeld and my much respected friend Joseph Walford of Woodbridge aforesaid Ironmonger, Executors of this my will.

Item. I give to the said Joseph Walford twenty pounds for his trouble desiring he may be moreover liberally paid all such costs charges Damages and Expenses he shall sustain expend or be put into in or about the due Execution thereof and do hereby revoke all former and other wills by me at any time heretofore made.

Witnesses, William Buckingham [tenant], John Russell, Samuel Pipe.

Will made 5 June 1798.

Proved P.C.C. London 17 April 1801.

'The Guichenets'

In dealing with the children of William (II) and Hannah née Gooding, following their marriage at Clopton on 22 September 1737, we have already had the advantage of seeing the wills of each parent; William who pre-deceased his wife by 27 years, had left everything to her anyway, so it is her will of 4 August 1798 which has first claim to our attention. The important point now is to appreciate that one of her sons – William (III) – (our ancestor) had died 16 years before she made her will, and so all her possessions went to the two other sons Thomas, of Woodbridge, and Francis, of London. Of her other children, a daughter Hannah had married William Wilson at St Vedast in Foster Lane, the City of London, in 1773, but as she is only represented in her mother's will by a small legacy to him, we must assume that she had died before that will was made in 1798; and two others had died as infants and had been buried not in Woodbridge but at nearby Hasketon – they were Sarah, buried 16 April 1739, and an earlier Thomas buried 26 December 1744.

The three older sons are like three fingerposts on a road sign. That of Thomas points firmly to nearby Woodbridge, that of Francis points to London, and that of the soon-to-be-dead William points to Shrewsbury. If, as we must, we are to follow our ancestor William to Shrewsbury, we cannot at the same time chase Francis to London, and for the time at least therefore we must be content to watch him and his coach disappear in that direction. But before jumping on our Shrewsbury coach we can, and will, linger a little to see how his brother Thomas gets along in Woodbridge.

When Thomas was born in 1749, his mother had been married some twelve years and was then 33, having previously had at least two other children both of whom had died in infancy. She had him baptised into the Church of England – not as a Quaker – and the year following his father's death he married Elizabeth Guichenet. As they were to have a large family – no less than 12 children including four who died in infancy – I am calling them all 'The Guichenets' after their mother's maiden name, and to distinguish them a little from their cousins. The first six were baptised at St Mary's Church, Woodbridge, and in the intervals between baptisms their father Thomas earned his and their living as a timber merchant, to such good effect that he became Chief Constable of the Hundred of Loes, and a County Treasurer of Suffolk. (According to British Museum Additional MS 19148 Pedigrees S.-S.H.E. Davy's Suffolk Collection, 72.[85] [But he may at one time have been a linen draper, like brother William in Shrewsbury.]) Though he was also to inherit from his mother, she did not die until all his 12 children had been born, so he and his wife Elizabeth (née Guichenet) must take all the credit, though no doubt Granny from time to time 'stood treat'; but she would have to do this on her own, for it is sad to note that Grandfather William had died shortly before the first of the 12 was born.

A few brief notes about these children may not be out of place. The first 'Little Guichenet' was baptised 13 October 1777, and before his early death was given the name Thomas (XI), which was not in line with the earlier tradition of naming the first-born after the grandfather. I strongly suspect that the 'Guichenets' were in fact living with Granny, in her house in the Thorofare – the main street of Woodbridge – which home she later left to Francis 'of London'. She left her other house in the Thorofare to 'father Guichenet' and indicates in her will that it had before her death been tenanted

24. Hasketon church.

by a non-relation. So the Guichenets either lived with her, or in the Hasketon property (which for the timber business would not be very convenient).

The second child George was born in September 1779, lived for only a few weeks, and was buried at Hasketon in the 'Dissenters Burial Ground'. His successor, also to be christened George, appeared in October the following year, and survived for a while. Next came Henry, baptised 6 December 1781, heir-to-be of his father's estates. Then Elizabeth, baptised 17 May 1783 but, as she is not mentioned in her Granny's will, must have died before 1793. Next William, baptised 18 May 1784, and then Francis (V) (13 November 1785) followed by Hannah (21 January 1787) and mentioned in Granny's will as the eldest daughter of Thomas (X). Whereas the earlier children were baptised in Woodbridge, this Hannah and her brother Francis, and indeed the four remaining children, were baptised at Hasketon, which may indicate that the family was outgrowing the Woodbridge premises. Hetty followed, but survived only a few months and was buried in the family burial ground at Hasketon on 15 March 1790, as was Kitty on 13 September 1791. But the next child – the second to be named Elizabeth after her mother – was baptised on 15 April 1792 and survived to be mentioned in Granny's will as the youngest grand-daughter. A last child, Samuel, was buried as an infant on 26 January 1796, at Hasketon.

The 'Guichenets' father, Thomas, entered into his inheritance following an award of the Hasketon Court Baron on 8 January 1802, on the death of his mother. He made his will on 8 June 1820, and, following his burial 'in his own land at Hasketon', it was proved at Canterbury in 1823 – a verbose hand-written document, not too easy to read in parts, but interesting in its provisions. It appoints his eldest son Henry as a co-trustee with John Spurling of Burge (a farmer) and a Woodbridge wine-merchant named Abraham Brook; Henry gets the farm and 97 acres of land at Hasketon. Francis has an annuity of £60 a year from an entailed principal of £1,200, payable from Henry's farm but, if Francis continues to live with his mother, she gets half his £30 a year. His daughter Susannah (who was baptised 'Hannah') now married to Joseph Chapman gets – but not for his use – an annuity of £40 a year from an entailed principal also charged to Henry, of £800, and passing to her children, if any, on her death. To his wife Elizabeth (provided she does not re-marry) Thomas leaves his house and premises in the main street of Woodbridge – the 'Thorofare' – including his 'counting-house, buildings yards, other premises occupied by William Walton, a malt house occupied by George Ely, a mill house and corn chamber', and all these on her death to pass to her son Henry and to his heirs and assigns. On her death, too, his son William to be paid, by Henry, £800 plus 5 per cent. interest. His daughter Elizabeth, now married to a grocer (James Martin of Woodbridge), inherits their other premises in the 'Thorofare' – a 'messuage, outhouses, buildings yards garden land and a barn', to be sold on her death for the benefit of her children when they reach twenty-one. His trustees are to prepare an inventory of all his household furniture, plate, china, watches, jewels, goods, and effects; his wife may use these until her death when all are to be sold and with the residue of his estate the capital is 'to be put out at interest', later to be equally divided between Henry, William, Francis, Susannah and daughter Elizabeth. Most of the rest of the will deals with action to be taken should Henry fail to make these legacy payments every half year, as directed, and how the grand-children are to be paid when they in turn reach the age of twenty-one. Thomas leaves nothing to his own brothers, for of course William our ancestor has been dead long since in Shrewsbury (1782) and indeed Thomas had been a trustee of William's will. Perhaps Francis 'of London' was by now dead also.

Undoubtedly this Thomas was a man of means – thanks to his inheritances from the distaff side; one would have to go back a long way in this our story to find a more warmly endowed Salkeld – perhaps as far as Thomas (IV) the sheriff who married Margaret Curwen, and lived with her at Rosgill and Corby Castle – six 'Thomases' ago.

Before leaving the 'Guichenets' we must say a word about Thomas (X)'s children. Their mother Elizabeth lived another seven years after his death, and was buried at Hasketon in February 1828. To Henry, the heir, we will come back shortly. Francis (V) lived on in Woodbridge and has a mention in White's *Directory of Suffolk* in 1844 (p. 260)[83] as 'Gent' living in Cumberland Street – an extension of the old Thorofare; he also attends the sale of Henry's estate, mentioned later. Son Thomas (XI) married Elizabeth Jones of Aldgate in London on 14 November 1817, and as an old man died on 5 September 1876 (leaving a daughter Elizabeth Jones Salkeld who on 3 September 1840 married Henry William the younger son of Abraham Brook, Gent of Woodbridge); Hannah, as we saw, married Joseph Chapman from Lubbenham in Leicestershire on 17 September 1814, and young Elizabeth married her Woodbridge grocer James Martin on 20 July 1820 but died 11 years later leaving, according to the *Ipswich Journal* of 11 June 1831, 'seven small children to lament the loss of an indulgent mother'.

As for Henry, his will of 3 March 1836, of Thames Ditton, Surrey, proved 17 October 1839, left to his wife Anne all the household effects including wines and liqueurs, £100 in cash, and the use of his copyhold estates messuages tenements and hereditaments in Woodbridge but during her life her consent in writing must be secured before any part of them was sold; thereafter his trustees (his brother-in-law James Martin excluded) are to be his friends Henry Wyatt of Long Ditton, Surrey, and Clement Dale of Raymond Buildings, Gray's Inn; they are to see to the payment of the various legacies provided for in his father's will and then to sell the estates as they see fit and out of the proceeds to pay certain further small annuities to his near relatives and then to organise payments at stated dates to the children of his brothers Francis (V) and William and of his late sister Elizabeth Martin.

The trustees duly arranged for the sale of the Hasketon estates, by auction, on 6 May 1840 at Woodbridge – see notice of sale – but this may have failed as Henry Wyatt later appeared at the Hasketon Court Baron (on 10 December 1840) and was himself granted tenancy; he later sold the estates not in Woodbridge to a farmer, William Walker, for £4,000 on 12 January 1842, the brother Francis (V) being present together with sister Hannah and her husband Joseph Chapman, and Henry's widow Anne Salkeld. The various Court Baron records of all these transactions occupy 54 pages, of which I have made a short summary (from the Ipswich Records Office); amongst other matters they reveal that at one stage Thomas (X) himself acted as attorney in a claim made in June 1783 by James Gooding of Millbrook St Mary Magdalen, Bermondsey, London (the only son of Mary Gooding the late wife of James Gooding and co-heir of Joseph Gooding). This claim was that they should have one third of the estates – which claim caused Hannah's sister Sarah to 'surrender' her moiety.

And so, perhaps with a sigh of relief, we can say goodbye to the 'Guichenets', their passion for property litigation, and complex wills, and take the road to Shrewsbury where our ancestor William (III) (brother of Thomas (X) the 'father Guichenet') has too long been awaiting our attentions.

Summary of Information in the Hasketon Court Baron Records

1764 – The record of the Court sitting on 18 May 1764 reveals: *on 23 January 1667* (nearly a hundred years previously) *John Bennet had surrendered his copyhold tenement in Hasketon* and his death was presented at the Court held on 10 October 1720 *to whom Joseph Gooding and his wife Sarah claimed under John Bennett's will of 17 April 1712* which will made them his heirs (but if they have no children, to *John Whayman his grandson by his daughter*) and *they were so admitted on 10 October 1720. Now (1764) comes Sarah the wife of Thomas Gooding and Hannah the wife of William Salkeld* the daughters and co-heirs of Joseph Gooding (now and his wife Sarah dead) each claiming the tenancy of a moiety of those possessions.

Sarah and Hannah duly hand over their copyhold tenancy to the lord of the manor and plead for their return whereupon Richard Wood of Melton claims them, to remove any entail; this in turn is challenged by a John Shaw who is denied by Richard Wood and John Shaw then challenges Sarah and Hannah and their husbands who defend their right and call Marmaduke Shaw who himself claims the right to tenancy. Adjournment till 4 p.m. when Marmaduke tho' called does not appear; any other claimants are called for 'but no person comes' so Court says John Shaw recovers his seizin from Richard Wood and claims for the bailiff to install him as tenant and so Hannah and Sarah and their husbands surrender their copyhold to the lord of the manor and then John Shaw surrenders his and then Hannah and Sarah plead for the tenancies and get them.

1783 – Court sat 10 June 1783. Refers to above 'common recovery'. *Hannah Salkeld now widow (1783)* and she and *the two Goodings* are admitted as tenants; then Thos. Salkeld of Woodbridge gentleman brings letters of Attorney under the hand and seal of James Gooding bearing date 23 August 1780 by *James Gooding of Millbrooke St Mary Magdalen Bermondsey Southwark waterman only son and heir of Mary Gooding the late wife of James Gooding* deceased which said that *Mary was one of the daughters and co-heirs of Joseph Gooding and Sarah his wife* 'and who were devisees intail named in the last will and testament of *John Bennett* heretofore of Hasketon in Suffolk yeoman . . . ' for divers good causes . . . do make *Thomas Salkeld of Woodbridge in Suffolk gent my true and lawful attorney* . . . claiming a third part of all and every . . . property of which John Bennett was seized and to whom I am entitled *as only son and heir of the said Mary Gooding wife of the said James Gooding* and pleads for admission to *a third part* for the use and behoof of Robert Cooper of Woodbridge gent as tenant and lkeld claims power of attorney to act in any proceedings necessary to secure this third part. *His claim to be for the use and behoof of Hannah Salkeld of Woodbridge* aforesaid widow her heirs and assigns – Signed James Gooding on 23 August 1780. And he was so admitted, for a fine, and Robert Cooper admitted as a tenant after usual rigmarole with bailiffs, etc., in which *Thomas Gooding and Sarah his wife absolutely surrender their moiety to Hannah Salkeld.*

1802 – At Court on 8 January 1802 Thomas Salkeld of Woodbridge gent comes to say Hannah Salkeld widow died since last Court, her will dated 4 June 1798 (portions cited) and makes Thomas Salkeld heir of those lands and claims tenancy which is granted as seizin for ever to the use and behoof of his last will and testament to be declared. Fine £34 11s. 0d.

1822 – Thos. Salkeld gent late a copyhold Tenant died seized of the Hasketon properties and now comes Henry Salkeld his son (by Abraham Brooks his attorney) who produces the probate of the last will of Thos. Salkeld dated 8 June 1821 proved P.C.C. on 23 May (1822) quotes will that Henry inherits (*subject* to annuity and legacies specified) 97 acres in Hasketon in tenancy of James Smith; (Thos. was admitted to tenancy 8 February 1802) seizin granted to Henry. Fine is £34 11s. 0d.

1840 – On 1 August 1840 Henry Salkeld copyholder had died seized – application proclaimed 'but no person came'. On to 10 December 1840, when Henry Wyatt of Long Ditton, Surrey esq. (by Thos. Crabbe gent his attorney) produces to the Court Henry Salkeld's will of 3 March 1836. This will of Henry's appointed two trustees, Henry Wyatt and Clement Dale of Raymond Buildings, Gray's Inn, to sell his properties when they can and meanwhile to occupy and use them, the premises being those to which he was admitted by the Court Baron on 6 October 1823 on his father Thomas's death; Wyatt was admitted by the Court, to his day (but no claim to be admitted as tenant by anyone else).

These courts were not in operation in Cumbria and must have been a shock to the newly-arrived Salkelds of Woodbridge.

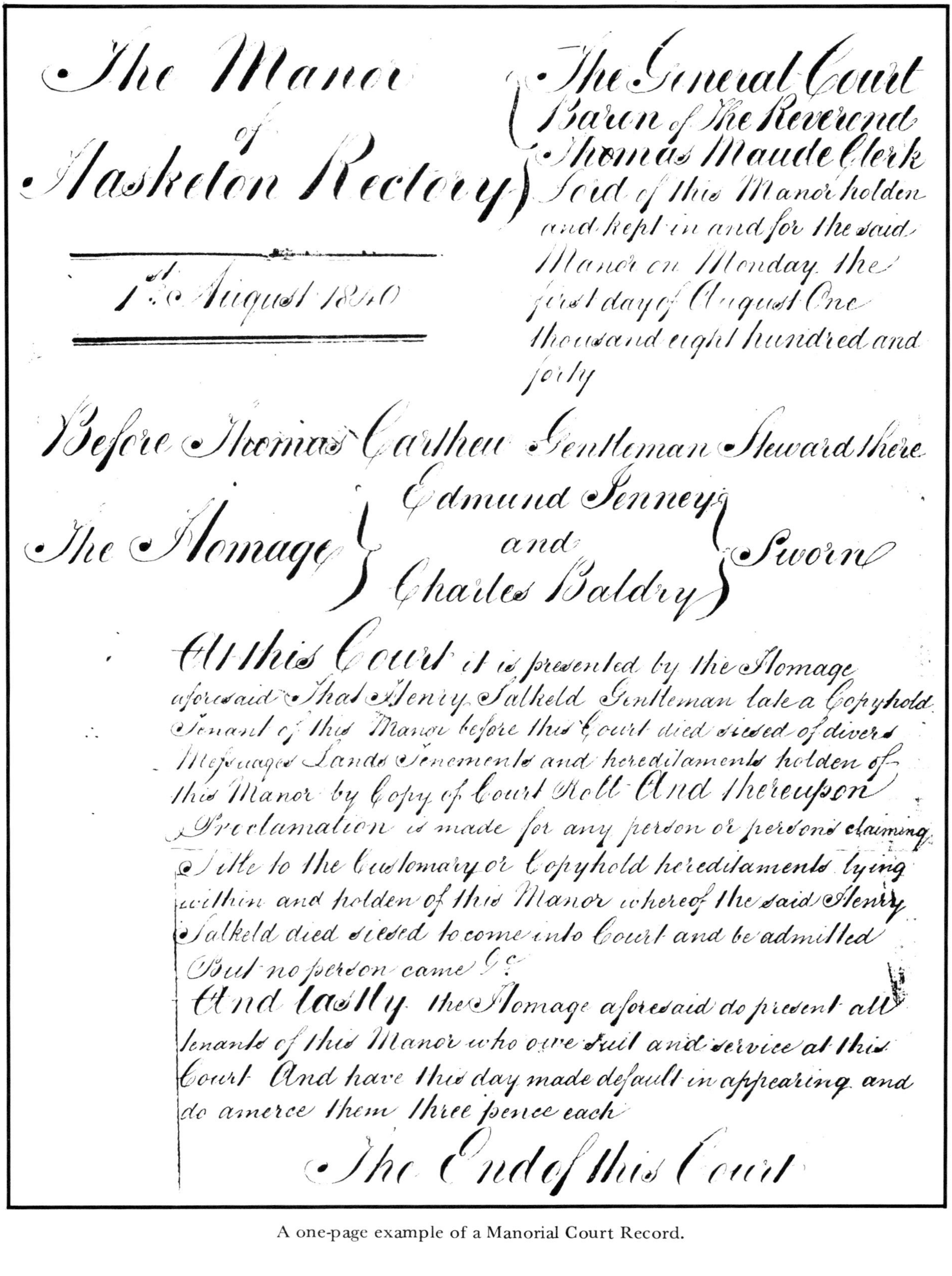

The Manor of Haskelon Rectory

The General Court Baron of The Reverend Thomas Maude Clerk

Lord of this Manor holden and kept in and for the said Manor on Monday the first day of August One thousand eight hundred and forty

1st August 1840

Before Thomas Carthew Gentleman Steward there

The Homage

Edmund Jenney
and
Charles Baldry

Sworn

At this Court it is presented by the Homage aforesaid That Henry Salkeld Gentleman late a Copyhold Tenant of this Manor before this Court died siesed of divers Messuages Lands Tenements and hereditaments holden of this Manor by Copy of Court Roll And thereupon Proclamation is made for any person or persons claiming Title to the Customary or Copyhold hereditaments lying within and holden of this Manor whereof the said Henry Salkeld died siesed to come into Court and be admitted But no person came &c.

And lastly the Homage aforesaid do present all Tenants of this Manor who owe Suit and service at this Court And have this day made default in appearing and do amerce them three pence each

The End of this Court

A one-page example of a Manorial Court Record.

25. The Salkeld home in Cumberland Street, Woodbridge.

Summary

Thomas's will proved 8 June 1820
Elizabeth died 24 February 1828
Henry's will 3 March 1836 – died 1839
Henry's auction 6 May 1840
Court application 1 August 1840 – none came
Henry Wyatt produces Henry's will 10 December 1840
Sold to farmer 12 January 1842. £4,000.

Auction at Woodbridge

When Hannah Gooding married William (II) Salkeld in January 1713 she brought with her the prospects of inheriting substantial estates in Hasketon and in Woodbridge; when she died, in 1801, her husband had pre-deceased her by 27 years and one of her elder sons – William (III) – was also dead, so she left her estates to her two other sons Thomas (X) and Francis (III). Thomas died and his will of 8 July 1820 provided that his eldest son Henry should inherit those properties which had been in his possession; so when Henry died in 1839 they were auctioned at Woodbridge. The notice of the auction which appeared in the *Ipswich Journal* on 25 April 1840 read:

TO BE SOLD BY AUCTION 6th MAY 1840 THE ESTATE OF
THE LATE HENRY SALKELD ESQUIRE DECEASED

Lot 1   A Freehold and Copyhold estate, cottage residence, garden, plantations, etc. and 97 acres of arable land and meadow land in Hasketon in the occupation of C. Churchill Esq.

Lot 2   A dwelling house with two parlours kitchen etc. stable pig-house and about ¾ acre of land in Cumberland Street Woodbridge and also all that messuage adjoining in the occupation of Mr. T. Salkeld (XI).

Lot 3   A malt office of 25 Coombs Street (Cumberland Street) in the occupation of Mr. Wm. Tebs.

Lot 4   A brick and slate malt office of 25 Coombs Street (Cumberland Street).

Lot 5   A messuage and outbuildings in Cumberland Street in the occupancy of Mr. James Noble, dyer.

Lot 6   A freehold dwellinghouse with a wharehouse yard etc. late in the occupancy of Mrs. Knight also a long established shop, dwellinghouse etc. in Cumberland Street Woodbridge in the occupancy of Mr. Thomas Comyn this portion of the lots is freehold.

Although this auction was held only four years before the publication of White's *History Gazetteer and Directory of Suffolk*[83] in 1844, there is no mention in that Directory of Coombs Street (Cumberland Street), or of C. Churchill, or Wm. Tebs, or James Noble, nor indeed of Mrs. Knight, which suggests that these publications in this period are liable to be incomplete. But White does record that 'Salkeld Fras. (V) gent' lived in Cumberland Street – no doubt the Francis born 13 November 1785 and a brother of Henry; White also notes under Hasketon that 'Mr. Salkeld' owns land there (p. 134).

Chapter Thirteen

A Shrewsbury Linen Draper

Sometime between 1760 and 1770 young William (III) Salkeld set out from his parents' house in Woodbridge, for Shrewsbury. Both parents were still alive, reasonably prosperous, and with good hopes of inheriting property which could in due course lend itself to exploitation by an eldest son; yet young William went, apparently into the blue, as it were 'to seek his fortune'. And it is far from obvious why he should have preferred Shrewsbury to,say, London – where his younger brother Francis was soon to move. Nor does his chosen activity give a clue, for he became, without doubt, a linen-draper, and so describes himself in his will. In that document there may be a vestige of a clue, for it reveals that he had 'an esteemed friend' Francis Moore, also a linen-draper, living in London at Cheapside, and indeed William makes this Francis Moore a joint executor of his will, and a joint guardian – with his own brother Thomas (X) Salkeld of Woodbridge – of his children. But this still leaves unanswered the question – What was the magnetic attraction of this pleasant county town of Shrewsbury, in the years 1760 to 1770? Maybe the draping of linen was at that time highly fashionable and regarded as a prestige occupation – but why in Shrewsbury? Owen and Blakeways *History of Shrewsbury*, two volumes, London, 1825, shows on p. 517 of vol. 2 that William's grave in St Alkmund's was dated 1782 'aged 45' so he must have been born 1737 and therefore 33 when he married.

Whatever the answer may be, there is no doubt that, once there, William found a girl he wanted to marry. Her Christian name – like that of his mother – was Hannah, but her surname was Cross, and she lived in the parish of St Alkmund's, one of the main Shrewsbury parishes. She was baptised on 23 September 1744; they married on 30 September 1770, when she was just twenty-six. The marriage was held not at St Alkmund's, but at St Chad's, the other main Shrewsbury parish church, though none of their children was baptised at St Chads thereafter.

The marriage entry – in vol. 3 of the St Chad's register (page 1793) reads:

1770 August 30 Mr. William Salkeld b, and Mrs. Hannah Cross p St Alkmund sp lic Wit. William Wilson, Thomas Clarke.

So his wife was a spinster (unmarried woman) and presumably not a widow, but the 'Mrs.'? – perhaps a teacher? At the relatively youthful age of 26, hardly the head of a family? A register search of her relations has not yet been made, but clearly needs to be. (Cross is a very frequently occurring surname in Shrewsbury church records, unfortunately.)

The married couple's home was on Pride Hill, in the centre of the city, and one supposes that they lived 'over the shop': all traces of that shop have now been obliterated by multiple stores just as the home of the early Salkelds of Rosgill in Cumbria has been obliterated by a huge grass silo!

As William's will of 5 January 1782 shows, they had five children, the eldest being

Harriet, then William (IV) (not our ancestor), then Charlotte, Maria and finally our ancestor Francis (IV), who was baptised from the Pride Hill home on 5 March 1781. Almost to the day, and only a year later, father William was buried – at St Alkmund's, 8 March 1781. His mother was still alive, and would be so for a further 19 years. Indeed he was only 45 when he died, and his wife survived him on Pride Hill for another 35 years, being buried 'aged 75', according to *History of Shrewsbury*, p. 517, in her own parish of St Alkmund on 23 September 1817. That she was not remembered in his mother's will of 1798 suggests that there was very little contact between these two widowed ladies, in their latter years; not perhaps surprisingly, as Shrewsbury is not, even today, an easy journey from Woodbridge. But the loss of what could have been a very substantial share in their Granny's will was not quite complete, for she left each of the five 'Shrewsbury' children £400, plus some jewellery and household linen for each of the little girls.

However, their father had instructed his executors (his brother Thomas (X) of Woodbridge, the friend Francis Moore who was a draper in London, and Joseph Carless) that they were to be guardians of the children who were to share equally in his estate. Their father left nothing to his own brothers nor to the last remaining sister Hannah, unless in the unlikely event all five of his children had died, when his two brothers were to share equally. Sister Hannah had married William Wilson (who incidentally had been a witness to her father's wedding) in the church of St Vedast in Foster Lane, London, in 1773, and no doubt was considered as provided for.

Of all these Salkelds, it is the son Francis (IV) who is Lilian's ancestor, and Francis was shortly to leave Shrewsbury and his mother, for Runcorn; but before we go with him we must leave on record a little about the other son William (IV), who having been born in 1771 was just 10 years older than brother Francis. From the Shrewsbury Burgess Roll (edited by Forrest in 1924)[86] we learn that William was himself a Burgess of Shrewsbury by 1806, had a thriving wine lodge on Pride Hill, and no doubt saw a lot of his mother and three sisters Harriet, Charlotte and Maria, the last two having been born in 1796 and 1778 respectively, on Pride Hill where their mother Hannah continued to live until her burial at St Alkmund's in 1817. Though she had been married in St Chad's, she was clearly of the parish of St Alkmund.

William (IV), the Burgess of Shrewsbury, born in 1771, at the age of 21 took to himself a wife Fanny and they had five children – William born in 1793, Francis in 1794, Thomas in 1799, Maria in 1803, and John Chance Salkeld in 1805; but by 1812 he was no longer on the Burgess Roll and may well by then have died. (Who was Fanny? The only clue I at present have comes from the Christian name of her son who went to Shrewsbury School – John Chance Salkeld, which does suggest that she might have been a Miss Chance. [The Chad register, p. 1826, records that Miss Chance (a niece?) married Evan Evans of St Martin, Birmingham, there on 22 May 1786 – the only Chance mentioned in Chad's register.]) There does not appear to have been any major financial crisis, for we learn from the Shrewsbury School records that John Chance Salkeld was a pupil there in 1821, 1822, and 1823.

Admission to the Burgess Roll required that the candidate had either been born in Shrewsbury, or was descended from a Burgess, or had served an apprenticeship to one – or it could be purchased for £5. Membership gave the right to trade in the town, to free education (or a place at the Free Grammar School) for sons, to pasturage in the Quarry and elsewhere, and to a vote at elections. William last voted apparently in 1807. As we have seen, William (III) his father from Woodbridge had been a draper – and said so in his will – but an examination of the Roll of the Drapers Company of Throgmorton[87] Street in London finds no mention of a William Salkeld, draper, though it does record the following Salkelds who had the Freedom of the Company after serving a seven-year apprenticeship – John, bound 1423; Charles, freedom in 1573; George, bound 1687; Charles, bound 1732 (and still living 1772); and Thomas, bound 1791, freedom 1798; from the dates I strongly suspect that this last – Thomas (XI) was the son of Thomas (X) and Elizabeth (née Guichenet) of Woodbridge, who had a draper's shop there, and who with his inheritances was a man of parts, a landowner in Hasketon, a County Treasurer, Chief Constable of the Loes Hundred – and uncle of our ancestor Francis (IV) soon to be of Runcorn.

Young Thomas (XI), his eldest son, born 13 October 1777 at Woodbridge, was however in no hurry to marry after completing his indentures as a draper – for it was not until he was 40 years old that he married Elizabeth Jones of Aldgate in the City of London, their wedding being on 14 November 1817. Woodbridge was, by then, little more than a day's trip from London, but Shrewsbury was a more tiring and expensive journey. For instance in 1829 the Royal Mail coach left the *Lion Inn* in Shrewsbury, for London, every morning at a quarter before twelve, arriving at the *Swan with Two Necks*, in Lad Lane, by 6 a.m. the following day!

THE WILL OF WILLIAM (III) SALKELD OF SHREWSBURY,
5 January 1782, LINEN DRAPER

To my dear brother Thomas (X) Salkeld of Woodbridge, Suffolk, my esteemed Friend Francis Moore of Cheapside London linen draper and my esteemed friend Joseph Carliss of Shrewsbury, Druggist, all my personal estate upon trust, the interest to pay my debts, funeral expenses etc., the result of the sales of effects, the capital to be invested in land and not in the Funds and one fifth part of the interest to my wife Mrs. Hannah Salkeld junior.

The trustees to be Guardians of my children, the remainder of my Estate to be divided equally between my five children Harriet, William (IV), Charlotte, Maria and Francis (VI) share and share alike, the share of my sons to be paid them at their age of 21, the share of my daughters to be paid them at the age of 21 or day of marriage.

In case all my said children shall happen to die before their respective portions become payable then I give and bequeath all the rest residue and remainder of my personal estate to my two brothers the said Thomas (X) Salkeld and Francis (III) Salkeld of London to be equally divided between them.

Execs: Thomas (X) Salkeld, Francis Moore and Joseph Carliss
Witnesses: S. Milward, Thomas Loxdale junior

Chapter Fourteen

The Salkelds into Cheshire

At Daresbury church there is a large 'table' tomb to the right of the main entrance, in excellent repair, and inscribed as follows:

> Here lieth the body of Luke Jones of Preston departed this life October 8th 1800 age 24 years. Francis Salkeld who departed this life October 26 1866 aged 85 years. His end was peace. Elizabeth Salkeld the beloved wife of the above who departed this life March 8 1849 aged 74 years. Much and deservedly regretted. Francis Salkeld son of Francis and Elizabeth Salkeld of Runcorn who departed this life August 28 1808 aged 3 years 5 months, also two boys who were stillborn. Thomas Salkeld their son who departed this life July 26 1820 aged 8 years 5 months.

There is a big space left, with no further entries.

Who was Luke Jones and why was he buried in a Salkeld grave? Why were there only Salkeld infants mentioned? But above all, where had this Francis come from? The history of Francis's *ancestors* I have already collected together into preceding chapters. The last chapter mentioned Francis's family, and those whom he left behind in Shrewsbury, in the shop or shops they owned on Pride Hill, where Francis had been born on 5 March 1781.

The first point to note is that Francis's own father died only a year after Francis had been born, and was buried on 8 March 1782 in St Alkmund's, Shrewsbury, thus leaving Francis's mother Hannah to bring up the family. There was already, besides Francis, an eldest brother William, born 1771 and therefore 10 years senior to Francis; some say there was also another son Joseph, but if so he is not mentioned in their father William's will which was written on 5 January 1782.

Francis grew up, fatherless and very much the younger brother, in the shop on Pride Hill, and was no doubt watched over by his guardians who included his uncle Thomas, gentleman, of Woodbridge in Suffolk, who had his own large family and wide interests, but who may well have found the journey from Woodbridge to Shrewsbury rather too far to permit frequent calls on this young nephew. It would be of great interest to find just what it was which persuaded Francis to move, at the tender age of 14 (to be exact, on 5 April 1795), to Runcorn, some forty-five miles north of Shrewsbury. His father had been a draper – as was his uncle in Woodbridge; and his brother was to become a successful wine merchant in Shrewsbury. It is true that, many years later, Francis described *himself* as a 'retired grocer' (in the 1861 census) but, as we shall see, he developed many other outdoor interests, and, in particular, his canal operations scarcely fit in with the image of a small shopkeeper of those times. I suspect that his brother William, who in the year of Francis's move to Runcorn would have been 24 years old, may have made the necessary enquiries to locate a suitable employer under whom his young brother could serve, but this is merely a guess. What is certain is that on 3 October 1797 Francis was bound apprentice to Mr. Morrison, in Runcorn, for six years. But on Morrison's leaving Runcorn, Francis entered into an agreement to serve Messrs. Wright, George Jackson and Samuel Sherlock for six years from 1 April 1802 –

just a year after his marriage in 1801. Samuel Sherlock had an interest in the local Runcorn brewery at that time.

With one third of his indentures to run, and whilst still at the 'tender' age of 20, Francis married a widow with a two-year-old daughter Catherine. (This I learnt from a search of a Salkeld Family Bible kindly lent by the daughter of the late John ('Uncle Jack') Salkeld, a son of Arthur Salkeld by a second marriage.) The widow's maiden name was Kirkham; she was the eldest of a family of three boys and three girls, born between August 1774 and September 1791, to Thomas Kirkham and Sarah his wife (who were born in 1750 and 1749 respectively, and were buried in Daresbury on 5 February 1820 and 24 December 1824, respectively). Father Thomas Kirkham was probably a farmer or a farm-worker. He must not be confused with a Thomas Kirkham who is shown in Jos. Foster's *Index Ecclesiasticus* as being a 'Reverend' and priest in charge of nearby Croft, in 1839 – 19 years after our Thomas had died; nor could this parson be a *son* of our farmer, as the three sons were named Richard, John and William, born respectively in June 1776, April 1778, and April 1780. To complete the Kirkham picture, Elizabeth's two sisters were the youngest of the family, and named Sarah (born May 1783, died Liverpool, December 1838) and Mary (born September 1791 and died St Helens, 2 June 1864). Her brothers all died before she did, their deaths occurring on 9 April 1840 (Richard, buried Daresbury), 2 January 1828 (John, buried in 'Mr. Kenwright's vault' in Stoke-on-Trent), and on 22 November 1824 (William). Elizabeth, as we shall see, died on 8 March 1849 'at 11 a.m.', at the respectable age of 75, with, of all her family of Kirkhams, only sister Mary still living.

The first really big event in Elizabeth's life must have been her marriage to young Luke Jones, commemorated by the aforementioned Bible embossed on the front simply 'Luke & Elizabeth Jones 1800' with a pattern.

On the inside front cover are details of Thomas and Sarah Kirkham's family – as above – followed by details of the Salkeld family as produced by Elizabeth, and kept more or less up to date. This Bible is now in the possession of Jack Salkeld's daughter Mrs. Elizabeth Jones of Tarvin near Chester. Despite its most informative contents the Bible does not record the date of Elizabeth's wedding in the year 1800; as it was to last so short a time, with young Luke dying in October 1800, that same year, this is indeed a loss. So is the entry on the reverse of the second page, of the birth of 'Catherine Jones born September 179x', the x here standing for an indecipherable figure, This vagueness about dates, when placed in the context of the Bible's other entries, suggests the possibility that Catherine was Elizabeth's daughter but born out of wedlock, and that the wedding in 1800 put all right again. Be that as it may, the record goes on then to add that the young Catherine in due course married a surgeon Thomas Case who died in 1849 (9 November), and that she died, childless, on 23 January 1851, some two years after Elizabeth her mother had died.

What caused the so early death on 8 October 1800 of Elizabeth's young husband Luke Jones is not on record; he was buried in the grave in Daresbury Churchyard on 11 October 1800, at the age of 24, Elizabeth being two years older. Nor do we know how she first met young Francis Salkeld, nor indeed the date or place of their marriage, though as their first child Hannah was born on 3 May 1802 the wedding must surely have been in mid-1801, with Francis just 20 years old and still indentured to employers in Runcorn. (At age 21 he would inherit £400 from his Woodbridge grandmother's will.) His bride was three-and-a-half years his senior. He may at this stage have been a non-Conformist, for there is an entry in the Bible that he was *christened* on 13 April 1811 in Runcorn, by the Rev. Mr. Kyte, his godfathers being Ralph Green and his wife's father Thomas Kirkham – with Mrs. Kirkham his mother-in-law as his godmother! On the date of his christening therefore, Francis was a married man aged just 30, with a step-daughter (Catherine), a wife three years his senior, a son and two daughters alive, and another son having lived for only three years. He and Elizabeth were to have three more children, excluding two stillborn. A photograph of a portrait of Elizabeth, painted by an unknown artist sometime in the period 1825-35 (judging by her dress), shows her as she was some ten or more years after her last child had been born – as a rather frail little body wearing a mob-cap and seated in a large chair nursing a sleeping white cat. This picture is of very special interest as being the *oldest* extant 'likeness' of any member of the Salkeld family since the alabaster tomb of Sir Richard Salkeld and his wife Lady Jane was placed in Wetheral Church in about A.D. 1501. The original painting is in the possession of Miss Elsie Guest (a descendant of Francis and Elizabeth) of Prestatyn, North Wales, who very kindly had it professionally photographed in 1979.

Although describing himself in the 1861 National Census as a 'retired Grocer' ('with one servant'), Francis had many other interests, being at various times an operator of canal-boats, the manager of 'Salkeld wharf' which he built, the owner of a brewery in Runcorn, hotel-owner (*The Navigation*), a farmer (Pool Farm) and a considerable landowner with property at his death – including Pool House and Pool Dale – stretching up to the village of Halton. Some of this land he sold to his son-in-law John Hazelhurst (husband of his daughter Sarah, married 7 January 1830) who built 'The Grange' on it for his own son Charles Hazelhurst. The Grange later was to be the headquarters of the Runcorn Urban District Council – the Town Hall in fact; it stands in extensive grounds into which the buildings now penetrate. The Hazelhursts who occupied it came from Beaconsfield, once a large house on Weston Road on the way from Runcorn to Weston village; they were important employers of local labour in the Camden soap manufacturing works in Runcorn.

Thoroughly to understand the factors which were to determine the rise and fall of the canal industry in this area would require a separate study of the famous Bridgewater Canal, completed in 1773 to link the Duke's coal mines at Worsley near Manchester to Runcorn and the River Mersey (to be linked later with the Mersey and Irwell and with the Trent and Mersey canals). Canal development offered to Francis Salkeld and, later, to his son William Francis Salkeld a source of much of their wealth. Francis was soon operating a fleet of canal boats which carried Cornish china-clay from the docks and wharfs at Runcorn into the Potteries, bringing back to the Port of Runcorn their manufactured pottery for export in larger (ocean-going) ships. In particular he set up, with W. R. Crockett of Little Onion Hall, Lichfield, a partnership under which Crocket supervised the Potteries end of the business, and Francis the Runcorn end; this partnership was terminated in November 1830, by which time the boats were bringing coal back from the Potteries. Interestingly, the canal route passed through Preston Brook (O.S. map ref. 5680) where the Bridgewater Canal and the Trent and Mersey Canal met, and no doubt Francis would often proceed from Runcorn to this Junction on his horse, calling in on his wife's relatives who lived thereabouts, and strengthening his contacts with those who worshipped at Daresbury Church (four miles from Pool

26. Pool Dale, Runcorn.

Dale), at the top of the hill; he and his wife are, as we have already said, buried in that churchyard. All this business he handed over eventually to his son William Francis who, born in Runcorn on 3 August 1809, became by 1820 his only surviving son. Born at the house 'Pool Dale' which his father had built, William Francis later lived in another of his father's houses – Pool House – in Runcorn, and extended his father's interests. But before going into any detail about William, we must first finish our tale about Francis his father.

The managers, whom Francis needed to operate his businesses, themselves needed houses, and these Francis built for them in Halton Road, Runcorn – just beyond the Gas Works, a practical if not perhaps a very salubrious site! His brewery, and his hotel *The Navigation* adjoining, he rented to son William, who used the hotel mostly as a bottle store.[88]

In his will, dated 30 September 1850 (probate granted 16 years later, following his death on 26 October 1866), Francis appointed as his executors his son William Francis and his son-in-law John Hazelhurst. To his youngest daughter 'Betsy', who, born 26 October 1818, had married Joseph Hall of Warrington on 17 December 1844, he merely left his gold watch. She died on 18 June 1898, at the age of eighty. To his son-in-law John Hazelhurst, who had married his daughter Sarah (born 13 June 1807) on 7 January 1830, he left his silver snuff-box; she died 8 May 1891, at the age of 84; popularly known as 'Aunt John'; she lived alone in Roche House, in the High Street, from her husband's death in August 1885. (One of their two sons took as his second wife the Hon. Blanche Devereux, sister of the 16th Viscount Hereford, but they had no children and she died in 1923.) Francis had named one of his flatboats 'Sarah' and this in course of time became the property of William Francis. Francis also left other property to Sarah, and to his daughter Maria (born 26 April 1815 and married on 25 October 1832 to John William Webster of Bury St Edmunds), and to the children of his late daughter Hannah (who on 15 June 1824 had married John Ellison of Bowden and died there in January 1840) – the children's names being Elizabeth, Thomas, Frank, and Harry. All the residue he left to William Francis his son, with instructions that his farm 'Pool Farm' was to be sold to meet 'debts owed to John Rowland'.

This grand old man was, as we have seen, born at Pride Hill, Shrewsbury, on 5 March 1781 – at 10 a.m. – and died 26 October 1866, aged 85, in the home he had built in Runcorn known as Pool Dale. But his will does not disclose two sadnesses in his life – the death from measles of 'very young' Francis on 28 August 1808, his second child and but three years old; and the accident which occurred on 26 July 1820 when his fifth child Thomas – born February 1812 – fell off a hired pony in Greenway Road, Runcorn at 5.30 p.m. and was killed by the fall. This is the Thomas Salkeld whose name appears alongside those of Francis and Elizabeth, and Luke Jones, on that windswept grave in Daresbury churchyard. We must not forget that the author of the *Alice* children's stories – Lewis Carroll – was also born at Daresbury (at the now demolished Old Parsonage) on 27 January 1832 and lived there until 1843, perhaps, as a small boy, meeting some of these Salkelds who worshipped in his father's church.

New canals continued to be built until about 1827, especially in the south of England, but by that date the threat of competition from the expanding railways began to make itself felt. One of the many handicaps of the canal system in England was that the 70 ft. boats with their 7 ft. beam and $3\frac{1}{4}$ ft. draft carried only 30 tons at less than an average of three miles per hour, for even up to the First World War they were mostly horse-drawn; the canal *barges* with twice the beam could carry up to sixty tons, though perhaps more slowly. To go faster endangered the canal banks, and the use of tugs or power boats in place of horses was seldom economic and never so if many locks had to be negotiated. Despite all this, it is true to say that most of these canals prospered, year by year, beyond 1867 – their centenary as a system. Certainly the rise of Runcorn as a town and port, in the 30 years from 1831, was due to them, and the period 1845-6 was one of great prosperity to the canal community at Preston Brook. For a detailed account of the many problems raised by the growing competition – from other canals but mostly from the railways – the book *After the Canal Duke* by F. C. Mather (Oxford 1970)[90] is very informative, showing as it does the continually changing commercial scene; a few examples follow:

   p. 123-4 – Competition for loads to the Midlands, between five carriers on different canals – including the Weaver Navigation and the Ellesmere and Chester Canal – using different seaports to start from.
   p. 129 (and p. 132) – Price cutting by carriers in 1837.
   p. 133 – New railway opening, threatening the canal route via Preston Brook.
   p. 258 – Too many loaded sea-vessels arriving at Runcorn in 1850 leading to a shortage of canal boats in this and several later years.

At this competitive period it must be remembered that Runcorn was not served by any railway line (until the railway bridge over the Mersey was built – it was started in 1863 and completed in 1868), so that goods arriving at Liverpool had to be re-shipped to the docks at Runcorn if they were to use the canal systems, or else they were sent to other ports such as Fleetwood or Bristol. The greater Manchester Ship Canal was not in existence, its 35 miles not being constructed until 1885-94, so that Manchester had to use the canals here described, or choose the famous rail link to Liverpool.

The canal owners, and their customers for canal carriage, were waging a losing battle, but even by 1906 the railways owned no more than 1,138 miles of the 3,902 miles of canal and inland waterway – which total includes some 1,500 miles of canalised rivers; nor was there much change in these figures by 1928.

Early Runcorn

Francis Salkeld came to Runcorn from his parents' home in Shrewsbury in April 1795. William Francis, his son and heir, died in Runcorn in April 1897; these two direct ancestors spent this one hundred year period in Runcorn. The first half of the period I take from Mr. William Bagshaw's *History Gazetteer and Directory of Cheshire* (Sheffield 1850)[91] and much of the second half from the *Journal* kept by Richard Lea between 1837 and 1891, given to me by Miss Elsie Guest.

In 1801 (the year of Francis's marriage) the population of Runcorn – including Daresbury, Halton, Moore, and Weston – was 4,860 souls; today (1987) it exceeds 36,000. It probably owes its position to the fact that the winding River Mersey is at its narrowest at this point. But the town did not prosper, and in 1656 was described as 'a very poor village with a fair church on the banks of the river' remained in obscurity until the opening, in 1773, of the canal cut by the Duke of Bridgewater, connecting his collieries at Worsley, and Manchester, to the River Mersey and thereby opening up commerce and trade in both directions. In 1803 the proprietors of the Mersey and Irwell

27.   A View of Runcorn, 1835-46.

Navigation opened a canal to Latchford. Vessels drawing up to sixteen feet could be admitted at spring tides; quays and warehouses were built and 'powerful steamers ply every tide between Runcorn and Liverpool which tow ships with cargoes to or from the docks or canals, free of charge'. This also opened up the markets for the sandstone quarries at Runcorn. Soap manufacture, ship building, tanning, iron foundries and rope manufacture, etc., prospered, and by 1841 the population had increased to 12,700 persons.

At this time there was no means of crossing the Mersey at Runcorn (save by the 'man-managed' passenger ferry), until the completion of the railway bridge, with a footway at one side, in 1868; the well-known transporter bridge with its travelling car slung from the single span was not opened until 1905, to be replaced in 1961 by the permanent high-level roadway which has left no trace of its forerunner. The site of the original ferry was alongside the original baths, themselves opened in 1922. The Runcorn Savings Bank (founded by a Salkeld) and the Post Office are both in the High Street, as is the Town Hall (built in 1831). In this street lived the Hazelhursts – John, Thomas, and William, of the Camden Soap Works, and Charles lived in Waterloo House, in 1847 (John, son of Thomas, married of course Sarah Salkeld, a daughter of Thomas).

Of Weston, some two miles from Runcorn, Bagshaw says:[91]

> Opposite Weston is the widest part of the Mersey; and when the tide is up, and the numerous vessels are clearing out or coming in, the scene has a very pretty and animated appearance. To the right is seen the Mersey, there expanding like an immense lake, dotted over with vessels carrying salt and other merchandise to Liverpool and other places. On the left are the bold acclivities of Overton and Helsby, and in the front is a fine view of the plain of the Wirral, bounded by the Dee, and the extreme distance by the Welsh mountains . . . In this township are several extensive quarries of free stone, worked by Mr. John Tomkinson, who employs upwards of 150 men, and at some periods has employed as many as 700. The stone is conveyed by a tramway from the quarries to the river . . . West from the Village is Weston Point, a hamlet of several houses and a neat church, one of three built by the Trustees of the Weaver Navigation for the accommodation of watermen. This is the point of terminus of the Weaver Navigation.

As for the transport in 1850, an omnibus ran daily from the *Royal Hotel*, Runcorn, to Northwich, 'meeting the Liverpool steam packet'; another left the ferry house at Runcorn Gap at 7.30 a.m. for St Helens where trains departed daily (five a day), the bus returning at 10.30 a.m. and 5.30 p.m. A steam packet to Liverpool called at Weston Point, arriving from Liverpool one hour before high water; another ran to Manchester by the Mersey and Irwell Navigation, every morning and afternoon except Sunday, taking passengers to Warrington, Eccles, etc. From Manchester a packet at 7.30 a.m. and 1.15 p.m. by the Bridgewater canal 'takes passengers to Preston Brook, Warrington Lymm and Altrincham' etc. Goods by water to Liverpool, Manchester and Chester by the Mersey and Irwell canal; by the Bridgewater canal to Manchester, Liverpool by Preston Brook, and by the Anderton Co. from Runcorn to Macclesfield, Northwich, Congleton and the Potteries; and by the North Staffordshire Railway from Runcorn by water to the Potteries. Mary Lownds from her house on Mill Brown, Runcorn (near Pool Dale) 'carried to Warrington'.

Richard Lea describes Runcorn in 1839 as 'a mere fishing village' with some shipbuilding in four named yards. Mr. Charles Hazelhurst lived at the Grange (built for him by Francis Salkeld). The town had one large windmill. The old parish church had a tower with four bells, which included two cracked ones, and pealed 'ding dong smack wop'. The 'Westminster Cocoa Rooms' occupied a site near the Duke's warehouse, and the tannery now worked by Mr. Ockleston was then known as 'Salkeld's Wharf'. Mr. John Wright had another tannery in the High Street. In 1839 there was only one police constable ('Old Harding').

The five-and-a-half acre cemetery in Greenway Road was opened in 1861; a cryptic entry by Richard Lea, 19 August 1875 'Ma hurt her great toe with a weight and had to have leeches' throws light on the state of medicine in Runcorn. And the effect of the railway on the postal services is illustrated by the entry '1 Feb. 1887. From this date the mail cart ceases to run as the mail bags are now received at Runcorn Station at

28.   Runcorn Docks and the Bridgewater Canal.

3.15 a.m. On Sunday night the mails are sent by cart to Warrington, Samuel Yarwood contractor, 15s. for the journey to Warrington'.

We continue our account of the Salkelds in Cheshire with the observation that if we were correct in describing Francis Salkeld as a 'grand old man' when he died at the age of 85, then we must coin a still grander phrase to fit his son William Francis, who was born at Pool Dale on 3 August 1809, and who died in Pool House (both built by his father) on 28 April 1897. For William Francis lived to the age of 87 – two years longer than his father – had more children than his father, and in addition to keeping going his father's businesses, he expanded them and created quite new ones as well.

Genetically, boys (as distinct from girls) were having a hard life in this Salkeld family, for by the time that William Francis had reached the not very great age of 11, there had been two stillborn boys, another boy (Francis) who had died of measles at the age of three, and another boy (Thomas) who had died at the age of eight from a fall from a pony – leaving William Francis as the sole male heir of his father; true there were four girls – two born before and two after William Francis, all of whom eventually married and so provided father Francis with sons-in-law in plenty; but all this clearly placed William Francis in a special position, as heir apparent, in the household. We have no portrait of him, beyond what can be gleaned from his activities and interests, and from documents left by a few who knew him.

We can be sure that he learnt to ride at an early age, to be able to accompany his father on canal business, and though he did not marry until he was 32, when he did, he chose a young girl of 20 who lived at Latchford near Warrington. Her name was Elizabeth Hall and she is said to have been a farmer's daughter from Preston Brook, at that time an important canal operating centre. Whether she came from Latchford or from Preston Brook, may be a matter of what one understands as the meaning of 'came from'. Both are on routes connected with the same canal, and she may have been born at one and have been living, before her wedding, at the other.

They were married on 3 August 1841, on William Francis' thirty-second birthday, and they lived at Pool House, alongside his father at Pool Dale. Over a 22-year period they were to have eight children, the period starting with the birth of a daughter Elizabeth Hall Salkeld on 29 May 1842 (known as 'Aunt Libby' – she did not marry, and died 27 February 1893 aged 50) and ending with the birth of Frederick Charles on 4 June 1864, 23 years after their marriage. (This son entered the church and married, in Ceylon, Frances Sarah Graham; they had four daughters Olga, Eva, Brenda and Dagmar, and two sons William Francis and Percy; Francis recently lived in Brighton.) Within this 22-year period we find also the birth of Francis on 23 May 1844, who died of consumption 10 years later; of William, born on 31 October 1848, who died of whooping cough eight years later; and of little Rosa Ann, an infant born on 6 May 1857, who died three days later. To simplify my tale I have deliberately taken these out of order, so that I could now concentrate on the three 'major' children Jessie Maud, Arthur, and Joseph Hall Salkeld, of whom Arthur, our direct ancestor, will be dealt with last.

Jessie Maud was born on 13 June 1846, and, when 26, on 3 September 1872, married a Runcorn man William Edgar Lea, son of Richard Lea who had been born in September 1821 and who had married Hannah – a girl from Hertford – on 13 March 1848. William Edgar was born in 1849, by which time his father Richard had founded the Runcorn firm of Lea and Son, hardware dealers, who later developed into heating engineers; Richard died after 1891, leaving a most interesting diary ('journal') which I have been given by my cousin Elsie Guest; before his death Richard was also responsible for the Runcorn Post Office. His father John Lea (born 1782, died 1821) was a farmer and builder. William Edgar Lea and his wife Jessie Maud (Salkeld) had two sons and two daughters. The eldest, Julia, married Charles Worral who died in 1933, she being alive in 1980, with no children; the second, Francis Richard Lea, married Maud Orme and died 1966, she having died without issue in 1955. The third, Edgar Lea, born 1873, married Nora Harrison in 1918, and they had two girls Brenda Noreen and Frances Margaret; Edgar Lea died on 27 December 1972, in his one hundredth year, having journeyed into Runcorn frequently from his home in Prestatyn even in his last years to supervise the ironmongery business. The fourth child was born 31 October 1877 and christened Eleanor Lucy Nora; in 1910 she married Walter Guest and they had two girls Doris born 1913 – and Elsie, born 1912.

Before turning to Arthur Salkeld, a little must be said about his brother Joseph Hall Salkeld who was born 11 January 1854 at Pool Dale and later lived at Pool House; he remained a bachelor and made himself responsible for the clerical side of the family estates, collecting rents and running agencies for his father William Francis, and for the Hazelhursts, from whom he inherited, as a 'cousin'. He was buried in his father's grave in Runcorn parish church on 16 July 1926.

Gradually William Francis saw the wisdom of withdrawing capital from the 'canal stakes', and he embarked on a policy of selling the Salkeld interests to local organisations such as the Runcorn Urban District Council and the Runcorn Waterworks. With his father's other interests he still had plenty to do, and in the *History and Directory of Cheshire* published by William Bagshaw in 1850 (p. 583)[91] he describes himself as 'Salkeld Mr. Francis, Farmer'. But he was more than that. He started the Runcorn Savings Bank; he founded a private company to supply water to Runcorn, Halton and Weston, in 1854; in 1858 he founded the Runcorn Cemetery to supplement the parish graveyard; with his friends he built the Runcorn Public Hall. (At the centenary celebrations in 1938 the Runcorn Council published an account of all these activities.)

An interesting link in the above is given in a letter to Lilian Moore (née Salkeld) from Edgar Lea, dated 26 February 1968, describing how his grandfather William Francis Salkeld, as Actuary of the Runcorn Savings Bank, had on 9 March 1881 made out little Edgar's first savings bank book; this first deposit was for £1 16s. By 1887, including interest and later small deposits, it was in credit to a total of £4 11s. 5d. Edgar adds 'I think it was more a spare time hobby for Grandpa as he had so much to do with Waterworks, Burial Board, Public Hall, etc. Seeing the late times the Bank was open' [to eight o'clock in the evening] 'he would have some lonely walks to Pool House with poor gas-lights in those days, none after Union Street'.

And so, in the fullness of time, William Francis Salkeld's long life came to an end, in Pool House, on 28 April 1897. He was buried in the family grave at Runcorn Parish Church, and not in the wind-swept tomb in Daresbury churchyard where lie his beloved father and mother. At the Probate of his will on 30 July 1897, in London, his effects totalled only £288 8s. 11d. and his executors were given as:

Arthur Salkeld, Salt Agent
Joseph Hall Salkeld, Alkali Agent

Joseph Hall continued to live on at Pool House until his own death in 1926.

Chapter Fifteen

Arthur Salkeld and Family

In our study of the Salkelds in Cheshire we turn now to Arthur, the remaining child of William Francis Salkeld and his wife Elizabeth – remaining in the sense that, as our direct ancestor, we have kept him to the last. Born at Pool Dale, Runcorn on 15 February 1851, he was the fifth child, but, with the early death of his brother Francis in March 1854 of consumption, and of brother William in January 1857 of whooping cough, he became the eldest son. There are photographs of him as an adult, generally amongst a group of relatives; a good-looking slightly stocky but well set-up man who could dress very smartly when the occasion required; regular features, a firm chin and slight sideboards complete the picture. Little detail has survived of his early years until his marriage, on 28 July 1880 at the age of 29, to Clara Ellen Morris, a delightful lady five years his senior, about whom we shall have a good deal to say. The Morris family were well-to-do business people from the Macclesfield area of Cheshire; how and where Arthur met them, we do not know, but would very much like to.

On marriage, Arthur had to leave the home where he was born, and set up his own establishment, which was at Number 12 Waterloo Road, Runcorn, a terraced house of modest size and almost no garden. It stands yet, peeping from under one of the great arches of the concrete road bridge which today spans the River Mersey in place of the Transporter Bridge shown in older views of Runcorn.

After the marriage, Arthur wisely – in view of the age of his wife – wasted no time in starting his family, their first child, my mother Mary Elizabeth Lilian Salkeld, being born at 12 Waterloo Road on 20 May 1881. Numerous photographs show her generally as a small girl in the protection of a formidable old lady, her grandmother Morris; a little later they are accompanied by a thin pale child Edith Ellen, born only 15 months after Lilian, and who lived for only 16 months. The mother Clara Ellen survived these shocks (and busied herself with social work, 'helping unfortunates'), but died at Runcorn on 3 April 1890 at the age of 44, their only surviving child Lilian being nearly nine years old. Clara Ellen's will was made, at 12 Waterloo Road, on 11 March 1882, bequeathing all to her husband Arthur and appointing him her sole Executor; her witnesses were William Wright and George Livesley; Probate was in London at the High Court, on 16 August 1895; why there was a delay of just over five years in securing Probate, I do not know.

Some insight into Clara Ellen's character is obtainable from a letter written by Edgar Salkeld Lea to her daughter Lilian on 26 February 1968; after referring to his grandfather William Francis he continues:

> I liked your mother, our Aunt Clara, so one day I decided to pay her a visit on my own (you might have been an infant at that time and that could have been an extra attraction). Anyhow I called and was asked in and I suppose made a fuss of and probably stayed for afternoon tea – can't remember. Then I went home to 'Belvedere' opposite the River Mersey. I could not have been over 11 years old (as we left Belvedere when I was 11). When your father [Arthur] got back from his

29.   12 Waterloo Road, Runcorn.

office they wondered whether mother had sent me with a message. In case it should be so, Uncle
Arthur took the trouble to call upon my parents to see if I had lost any message . . .

This would have occurred in about 1883 when Lilian was about two years old.

Elsewhere, in a letter to me in November 1978, Elsie Guest says that her mother
(Nora) 'thought Clara Ellen the most wonderful lady she had ever met, loved her even
more than her own mother and knew her when playing with Lilian her cousin when
both were children'. This same letter contains interesting details of the Lea family, the
most relevant for this study of the Salkelds being that William Edgar Lea (born 1849)
was brought up by an uncle in Tarvin and when in August 1872 he married Arthur
Salkeld's sister Jessie Maud Salkeld he took over his father's shop and engineering
works in Runcorn whereupon his father (Richard Lea) looked after the Runcorn Post
Office and later retired to Hope Villa, Little Sutton, where he died, and was buried at
Tarvin. This helps to explain some of the references which Richard makes in his
aforementioned journal 1837-91 which I have used in compiling my comments on
'Runcorn'. Elsie Guest adds that her mother 'used to talk to me about seeing the Salkeld
family at Trinity Church [Runcorn] in the pew opposite to the Lea's pew, and of going
to Pool House to see her grandfather William Francis Salkeld, and Arthur'.

But the married life of Clara Ellen was to be of little less than ten years' duration;
when Lilian was just short of nine her beloved mother died. (It is said of tuberculosis
contracted after visiting a sick friend.) She was buried in the grave of her second and
last child the little Edith Ellen, in Runcorn Cemetery, and not with her husband, and
at the early age of forty-four. Arthur returned to his home; he was still only a young
man of 39, and for the next three years lived in Pool House with young Lilian. Until,
on bonfire night 1892, at a party in the conservatory, he proposed to Lilian's governess,
Miss Jessie Tinkler Crosby, a farmer's daughter, born in Hallwood May 1867, and thus
25 years of age. They were married on 19 May 1893, the day before Lilian's twelfth
birthday, and the birth of their first child Francis John Salkeld on 19 February 1894
saw the start of a new family of seven children; Lilian stayed in her father's house, and
seems to have been able to get along well enough with her stepmother, until her own
marriage to Joseph William Moore in June 1905.

Our narrative now splits into four: first, to say more about Clara Ellen, and her own
girlhood before marrying Arthur; second, to outline the rest of Arthur's career; third,
to describe the seven stepchildren; and fourth, to trace Lilian's own career. We shall
take them in that order.

Before Clara Ellen married Arthur Salkeld on 28 July 1880 she had spent the first
34 years of her life in the bosom of her 'family Morris', latterly at a very nice house in
Rainow, near Macclesfield, still known as 'Kerridge End House'. Her father John
Morris (whose will of 17 July 1868 was proved at Chester 17 September 1868) had died
when she was a young spinster of 22, but her mother Jane, a daughter of Robert Hughes,
had been born in 1810 and did not die until 1895, five years after Clara Ellen's own
death. Robert Hughes had other children – John, Robert, Elizabeth Ann – and in his
will had left shops and houses in Hughes Street and Brook Street, Chorlton upon
Medlock, in Trust for his daughter Jane (*before* her marriage to John Morris) and to her
children if any thereafter.

Jane Hughes and John Morris had married in about 1835, when John (born 16 March
1809) was 26 and she a year younger; they were to have three children – all girls –

including their youngest Clara Ellen; the eldest was christened Sarah Jane, and the second, Mary Elizabeth Lomax. Father John appears to have worried about the three daughters, particularly whether they would find husbands to support them after he had gone, and in his will leaves £1,000 to any daughter who marries, 'for her separate use'. Clara Ellen, as we know, did marry (Arthur Salkeld), and Mary Elizabeth Lomax was engaged to marry when she died in 1881. For good measure Sarah Jane married twice – firstly to John Bell, who died with no issue and was buried at Whalley parish churchyard – and then to George Owen (a son of Mary the sister of John Morris). Her will of 14 December 1915 (she died 17 March 1916 at 122 Raby Street, Moss Side, Manchester) directs that she, Sarah Jane Owen, be buried in the grave at Whalley of her *first* husband John Bell, and that her second husband George was to be paid the not very princely sum of £1 a week 'as long as he does not interfere with her instructions!' (i.e. contest the will). George appears to have complied with this condition; he died 11 January 1921 at 62 Eastbourne Street, West Derby, near Liverpool. Known to Lilian Salkeld and others as 'Aunt Jane', this formidable lady appointed Arthur Salkeld, Joseph William Moore, and Francis John Salkeld as her Trustees and Executors; the gross value of her estate was £2,756. Her headstone was to be carved 'Until the Day dawns' and no flowers were to be placed on the grave.

As neither she, nor her sister Mary Elizabeth Lomax Morris, had produced offspring, it is easy to understand her interest in and affection for the children of her sister Clara Ellen – and as little Edith Ellen died 16 months after birth, this really meant Lilian. Sarah left two-thirds of the residue to Lilian's children, whereas the children of Arthur's second marriage shared the remaining third between the six of them. In the event this meant £231 to each of Lilian's boys, plus a silver tea-service to her youngest son John Moore, and other bequests to daughter Joan and to Lilian and her husband. But Sarah's Trustees had to work for their money, because the small house at 122 Raby Street was apparently in a very untidy state when she died. Clara Ellen does not appear to have been a recipient under her sister's will, but she had in fact inherited, as did Lilian, under a settlement from the estates of her grandfather Hughes.

All the above connects directly or indirectly with John Morris and his three girls and their Hughes mother. But it should be added that John was but one member of a family of seven children, whose parents were John Morris 'senior', and wife Sarah; not in date order, the children were Mary (mother of George Owen), Elizabeth (will 3 April 1897), Sarah, Hannah, Alice, John (of whom we have just been dealing) and most important, John's brother Edmund. Most important, because Edmund had two girls and two boys – Edith Ellen, Alice Amy, Edmund Rothwell and Arthur J.; they too inherited under the 1847 Settlement of their grandparents (which penetrated through to Lilian on more than one occasion, as benefactors died) and, being not unlike each other in appearance, add to the confusion when studying the few Morris photographs which have survived. In particular, a painting of John Morris and his wife and three daughters is full of interest.

John, his wife Jane, and their daughter Mary Elizabeth Lomax Morris, are all buried in a 'table' grave opposite the main (tower) entrance to Trinity Church Rainow, inscribed

> Sacred to the memory of John Morris of Kerridge End House, Rainow, who departed this life July 18 1868 aged 59 years also Jane beloved wife of the above who departed this life April 20 1895 aged 85 years also Mary Elizabeth Lomax Morris second daughter of the above who fell asleep in Jesus June 17 1881 aged 41 years. . . .

Several relics have survived to remind us of Lilian's mother Clara Ellen and the Morris and Hughes family; these are: A bone or ivory card case, heavily carved and on the hinged lid a small oblong silver plate inscribed 'John Morris Junior'; this I have given to my daughter Gillian Dunsterville, as my mother Lilian left it to me. I made this gift in 1975.

Two 4 inch by 3 inch silhouette wooden-framed miniatures, one facing left, the other facing right, one (left) with the gold edging obliterated with black to indicate decease, which are in my opinion – they are by P. Skeolan Manchester and dated 1848 and marked Morris – very relevant to the above, but must be of an earlier generation to be dated 1848 – the sitters would have been *born* about 1825-30?, perhaps sisters of John Morris?

A copybook, entitled 'Thomas Morris Book December 10th 1812' on the inside front cover the words, in a shaky handwriting – 'This was among Aunt Elizabeth's things, evidently kept because they were proud of it. Written by Thomas Morris, born 1800, eldest brother of your grandfather, he died 1821 – you boys may be interested in it.'

I am sure that the Aunt Elizabeth referred to was Elizabeth the daughter of John Morris *senior* and his wife Sarah, and that the 'boys' were Edmund Rothwell and Arthur J. Morris; but as this Elizabeth did not die until 1897, it could not have been Jane Morris who wrote those words, as she died in 1895. Let us say that it was probably another of John Morris's sisters.

The book itself is interesting, written in very beautiful copperplate uniform writing; we have – p. 1. 'Trade furnishes employment for mankind' repeated six times and signed 'Thomas Morris, written at the age of 12'. p. 2. 'Resignation' – 'When even at last the solemn hour shall come, And wing my mystic flight to future worlds. I cheerful will obey; there, with new powers, Will rising wonders sing; I cannot go, Where Universal Love not smiles around.' Succeeding pages have 'Acquisitions in learning procure advancement' (five times) 'Christmas' (three times) 'Learning is valuable' (four times) 'Gaming is a wicked custom' (five times) 'Youth should endeavour to avoid disgrace' (six times) and finally 'Penmanship' (four times). The writer of these great thoughts was clearly a brother, Thomas, of John Morris *senior*, and therefore an uncle of John the father of Clara Ellen.

Another relic (in my bookcase) is a two-volume 1861 edition of Chapman and Hall's *Pickwick Papers*, by Charles Dickens, both volumes inscribed 'March 16th 1862 a birthday present from his affectionate wife Jane Morris'.

And the last relic – perhaps the most interesting of all – a piece of paper written on both sides, with a summary of the rules laid down by 'Mamma' for use by her daughters when entertaining young gentlemen at Kerridge End. The writing is that of Sarah Jane. The main theme applies to young men with an income of less than £150 a year – they are not to have the drawing-room fire lit especially for a visit, unless it would have been lit anyway! The date of this masterpiece was perhaps 1870 – a year or two after the death of their father.

Before leaving the Morris family, perhaps a little more should be said about Kerridge End House, their family home. We do not know whether John Morris owned it or merely rented it; for the house was built in 1837 by John Mellor, a timber merchant, as his home (see[93] *The Story of Rainow*, Wilfred Palmer and Rainow W.I. 1975, and Volume III of George Ormerod's *History of Cheshire*, 1819). John Mellor died in 1846 and his son John succeeded to the business, and, incidentally, built the church to replace the chapel, in that same year. John Mellor of Kerridge End is also on record as builder of a reservoir on land he owned at the top of Bull Hill, in 1893, but we also know from the before-mentioned tomb in the churchyard that John Morris was in occupation of Kerridge End House in 1868. Other records show that the extensive yard buildings to the right of the main mansion were in use by a blacksmith William Maybury in 1850, 1860 and 1874, followed later by a wheelwright Peter Barber; coal supply, and woodworking, were also practised. The upper rooms of the stone building, and the attics of adjoining cottages, were also used for hand-loom weaving by James Swindells; but the mansion itself would in no way be rendered unattractive by these homelike activities, standing as it does well back from the road and from other buildings. One needs but little imagination to visualise the Morris family, served by local girls in maids' uniforms, taking tea on the lawns with father John and mother Jane, and discussing the supply of eligible young men in Rainow!

We have not said how these Morris men (John and Edmund) earned their living, to support their families in such style. I believe the answer is that they were in the nearby Macclesfield silk industry, but from the men's style of dress they must have been managers or buyers of this booming material, rather than supervisors or operatives, and so would drive each day into that town, to work, a mere two miles away. Kerridge End (O.S. ref. 945751) was but 1.2 miles down the now A5002 road from the bridge over the Macclesfield canal. This canal was built by Telford in 1825-7, including a 20-arch aqueduct at nearby Bollington, and opened in 1831 to traffic; the industrial area of the town is centred on this canal, which linked Manchester directly with the Potteries and so cut out the Preston Brook linkages. It is conceivable that Arthur Salkeld, or perhaps his father, met the Morris brothers on canal business connected with their silk interests in Macclesfield, otherwise it is not very obvious how Arthur and Clara Ellen, living respectively in Runcorn and in Kerridge End, should ever meet.

(Front sheet) – 'Mamma's Rules' – S.J.M.

(Inside sheet) –

Rule 1st

Mamma will give her consent if anyone of us ask it to our marriage with a man *in the certain* receipt of £150 per annum. Under £150 Mamma will not consent.

Rule 2nd

If anyone of us become engaged and have to wait an uncertain time before the man is able to command his £150 Mamma only consents to the engagement by him and us complying with her household arrangements.

Viz

The gentleman only to have tea and supper once a fortnight and *he does not sleep* in the house unless *unforeseen bad weather prevent his returning* home.

The whole of his society may be exclusively given to the one he loves during the time of his visit unless both agree to the more general.

If a fire is in the Drawing Room it is given up to them the fire is not to be lighted on purpose for them unless what is considered a valid reason is given for its being requested to be lit. The reason to be considered as valid by the whole family.

In cold weather if no fire is in the Drawing Room that we leave the Dining Room to them alone for *one hour* or *more* if a reason is given for an extension of the time being asked for.

Lastly

That the gentleman is content and we also to his having a *plain tea with no extras* but what the family might have had no visitor being present.

One exception is made to these rules that if Mary engages herself on £100 a year that for 18 months she has the same privileges as S.J. had for that period with J.B. then if his income has not increased so that marriage is humanly sure in a 12 months Mary and he fall back to the first rule of this paper.

Comments by J.G.M.

S.J. was Sarah Jane Morris who later married 'J.B.' (John Bell); Mary was the second daughter Mary Elizabeth Lomax Morris, who did get engaged but died at the age of 41 still unmarried, and is the only one of the three to be buried with the parents in Rainow churchyard. One hopes that it was not Rule 1 above which produced this sad result, but clearly when these rules were drafted and agreed, there had been a problem over Mary – she died in 1881, perhaps these Rules were written about 1870 – not very long after their father John Morris had died and left Jane with the responsibility of looking after the three girls on a not very large income.

The words in italic type were underlined in the original.

Letters to Lilian Moore

1. – From Arthur Salkeld her father. From 'Moranedd' 14 March 1913.

My dear Lilian

Enclosed find cheque for Bank and Saving Bank int; please send receipt for same. I also hand you herewith Uncle Joe's letter which may interest you. Strange I am just winding up a trust-deed that has been going on for twenty years or more, the original Trustees were 'big pots', the lady a well known Runcorn beauty, her father died and left her some £14,000. She married a big pot of Runcorn and he (the husband) and a certain cotton manufacturer were the lady's Trustees, they lived happily and luxuriously in Runcorn, and when her husband died she was horrified to find that he had spent all her money. The other Trustee, a wealthy chap, blamed himself and came to the rescue, and another Trust was started out of the husband's prospective property and cash paid down by the other Trustee. That has been going on until she passed away and the children were of age and now the solicitors have wound it all up, and I come in as a Trustee of one of the Guarantors who placed down money at the time (many many years ago) to pull the thing through. It was funny having all the old things brought up again, and shows how easily money melts away if not properly handled by careful folk.

I don't know if Joe is going anywhere this Easter but if he would like a change to the seaside, tell him we shall *be delighted to put him up*. The weather here has been simply lovely lately, and as there will be high tides at Easter it's worth while coming down to get a good breath of pure air free from alkali. We know it's useless asking you or I am sure the change would do you good and *all* vestige of infection has gone, house has been cleaned down and dis-infected so that no one could take any harm. I have not had the transfers yet, but of course when I do I will sent them to Uncle Joe for signature.

We are all very well and hope you, the kiddies and Joe are the same. With our united love to each and all

Your affectionate

Dad

Note by J.G.M.

The complexities of Lilian's Trusts are mentioned elsewhere, including her modest inheritances and her change of Trustees, but it is obvious from the above letter from her father that he had some fears that her husband might get control of her investments and sell them and he is here warning her of the evils that husbands can do! That she is not really invited to spend the Easter of 1913 in North Wales, although her husband Joe (Moore) is, was doubtless because at that time she had Denzil (born 1907) and

Grange (born 1910) though not yet John, to look after – referred to by her father as the 'kiddies'. The 'Uncle Joe' referred to was of course Joseph Hall Salkeld, who lived as a bachelor at Pool House and died in July 1926. Arthur himself died in June 1920, seven years after writing this letter, but had been living at Penmaenmar on the North Wales coast since 1911, with his second wife Jessie Tinkler but before his death moved to the Waterloo district of Liverpool, and she died there in 1938.

[The reference to disinfecting the house in Wales, in 1913, suggests that there has been a recent death there, though of course it may only have been a non-fatal bout of ill-health; I cannot identify any close relative of Arthur's who died that year.]

2. – From Amy Morris, at Eccles near Manchester, 21 May but exact year unknown – probably the late 1920s. She was one of two daughters of Edmund Morris, brother of John the father of Lilian's mother Clara Ellen.

Swiss Cottage, Albert Road, Eccles. 21 May

My dear Lilian

Many thanks for your letter this Spring. I was very interested to hear about you and your family. Please tell Mr. Moore he need not have feared it was too long. I have waited to answer till I knew my plans. Now I am here in my cousin's house and go on May 31st to Lockyer's Private Hotel, Marine Road, Colwyn Bay, probably for the whole summer. I am glad you had a good time at Barmouth. I have stayed three times and driven and cycled through all the country round, also boated a good deal there.

I have quite decided that it is impossible for me to try housekeeping again, between the great drawback of my deafness and the scarcity of maids and small houses so I am sending my furniture to Capes and Durons' sale rooms to be sold next Thursday. I only wish I had done it years ago when prices were better, for storing is very expensive now. A number of old things that belonged to my grandparents I am sending to my brother Arthur at Wealdstone. I am spending hours going through papers before tearing most of them up and enclose two that may interest you. Also an old sampler in case you may like old family relics. I have sent two others to my brother.

It is very trying work giving up all ideas of having a house of one's own and parting with the familiar possessions of a life-time, also 'living in one's boxes' is tiresome, still it seems to me the best thing to do.

The night-dress case comes with the very best wishes for your birthday, hoping that it may be a happy one and that you are all well. Another long letter will be most welcome when you have time to write. I shall be glad to hear of you all. Too busy I have so many letters on hand to send a long one this time.

Much love to yourself and children and kind regards to Mr. Moore

Your loving cousin

Amy Morris.

Please do not send the papers back.

Note by J.G.M.

I know that Lilian and 'Mr. Moore' – my parents – both visited her at Lockyers Private Hotel at some later date and reported that the old lady seemed happy enough there. Because not mentioned, her sister had presumably died, and only one brother apparently remained. The cousin she mentions as her host I cannot identify.

Arthur Salkeld

When we left Arthur Salkeld, to give ourselves room to say something of his first wife (Lilian's mother), he had just made his second marriage, to Lilian's governess Jessie Tinkler Crosby, and their first child Francis John Salkeld – Lilian's favourite half-brother – had been born on 19 February 1894. He was followed on 14 Sepember 1896 by a daughter Elsie Crosby, both of whom survived to ripe old age, but the third child Arthur Lionel born (on Lilian's birthday) 20 May 1899, lived only into the fourth month of the new century. Jessie Irene came next, born 15 June 1901 – she married Frederick Baker and they had a son David. Next came 'the twins', Gladys Dorothy and Sybil Margaret, born 15 April 1905, the former dying a spinster in December 1970, the latter marrying Sidney Cogswell, having a child Jean, and being buried on 23 November 1950 in Hounslow, London. Finally, on 2 February 1908, came their last child Joseph William, who married Natalie and had a son Carl. Their mother Jessie Tinkler died on 27 November 1938, at 17 Marlborough Road, Waterloo near Liverpool (where she had lived for most of the years which followed her husband's death on 8 June 1920) and was buried in Runcorn Cemetery on 30 November. The eldest daughter Elsie married Mr. Crowdy who managed the gas works at Kendal, and they had a boy Michael. [One wonders whether, as a life-long resident of Kendal, she knew of its place in our earlier Salkeld history?] There was a time when she and Lilian were close friends, until distance and time made this too difficult. She still (1984) lives in Kendal, and my sister Joan Moore keeps in touch over the years. We visited her in June 1983 in her modern bungalow at Bellingham Road, Kendal.

Elsie's brother John ('Uncle Jack'), in 1927 married 'Lil' Owen of Cemaes Bay, Anglesey, where perhaps he was on holiday. Born 20 January 1893, she was a little older than Jack. At first they lived at Riverside, Trentham, in Runcorn, and through the good offices of my father he got employment as a draughtsman in Castner-Kellner Works at nearby Weston Point. They had three children – Jessica Elizabeth born 10 July 1928 (who married George Jones of Mosseley Hill, Liverpool in 1957 and had a son William), John Hall Salkeld born 18 January 1932 (who married a French girl Aliette of Cannes in 1960 and had a son the following year) and William Owen born 10 March 1933, their last child. When 'Uncle Jack' retired in 1956 the family moved to 3 Archerfield Road, Mosseley Hill; mother 'Lil' died theand was cremated at Anfield; her husband survived her by three years, being buried, after an accident outside his car, on 26 December 1977. He especially will be remembered for his sense of fun and happiness, and for his likeness to the Crosby rather than to the Salkeld physique and face.

So much for Arthur Salkeld's second family. How did he support them – and the sole surviving daughter Lilian of his first marriage – over the period from his own marriage to Clara Ellen Morris in 1880, to, say, his 65th birthday in the war year 1916? He had inherited modestly. But he had no truly professional training, as is evidenced from his description of himself as 'book-keeper' on Lilian's birth certificate. By 1897, for the probate of the will of his father William Francis Salkeld, he describes himself as 'Salt Agent of 12 Waterloo Road, Runcorn'. When he had to operate in the 1902 Indenture, regarding his daughter Lilian's inheritance from Jane Morris, he had become simply 'manager' and he signed before his co-trustee Joseph Hall Salkeld who is a 'managing clerk'. But on his daughter Lilian's wedding certificate he described himself as 'Secretary of Public Company' and on his own last will and testament, on 17 June 1916, at Blaenymor, Penmaenmawr, as 'Chief Clerk'. Though he may, in his early working life, have helped his father William Francis in duties connected with the family canal boat business, this as we have seen earlier, though at one time a splendid source of income for the family, was becoming inadequate soon after Arthur had been born. But the salt for which he was an 'agent' in 1897 was no doubt carried still on the canals, as also by rail. The move of his residence from Runcorn to Penmaenmawr was I have been told because he had the offer of a job there, as manager of the slate quarries. He was there from 1911 to 1919 but before his death he had moved to 'Wintersfield' in Waterloo, Liverpool. He died on 8 June 1920, and was buried three days later, in a fresh grave – not that of Clara Ellen – in Runcorn Cemetery where later Jessie Tinkler joined him, as did their daughter Gladys.

As to his relationship with his daughter (my mother, Lilian), I think this could fairly be described as coolly affectionate, but tinged, after her marriage, with a little suspicion of the influence her husband was then in a position to exert; but of this, perhaps some discussion later; for understandably she – and indeed also her husband – became anxious to get full control of Lilian's modest inheritances of stocks and shares, mostly railway investment inherited from Jane Morris, for which Arthur was joint trustee with his 'clerical' brother Joseph Hall Salkeld. The first major sally in this 'battle' was made by Lilian before she was married, and is described at length in an Indenture dated 7 June 1902, soon after she was twenty-one. The second, another Indenture, dated 22 November 1921, followed Arthur's death as a Trustee, when fresh Trustees were appointed.

My own contact with Arthur Salkeld was strictly a paper one, being confined to a letter he wrote from Pool Dale, on 7 May 1910 – when I was 16 days old. It accompanied a silver mug, with the letter 'J' engraved on the side; I have since given the mug to my grandson James Dunsterville, with the original letter, of which the following is a copy:

My dear Master Joseph Grange Moore

Allow me to congratulate you upon your entrance to this sublimary abode and hope that you may long be spared to become a man of merit and an honour to your parents in years to come. You bear two good names that should assist you while here, and I trust with the blessing of health you may grow as big and good as your forebears. May I hope that you will please accept the Cup which I venture to send herewith and that when you have developed your muscles somewhat, that you will kindly do me the honour of taking drinks out of it, to sustain the life which you have just entered upon. Wishing you most sincerely a long, happy and useful life, believe me to be

Your Godfather – Arthur.

On 17 June six years later he made his will, at Blaenymor in Penmaenmawr, appointing as executors and trustees his wife Jessie, his brother Joseph Hall, and his eldest son John; he left to his second wife his chattels and £400, all his property to be sold and the proceeds to be invested, she to have the income and after her death both capital and income to be shared between his six children of the second marriage – Lilian not being mentioned. He died 8 June 1920, Jessie surviving him until 27 November 1938.

This book set out to describe my mother's Salkeld ancestors, and something of their times. With *this* page we have now reached as far as my mother: to complete the task I will continue the record up to *her* death, in 1973.

Mary Eizabeth Lilian Salkeld (Lilian for short) was born at 12 Waterloo Road, Runcorn on 20 May 1881, the elder daughter of Arthur Salkeld and his wife Clara Ellen née Morris. I have been able to find a number of photographs of her as a very little girl, and as one growing up, and then engaged, and later as a parent. Most of them show her looking straight into the camera lens with a very unsmiling seriousness, no doubt due to the attitude sitters had towards being photographed, and 'keeping still'. But I suspect that that is not all the story – for Lilian had experienced more bereavements than most girls of her age – for example her little sister Edith Ellen died when Lilian was only three-and-a-half years old. In the dreadful year when she was nine she lost first her beloved mother and a year later her 'Aunt John', and before she was 20 had lost also her grandfather William Francis (and his sister Elizabeth), and her half-brother Arthur Lionel of whom she was very fond. Moreover, she was markedly older than even the eldest of her step-brothers and sisters (13 years in fact) and so would not be able to 'join in' as easily as the eldest child of the usual family, and would have to rely on school-friends such as Elsie Haywood of whom she often spoke. Schooling was by local governess and later at the Queen's School in Chester, with private instruction in music by her step-mother's sister Miss Crosby and in singing and painting by Miss Pierpoint, a sister of a well-known singer Bantock Pierpoint. (Lilian was confirmed, on 2 April 1897 (?), in Chester Cathedral, by Bishop Jane, when nearly sixteen.) But the daily journey by train from Pool Dale to Chester proved too much for Lilian's health and instead she became a pupil at a Southport boarding school. However, whilst a boarder there she contracted an infection in her arm, for which the school was thought responsible, so she rejoined the Queen's School at Chester but this time as a boarder during the week, returning home for most weekends, except for special events. She was very happy with this life; caught smoking once in the train, with her friends, she promised not to smoke and kept that promise all her life.

She helped her step-mother a lot, and if she had not married, had ideas of training as a nurse.

She became a proficient painter and pianist and as a singer took part in *Tableaux Vivants* organised by Miss Pierpoint and supported by the Runcorn Orchestral Society, some eighteen strong, in the Public Hall, Runcorn on 17 and 18 November 1903, with a further 24 performers and others, including Nora and Edgar Lea. On the first night, in the Tableau *Queen of Hearts*, she scored a personal triumph by rapidly reversing the wooden spoon when it proved too big to go into the legendary strawberry-jam pot. But the oldest record of her amusements is a simple folding programme with pencil attached, of a Bachelors' Dance at Runcorn on 17 December 1902; filled at each of the 23 dances. Miss Salkeld danced the Lancers to the *Country Girl* music, and the *Interval Waltz* and a second waltz *Whisper and I shall hear*, with a 'J. W. Moore'. In the diary which he kept for most of his life, this young man records on 7 February 1904 that it was the third anniversary 'of his first seeing Lilian'.

Socially 1904 started well, with another dance in the Public Hall on 8 January, when Lilian and this young man danced the Lancers and several waltzes. It was Leap Year, as the programme pointed out, and the music included *Floradora*, *Trial by Jury*, *Country Girl*, *Blue Danube*, *Whisper and I shall hear*, *Gondoliers* and the *Belle of New York*. She requested 'the pleasure of Mr. J. W. Moore's Company on Saturday, 23 January at Pool Dale, for Progressive Whist' on a neat little card and, of the 24 games, they were partners for the first, fourth and sixth, Miss Crosby rather 'hogging' the others. His diary says 'most enjoyable affair – won cigarette case prize'. In March and April she gave him some of her drawings and paintings and he followed her on a visit to

Criceeth in June; (he by boat from Liverpool to Redclyffe House, Church Walks, Llandudno, before joining her at Criceeth on 9 June 1904). There, on the 10th of that month, they became engaged, 'for a year'; further holidays in August and September, this time at Buxton, and the year ended with another bachelors' dance on 2 December at which the diary records 'Great success– Lilian looked and was charming'.

The banns were called by the Rev. Oliver, at Trinity Church on 14 May 1905 but it was then found that Pool Dale was in the parish of Halton and they had to be re-called there, and on 21 May; visits, shopping in Liverpool, purchase by Lilian of a house in The Holloway (No. 13) and removal of furniture from Pool Dale and from J. W. Moore's lodgings at 60 Greenway Road to it, and the wedding was very close. What better account of it than that given in the *Guardian* of 10 June 1905?:

> The marriage was solemnised at the Runcorn Parish Church, on Wednesday [11.30 a.m.], of Mr. Joseph Wm. Moore, eldest son of Dr. Jos. Moore, [given as] of Northwich, and Miss Mary Elizabeth Lilian Salkeld eldest daughter of Mr. Arthur Salkeld, of Pool Dale, Runcorn. The officiating clergyman was the Rev. E. S. Oliver. The bride, who was given away by her father, was charmingly attired in white crepe de chine, trimmed with orange blossoms, with chiffon artistically arranged in lovers knots. She wore a bridal wreath with veil. She carried a shower bouquet of white lilies, white roses, stephanotis and spireas, with streamers. The bridesmaids were Miss Moore (sister of the bridegroom) and the Misses Elsie and Irene Salkeld (sisters of the bride). They wore dresses of white silk, with yellow ribbons and white picture hats. Miss Moore carried a handsome shower bouquet and the two children carried baskets of flowers. Mr. G. Moore (brother of the bridegroom) was best man, and Mr. Oswald Smith groomsman. Mr. F. R. Boraston presided at the organ and played appropriate selections. After the ceremony a reception was held at Pool Dale. The guests included Mr. and Mrs. Salkeld, Mr. J. H. Salkeld, Mr. O. Salkeld, Miss E. Salkeld, Miss I. Salkeld, Mr. W. E. Lea, Mrs. Lea, Miss Nora Lea, Miss J. Lea, Mrs. Owen, Miss Hughes, Miss Crosby, Miss Hill, Mr. Smith, Mrs. Smith, Miss M. Moore, Miss W. Smith, Miss O. Smith, Mr. O. Smith, Mr. E. Smith, Mr. Gerard, Mr. R. Brown, Mr. G. Moore, the Rev. E. S. Oliver, and Miss Ada Timmins. About 80 presents were received. The Honeymoon is being spent at Scarborough. The bride's travelling dress was of grey cloth with blue hat and feather boa.
>
> *Wedding Breakfast*
>   Cold Salmon. Cold Chicken. Cold Ducks. Cold Lamb. Tongue. New Potatoes. Jellies. Creams. Blanc Mange. Trifle. Plum Pie. Best Chocs. Lemonade. Wedding Cake. Little cakes. Tea and Coffee.

His diary adds 'Escaped speech caught 2.45 p.m. train to Scarborough. Reached 4 Crown Crescent 9.45 p.m.' and that in the following days they visited Oliver's Mount, the Castle, Spa, Forge Valley, sailed to Whitby and went by train to Filey. On 22nd they 'caught the 10.30 a.m. train arriving Manchester 2.30 p.m., bought a piano at Forsyths for 35 guineas and reached home 5.10 p.m.' Entertained Miss Crosby, Ada Timmins, Margaret (Moore) and Grange to supper, and back to the Works the following morning. Many more visitors listed in the following week.

In June 1906 they had a fortnight at Oban (Mrs. Christy charged 32s. a week) and sailed to the Kyles of Bute, Staffa and Iona – 'very rough'; on 14 September they went with 'Maggie' (his unmarried sister Margaret, who often stayed at their house) by train to Bala where they were joined by the eldest Moore sister, 'Nellie', and her husband Harry Smith who had a motorcar! The following year, on 13 July, they started a fortnight's holiday at Miss Lovatt's corner house 'Ivy Lea' on Princes Drive/Marine Drive, Colwyn Bay, which for the next seven or so years was to be chosen as the regular summer holiday base. In 1907 Miss Lovatt's charge 'for rooms' was two-and-a-half guineas per week; later, on 13 October, the services of Dr. Cullen and Nurse Ford were required, and their first child Arthur Denzil was born at 3 p.m. on Thursday, 17 October

30. 13 The Holloway, Runcorn.

31. All Saints' church, Runcorn.

1907, 'Joe' going back to work on his bicycle at 4.30 p.m.! The christening was on Sunday 24 November, by Rev. E. S. Oliver, in the afternoon, followed by tea at 13 The Holloway attended by Grange and Ada (now married and with a son), Harry and Nellie, Mr. and Mrs. Arthur Salkeld, and their boy Jack, who 'left at 6.30 p.m.'. In the Holloway home they had two helpers – one a cook at 2s. 6d. a week plus board, and the other a maid at 2s. a week plus board. Family income at that time was Lilian's own annual £120 plus Joe's £180 a year salary.

But in August 1908 they had the courage to leave Arthur Denzil with a nurse (Ford) and the two went off to the Lake District for two weeks – Ambleside and Windermere; and in June and early July Lilian and a maid spent two weeks at Miss Lovatt's at Princes Drive, Colwyn Bay – there and back of course by train – at a total cost including tips of £14 12s. 8d.! Perhaps the fares were extra. This was followed in September by a week at Mrs. Parry's house, 'Angorfa', at Pensarn.

The following April Lilian, Joe, and Nurse Joynson played whist on the evenings of 18 and 20 April and their second child arrived at 1 p.m. on Thursday 21, to be visited by his Salkeld grandparents on 1 May – 'Lilian up'. The new baby was christened Joseph Grange, on Sunday, 29 May, and in early July all four, plus Nurse Joynson and the little maid, spent two weeks again at Colwyn Bay: 'it was very hot'.

It was now being felt that the Holloway house was too small, Arthur Salkeld offered them Pool Dale for £800 and would take the Holloway house in part exchange, but on 2 November Joe Moore said 'no' – perhaps feeling it to be too far from the Works at Weston Point. Lilian at this time was having some heart troubles, and fainting, and was ordered to rest. The following year saw the purchase, from Mr. Clarke, of Kinderton House on Weston Road, just having been built, and named after Kinderton Hall near Middlewich where Joe had played as a child. The family Moore was to live there until Joe died in 1955, he having added extra rooms, more garden, and a garage in later years. The house was sold by auction at Wilson's Hotel, Runcorn at 7 p.m. on Wednesday 19 September 1956, with its total area of 4,228 square yards of land, and freehold, for the miserable sum of £1,550. With its six bedrooms, large garden, and old-fashioned kitchenette it was not a very attractive proposition at that time, but it had been a very happy home for the four children who had spent their young years there. It passed into the hands of the then occupant of No. 2 Highlands Road – the local post office, and later the local council built an ugly concrete wall cutting off most of the lower garden from the new council houses below the hill. (If it had not found a purchaser, and had stood empty through the coming winter, it would no doubt have been worth even less; already vandals had started to raid the rose garden.)

To return to Lilian, who with her family moved into Kinderton House in 1911. Two years later, on 16 November 1913, a third son, John, was born; came the First World War, with her husband on essential work at Castner's, but able to reach home on his bicycle most nights, their battles were more concerned with food-rationing than with bombs. A fourth and last child – Clara Joan – was born at Kinderton House on 19 October 1916.

For Lilian, then came endless schooldays – the three boys in turn attending as boarders at Wrekin College, Wellington near Shrewsbury, after short periods in local schools; and Joan in her turn boarding at Lowther College, North Wales. As these children gradually moved, some through Cambridge University, and John for a while

32. Kinderton House, Runcorn.

a day student at Liverpool University, and eventually into I.C.I., her role became largely one of provider of 'board and lodgings' in out-of-term times, and later, for wives and grandchildren, the question 'And when did you last have something to eat' as she opened the front door of Kinderton House, becoming almost a password as well as a welcome. In later years she had some ill-health, especially with a poisoned foot which all but called for an amputation, and some recurring heart trouble. Her husband retired in 1938 (having joined the Castner Kellner Works staff in 1897) and busied himself with his large garden and his Riley car; but it is not the purpose of the present book to attempt an account of *his* life and works, which were very considerable and require quite separate treatment from this account of the *Salkeld* family. They celebrated their Golden Wedding on 7 June 1955, according to the *Runcorn Guardian*, 'Very quietly at home'. Later that year he was afflicted with a developing cancer, and he died at Kinderton House at 2 a.m. on Wednesday 16 November 1955. The following year Lilian moved to a small flat at 24 Ormonde Road, just off the Chester-Liverpool Road, in Chester, being joined by her only daughter Joan; she took sufficient furniture from Kinderton House for their needs, and the rest was disposed of.

Freed from the burden of a large house, Lilian lived a very retired but enjoyable life (at 80 she attended Chester races) at that flat, until her death in a Chester hospital on 23 March 1973, in her 92nd year. She worshipped regularly at the Cathedral and at local churches and was buried in her husband's grave in Runcorn Cemetery on 28 March, all close relatives present except Denzil (deceased).

Appendix One

Salkelds at Agincourt

> And gentlemen in England, now a-bed
> Shall think themselves accursed they were not here . . .

Will Shakespeare's famous lines have no doubt done more to glamorise Henry's gallant butchery of the feckless French on 25 October 1415 than any number of history books. Of the 60,000 Frenchmen who were encamped across the path of the tired and half-starved English relics from Harfleur, the carnage produced by the English bowmen left 11,000 Frenchmen dead on the field, and more than a hundred princes and great lords were amongst the fallen. The English, grossly outnumbered, had to massacre their prisoners in order themselves to escape; too weary to make a pursuit, they made their way to Calais and England, taking for ransom the richest of the prisoners and the best of the armour and plunder. The battle had lasted for about three hours, with less than five hundred English casualties, most of them wounded not killed.

Were all the Salkelds of England 'now a-bed'? It appears not, two at least being recorded as present – a Robert and a John.

Robert Salkeld carried one of the 143 lances in the Duke of Gloucester's retinue, together with 451 archers; with him were such well-known Cumbrian names as Geoffrey Lowther, Robert Dacre, Walter Strykland, Hugh Lowther and Edmond Dacre. Elsewhere it is recorded that this duke was Duke Humphrey of Gloucester and that his total retinue was 200 men-at-arms, six knights, 193 esquires and 600 horse archers. No list of casualties is given.

John Salkeld was also a lance carrier, in the retinue of Sir de Harrington, which was a smaller group totalling some thirty men-at-arms, three knights, 26 esquires and 90 horse archers.

Factual information is hard to find. The recent popular book *Agincourt* by Christopher Hibbert (1964)[95] gives a military account but mentions only the names of the king's own retinue which included 15 minstrels. The most useful work is rare, being published in 1827 with the simple title *Battle of Agincourt*,[96] author Nicholas Harris Nicholas, a barrister and antiquarian; it is in this book that the above information on the Salkelds can be found, and the Society of Genealogists in London keeps it on its 'Army' shelves.

It would of course be excellent if Robert and John could be identified and put on my charts, but apart from such obvious conclusions as that they were probably aged between twenty and thirty-five – to be fighting there – and were therefore born between 1380 and 1395, and probably – from the names of their companions – did come from Cumbria, one can only guess; my guesses are in the main text of this book.

The other imponderable is – did they go or were they sent? Like other monarchs, Henry V had great difficulty in financing the Harfleur-Agincourt enterprise and no doubt called on his knights of the shire to rally round and bring their fighting men to do their service. The prospects of ransom payments from prisoners, and of loot, would also serve to attract strong and bold young Salkelds with nothing better to do.

I strongly suspect that Robert and John would have been able to tell their comrades in arms, at Agincourt, just where Corby (or Rosgill) was, and might perhaps have added that they had a common grandfather called Hugh (I), who used to live there.

Appendix Two

Lancelot Salkeld, the First Dean of Carlisle, and the Salkeld Screen

Visitors to the Cathedral of Carlisle are likely to admire the large carved 15th-century screen on the north side of the choir. It is called the Salkeld screen and is fully described by C. G. Bulman in *CWAA* 56, pp. 119-27,[97] who advances the theory that it was erected to mark the birth of a male heir to Henry VIII, the infant Edward born in 1537 who came to the throne 10 years later and died six years after so doing. This theory is disputed by C. M. L. Bouch (*CWAA* 57, pp. 39-43)[98] who[67] points out that only a year before the prince was born, his father had suppressed the Pilgrimage of Grace and 66 men from Cumberland had been hanged in chains to die – not likely to endear Henry to the burghers of Carlisle or to make them enthusiastic about erecting a screen to his son. Moreover the Priory of Carlisle was suppressed in January 1540 and four of the canons pensioned off. Not until June 1541 was it known that Henry had acted with unusual generosity by founding the cathedral church of St Mary at Carlisle, with a dean and four prebendaries, and endowed it not only with the possessions of the priory, but also with those of the dissolved priory of Wetheral and its fishing rights on the River Eden. Bouch considers that this excellent news was more likely to have been the incentive to Salkeld to mark the event with his remarkable screen. He was of course the new dean.

This Salkeld was named Lancelot, and though it is highly likely that he *was* descended from some part of the pedigree discussed in this book, I cannot find the detailed evidence for this. He was elected prior in 1532 but he disliked the doctrinal changes introduced under and after Henry, and resigned in 1548; he was reinstated in 1554 after Mary Tudor had become queen, and died in 1560. He was buried in the cathedral, with no other monument to mark the spot, some say having again been demoted – by Elizabeth I.

The screen was erected by him probably in 1541 and is a remarkable mixture of expiring gothic and classical revival; so much so, that it appears to be unlikely that local craftsmen could have produced it, and Bulman suggests that it is of Italian workmanship.

From the foundation of the new Church, the title of the establishment was changed from the Cathedral Church of St Mary – of which Lancelot was the last prior – to the Cathedral of the Holy and Undivided Trinity – of which Lancelot became the first dean. No other Salkeld has attained such eminence in Holy Orders. I wish I could trace his ancestors – who were his parents and when and where was he born? Nicholson and Burn (vol. 2, p. 303)[99] merely say 'He was of the house of Corby nigh Carlisle'.

He is said (*CWAA*, vol. 62, p. 355)[100] to have corresponded with the Clifford family, and the Surtees Society (172, p. 158)[101] *Clifford Letters of the 16th Century*, edited by A. G. Dickens, may be a possible source of information. The excellent *Victoria History of Cumberland* (2, pp. 149-50)[45] adds 'Lancelot Salkeld, a canon defamed in the report of the royal visitation, was made prior of the house for the purpose of its surrender. The priory was surrendered with all its possessions by Lancelot Salkeld, prior, and the convent on 9 January 1540. . . . Salkeld died Dean of Carlisle on 3 September 1560, leaving behind him a name for piety, rectitude and consistency second to none in the history of the diocese'.

33. Part of the Salkeld Screen, Carlisle Cathedral.

Appendix Three

A Salkeld Pirate

As the Salkeld saga moves towards the sea it is perhaps appropriate to mention that there was once a celebrated pirate of that name, who caused the authorities a lot of bother, and secured for himself mentions in the Calendar of State Papers (Domestic), starting with the following:

8 August 1609 – 'Sakell a pirate took a flyboat near Spain, now in prison.' [That was in vol. 1600-3, pp. 534-601.[102] Followed by]:

17 April 1610 'Deposition of William Young, taken prisoner by Captain Thomas Salkeld, a pirate; details of vessels taken and their owners imprisoned by Salkeld. He also took the Island of Lundy and called himself King of it. Escape of the prisoners under the guidance of George Estcott of Bridgewater.'

Unfortunately no more details are given; one would like to have known how he got out of prison to commit the attack on Lundy, or whether this second entry is merely a summary of the evidence available to the prosecution on the terse first entry. I have searched volumes to learn what happened next, but without result. It is a fair guess that he was aged between twenty-five and forty-five at the time of his 'maximum piratical activity', meaning that he must have been born in the period from about 1565 to 1585; for the longer period 1560 to 1589 I have baptism details of 103 Salkelds of whom seven were named Thomas but of these only two could, for various reasons, have become pirates by 1609-10; both came from the Cumbrian town of Brough! The elder, baptised 16 November 1572, would have been some thirty-eight years old, the son of Henry Salkeld of that town. The other, son of Edward Salkeld, was baptised 3 October 1578 and so would have been about thirty-two. Apart from the coincidence of surname, Christian name, and age bracket, there is absolutely no evidence that either of these Salkelds was the pirate, nor indeed that the pirate came from Cumbria in the first place. But he *might* have done! He was not an 'ancestor Salkeld' – 'distinguished relative', perhaps!

There is another reference to piracy in these State Papers, but this time the Salkeld concerned was on the side of the authorities. Volume 1653, p. 117[103] records that on 30 September 1653 Capt. Jno Salkeld wrote to the Navy Commissioners from the *James of London* at Tynemouth:

I regret the delay in sending the muster book but I was ordered by the Council of State to convoy some merchant ships to and from Dunkirk and then to carry and convoy a whole company of soldiers and a train of artillery for the Orcades and then more soldiers for reducing Lewes and the rest of the northern isles of Scotland and had no opportunity of sending. P.S. I have now come into this harbour by Col. Lilburne's orders to convoy a fleet of colliers.

A year or more later he writes from the *Colchester Hope* (on 30 October 1654):

Sends two minute books. Has been cruising upon the French coast and the Channel. Convoyed two ships from Hull to Hamburg. Met a small man-of-war belonging to Dunkirk and suspecting him to be a pirate took him into Dover.

Appendix Four

Mr. George of Thrimby Grange

There were several branches of the Salkeld family, first mentioned in the 13th century, but perhaps the best-documented and interesting is that resulting from the activities of one George Salkeld who was born in 1528 at Thrimby Grange, roughly halfway between Shap and Penrith, and became a very wealthy landowner.

His father, Rychard (V) Salkeld, was directly descended from the famous Sir Richard (I) Salkeld whose alabaster tomb, dated A.D. 1501, lies in Wetheral church, near Carlisle. His mother was Agnes, née Bellingham, an equally famous northern family name. He was probably christened at Morland church, though the church records do not quite go back far enough, but his later brothers and sisters undoubtedly were.

Thrimby Grange has itself a distinguished history. Nicholson and Burn[22] in a footnote say that Thirneby ('now corruptly called Thrimby') was shown in Domesday Book as amongst the possessions of Tosti, Earl of Northumberland and (p. 449) was a small village of but six families, holding in the fourth year of the reign of King John (1203) an agreement between William de Tyrneby and the Prior of Watton for one carucate of land together with pasture for 1,000 sheep. Later, in the reign of King Henry III (1216 to 1272) the manor was given to the Priory of Wetheral by John son of William de Thrimby, the gift including lands and a Grange. Later, the manor came to the Harringtons who held it in capite under the Richmond Fee of the Barony of Kendal. Thrimby Grange manor once owned the south aisle of Morland church (Whellan, p. 801)[13] but later this was given to the parishioners by Henry Viscount Lonsdale.

The *first* reference I have as yet found of the *Salkeld* interest in Thrimby is in Flower's Visitation to Yorkshire 1563-4 (p. 272)[9] which clearly records that Roger Salkeld (son of John Salkeld who dwelt at Goboroo (Gawbarrow)) 'dwelt at Thrymby'; this Roger must have been born between 1470 and 1500. Perhaps the *last* mention of the Salkelds and Thrimby is of the burial of Mr. Robert Salkeld of Thrimby at Morland church on 6 January 1610-11. Compared for example with the Salkelds who lived at Corby for over three hundred years, their stay of some one hundred and fifty years at Thrimby was a relatively short one.

Apart from having been born the eldest son of Rychard (V) Salkeld and so being heir to his estates, the biggest thing George did was to marry his cousin Barbara, who was heiress to nearby Rosgill (on Shap), Corby (near Carlisle) and Pardshaw (near Dean/Cockermouth); I estimate that George's marriage took place in about 1560, and as his father had died in 1559 we can assume that George was already the 'squire' of Thrimby when his wife brought all these inheritances to him. From then on he was referred to as 'Mr. George', but whether *he* continued to live at Thrimby is doubtful, because he now had several other houses, and his redoubtable mother Agnes dominated the scene at Thrimby until her death in 1578; she was buried at Morland on 29 June 1578, the parish register describing her as 'MISTRIS SALKELDE OF THRIMBIE GRAINDGE' – in capital letters, just like that!

George's wife Barbara brought to him in marriage not only these estates but also two girl children by a previous marriage – these were Madlayne who had been born shortly I think before Barbara's second marriage (and who later married Mr. Robert Salkeld of Thrimby and died in April 1585), and Frances, who died a spinster and was buried at Shap in 1582. My reason for believing that these two girls were *not* daughters of George is the way they are described in the will of Barbara's father Richard (IV) Salkeld of Rosgill (who was himself buried on 3 February 1574-5); he speaks in his will of his 'son-in-law George' but of the girls as 'daughters to my daughter Barbarye'. By that time however George had, by Barbara, a son and heir Thomas, and a second son Richard was baptised on 3 October 1562 – hence my belief that George and Barbara had married in 1560. I have a copy of the will of George's father-in-law Richard (IV), and it mentions no further grandchildren – though as I shall show later there were plenty; the inventory accompanying Richard's (IV) will is dated 6 February 1574-5 and runs to four foolscap pages, with exciting details of the treasures at Rosgill, Slegill and 'Corkbie', many of which – silver gilt goblets, cups and spoons, and much furniture – were bequeathed to George's young son Thomas but were to remain as 'heyrelumes' at Rosgill and at Corby – but more of Thomas later.

Although this will mentions only the two girls of Barbara, and the two sons (Thomas and Richard) of George, the Herald's Visitation to Yorkshire in 1563-4 by W. Flower, Norroy King of Arms,[9] credits George also with a boy Hugh and daughters Doraty and Jane – who must surely have been born after 1563. Indeed the church registers record the *baptism* of 'Doraty', at Shap, on 5 January 1571 and of her sister Jane, at Morland church, on 29 February 1573. But a further search of these registers reveals that, at Morland, children named Margaret (daughter of George Salkeld) and Francis (son of the same), were *baptised* on 23 July 1561 and 1 February 1568 respectively, while at Shap were *baptised* Alan on 20 June 1566, and girls Jane and Mary *children of Mr. George* on 31 March 1577 and 5 October 1579 respectively. Finally and for good measure, a George Salkeld *baptised* another Thomas on 10 April 1590, at Rosgill. It must at once be said that some of these children may have belonged to some other George Salkeld – but surely not the two underlined, because of the 'Mr.'.

We do know that Mr. George was buried on 1 August 1597 – a year of the great plague in Cumbria – but I can find no record of the burial of his wife Barbara. There is however a record of a George Salkeld marrying an Elizabeth Short of Rosgill on 12 May 1589 at Shap; this could have been George's second wife – he would then be 61 years of age – but on balance I do not think that this last Thomas – who would be the second to be so named (and alive) in this family – was attributable to our 'Mr. George'. What is certain however is that there would be plenty of little feet visiting Thrimby Grange in the years 1560 to 1597.

George had turned his attention to other matters also, for as major landowner he was appointed High Sheriff of Westmorland in the years 1577, 1579 and 1587, and a J.P. in 1596. He was also a King's Commissioner in 1580 with the onerous task of surveying the adequacy of the castles of the West Marches as part of the defences against the wild raiders from over the Border. At home he was much in demand as a wise councillor and witness of deeds and wills for his friends and relatives; thus 'John Salkeld of Thrimby' (probably Thrimby *Hall*) in his will of May 1563 cites George as one who had witnessed the bargain that John's son Oswalde should 'espouse marry and tayke to wiff Johanne Rigg daughter of Rigge of Little Strickland gentylman'; similarly Lancelot Salkeld in a will made at Addingham on 3 May 1574 cites his 'trusty and well-beloved maister – Mr. George Salkeld' and John Salkeld of Corby in his will dated 18 March 1595 makes Mr. George a 'supervisor'; (though I can find no instances where Mr. George has been an appraiser for an inventory – a job perhaps beneath his station).

So George died, and was buried at Morland, on 1 August 1597, leaving, by my calculations, up to twelve children – including Barbara's two – less any who had meanwhile died. Of these 12 children the most important was the already-mentioned Thomas (V), born I calculate in 1560 or 1561 and mentioned in his grandfather Richard's will and inventory of 1574, as George's heir.

This Thomas Salkeld married Thomazin, a daughter of Alan and Dorothy Bellingham of Helsington, who in 1569-70 were big landowners in the Hugill area; they had five children – two boys and three girls; the eldest boy (Richard of course) was born in 1592 but died without issue in 1630. Thomas (V) had an eventful and in many ways a sad life. He was Sheriff of Cumberland in 1598 and was probably the 'False Salkeld' described (in Bain's *Calendar of the Border Papers*, vols. I and II, pp. 1560-94)[47] as the deputy warden of Carlisle Castle who had to deal with the infamous rascal Kinmont Willie and his gangs – including having his eldest son Richard, then aged six, kidnapped as a hostage. But perhaps the saddest thing was his long and costly law-suit with Lord William Howard of Naworth for ownership of the remaining half of the Corby estates, a struggle which started in 1605 and ended in 1625 with Thomas nearly bankrupt and forced to sell his inheritance for £1,100. This is described in much detail in an excellent paper by H. S. Reinmuth, Professor of History in the University of Akron, and read to the Cumberland and Westmorland Antiquarian and Archaelogical Society (see their *Transactions*, vol. 66, p. 190)[104] at Kendal on 4 April 1964.

Of Thomas's brothers and sisters, we know that his half-sister Madlayne married Mr. Robert Salkeld of Thrimby Grange in February 1579 (at Shap), but she died five years later and was buried there in April 1584; Thomas's sister 'Mistress Mary', born 5 October 1579 (Shap), married Henry Dacre of the famous Dacres family on 7 November 1599; Heugh, baptised at Morland in October 1574 had a wife Mary and together they sued Sir James Bellingham of Levens over the deeds of the manors of Ormshead and Thrimby – Heugh and Mary were living at Rosgill in 1633 and had several children. Thomas's brother Francis died at the age of 14, and the remaining brother Rychard who was mentioned in his grandfather's will when about thirteen years of age (and was left one horse 'called graye thomson') died without issue when twenty-four.

So much for Mr. George and his children and grandchildren; he also had his brothers and sisters, born to Rychard and Agnes née Bellingham at Thrimby Grange and mostly baptised at Morland as the children of 'Richard and Agnes'. Morland was one of the very few churches at this time to include the mother's name with the father's in the baptismal entry, as in this example, and this has been a great help in unravelling these relationships.

Unfortunately I cannot trace a will for either of George's parents, but the afore-mentioned Flower Visitation[9] shows George, as 'son and heyr' and, in descending order of birth, a brother Charles, then Robert, then Cuthbert, then Edward, and finally

Richard; however the Morland parish register, while including all these, goes on to add William baptised 1525, and daughters Anne, baptised 1544, and Agnes in 1549. It will be noticed that the order of baptism derived from the Morland register differs slightly from that given in the Visitation records – and as already mentioned, some of these children may belong to some other Richard Salkeld of the period; the only one calling for mention here is Edward, born 1550, who amongst his own eight children had John baptised 1579 who became a priest and for his erudition and ability in discourse was named by the King 'The learned Salkeld'; a grandson of this John was John of Ulfculne, who bore arms at Taunton and is credited with the profound observation that 'None sat in Parliament but knaves and cobblers'.

So much for what I have been able to find – so far – in the literature, of George Salkeld and Thrimby Grange. In the marriage of Barbara and George, Thrimby probably saw the Cumbria Salkelds at the height of their wealth and position; in the loss through their son Thomas (V), of Corby to Lord Howard, Thrimby saw them on the beginning of the downward path. Today (1978) there are fewer Salkelds in the Cumbria telephone directory than there were Salkelds at Pardshaw in 1625 – and that was but a small side-branch of the then Salkelds of Cumbria.

INVENTORY OF GEORGE SALKELD 1599 (Corkby)
Probate granted to Thomas (V) Salkeld

	Sette downe by the p[er]sons	300^{li}
<In primis>[1]	all the Crope of Corne at Corkby <wi>th the tythe	60^{li}
<Item>	ij dosen and ij spones	ix^{li}
<I>t[em]	one duble gylte salte	viij^{li}
It[em]	ij sylver tunes	iij^{li} xiij^{s} iiij^{d}
It[em]	one sylver[2]	xxx^{s}
It[em]	vj ox<e>n	ix (?)
It[em]	iiij[3]	iij^{li}
It[em]	ij[4]	
It[em]	iiij slotes	vj^{li}
It[em]	ij worke nages	lvj^{s} iiij^{d}
It[em]	xxx^{ti} paire of sheites	xiij^{li} xiij^{s} iiij^{d}
It[em]	xx^{ti} Coverclothes	vj^{li}
It[em]	xij paire of blanckettes	iiij^{li} x^{s}
It[em]	iiij happens	xvj^{s}
It[em]	ij bede Coverins	vj^{li}
It[em]	ij old bed Coverins	xiij^{s} iiij^{d}
It[em]	vj fether bedes w[i]th pillowes and Boulsters	xv^{li}
It[em]	x matteresses & iiij boulsters	iiij^{li}
It[em]	xij pillover Coverins	xxvj^{s} viij^{d}
It[em]	in naperye iiij table Clothes and one dip bord clothe and ij dozen of napkins and iiij towells & iiij Cubberte	iij^{li} vj^{s} 8^{d}
It[em]	ij bord Coverins	xxv^{s}
It[em]	ij grene sqware table Clothes	xiij^{s} iiij^{d}
It[em]	j paire of grene taffitie hangins	xx^{s}
It[em]	iij paire of say hangins	iij^{li}
It[em]	ix Carpet quyssens	xxx^{s}
It[em]	in fyer vessell ij Caldrens vj pottes vj panes ij droppen panes j fryinge pan j Chassinge dishe iij spetes one paire of droppinge panes tanges ij paire morter and pestell	v^{li}
It[em]	in puder vessell ij basens & ewers vj dosen of puder and ij greate puder pottes iij Chamber pottes vj Candle stickes and iiij latten Candlestickes	vj^{li} xiij^{s} iiij^{d}

Probate to Thomas Salkeld

1 mutilated
2 illegible because of mutilation
3 ?? kine
4 illegible because of mutilation

Appendix Five

Mr. John Salkeld of Thrimby in Morland

Two Johns and their brother James (our ancestor) are all three specifically mentioned in the will of their brother Richard, dated January 1574-5, so there can be no doubt that they were the sons of our ancestor Thomas of Corby and Pardshaw (who married Elizabeth Curwen). They must not therefore be confused with the John, whose very interesting will and inventory is attached, and whom we now know was the brother of Richard of Morland and the son of Roger of Thrimby. But as George of Thrimby and Rosgill left no will for us to see (his inventory however has been found, and is attached, dated 1599, probate having been granted by then to George's son Thomas (V) the sheriff), and neither did Thomas his grandfather, we have only the excellent will of Richard (mentioned above) to give us a picture of the times unless we also include – as I now do – that of John the brother of Richard of Morland, who had died only some eleven years previously.

Several points in it are worthy of mention:

(a) John's natural heir would have been his eldest son Anthony, but we learn from the opening paragraph of bequests that Anthony has very generously opted out of the heavy responsibilities of running this considerable estate, in favour of the second brother Oswolde; a clue to why is to be found in the comment on p. 272 of Flower's Visitation's of 1563-4 that Roger of Thrimby had a grandson Anthony who 'was servant to Lord Sowche' – suggesting to those who know of his lordship's extensive travels that Anthony would have had very little time to spend at Thrimby – assuming as I do that this refers to the Lord Zouche who was a Commissioner at the trial of Mary Queen of Scots in October 1586 and who dissented from the other Commissioners' verdict of guilty of high treason. He was also Ambassador to Scotland and to Denmark, and died without male heir in 1625.

(b) The determination of the testator that his heir Oswolde shall 'marry the right girl' extends even to this being mentioned in his will, and the girl named; in fact the Morland church register shows that this wedding took place there on 29 August 1562 and as the will is dated 3 May 1563 – some eight months later – it looks as though the version we now have had not been corrected for the action so promptly taken by this dutiful son. But it was a very good choice, for Oswolde and Joan had at least eight children including three sons, in the period 1563 to 1583 – as the Morland register shows.

(c) A second inventory was taken, just four years after the first, and this would lead one to suppose that John's wife Anne had died shortly before its date of 19 April 1567 – but it does not specifically *say* that she was then dead, although it includes for money to pay 'charges (4s.) for suche thynges as was bought in the tyme of hyr sekeness'. The list of other debts is very informative. A close comparison of the two inventories is possible, from this information – giving for example a good idea of the value put upon an ox, a cow, and a horse, etc.

Will of John Salkelde of thrynby in the Parish of Moreland gentleman
[dated 3 May 1563]
*(Too early to be John the son of Richard who made his will in 1575 and mentioned
John and Jane.)

[to be buried] yn the lady poorche of morelande churche Aforesaide nighe vnto my father* there.
. . . And wheras Antony salkelde my eldeste Son of his owne naturall love fayvoure zeale & good
will, hathe geven grauntede Released And surrendreth vnto oswolde Salkelde my son his brother
And to the heires and Assignes of the same Oswolde for ever, All the estate title Entereste Clames
Customarye Rights or demandes w[hi]ch the said Anthonye hathe, or in Any tyme to come hereaft[er]
owght of Right to have Off and in All the messuages landes tenementes farmeholdes & mylne then
beinge in the tene[ure] & Occupacion of me the foresaid John Salkelde wyth all the Appurtenances
thereto App[er]teyninge or belonginge or beynge Any p[ar]te or p[ar]cells of the same Where vpon
I the said John Salkeld dothe give bequethe by this my p[re]sent last will and Testerment vnto
Anne Salkelde my wiffe the one halfe & moy[e]tie of All my foresaide messuages tenementes
farmeholdes & mylne w[i]th ther appurt[e]n[a]nces To have holde Occupie & enyoe the same
halfe & moitie of all my foresaide messuages tenementes farmeholdes and mylne wyth thappurt[e]n[-
a]nces vnto the said Anne Salkelde for & dureinge hir wedowheade, Also I give & bequethe vnto
oswolde salkelde my said sone the oder halfe & moitie of all my foresaide messuages tenementes
farmeholdes & mylne w[i]th ther appurt[e]n[a]nces To have holde occupie & enyoe the same
halfe & moitie of All the saide messuages tenementes farmeholdes & mylne w[i]th there Appurt[e]n[-
a]nces vnto the said Oswolde salkelde his heires & Assignes for ev[er],And lykewise After the
wedowheade of the same Anne my Wife I give And bequethe vnto the said Oswolde Salkelde my
sone his heires & Assignes for ever the Reuercyon of the one halfe & moytie of All the foresaide
tenementes farmeholdes & mylne w[i]th ther appurt[e]n[a]nces heretofor gyven & bequested vnto
the said Anne my wiffe for And duringe hir wedowheade To have hole Occupie & enyoe All the
p[re]misses vnto the forsayd oswolde salkelde his heires & Assignes for ever, According to the
Custome of the lordshippe of thrynby aforesaide, Also my mynde & wyll is that my saide sonne
Oswalde Salkelde, shall espouse marry and tayke to wiffe Johanne Rigge Dawghter of [. . .]¹ Rigge
of lytell Stryklande gentlyman Accordinge to the comandes and bargaine therof maide & promysed
before Richard Salkelde Thom[a]s fallowfelde esquyres george salkelde gentilman & oders, Also I
give & bequethe vnto hew salkelde my sonne my best horse or my best oxe whether of them as shalbe
Reserued frome the harryatt,('plunder'), It[em] I give & bequethe vnto Richarde salkelde my
brother one Calfe, It[em] I give & bequethe to michaell salkelde & bridgett salkelde childringe of
the said Richard to Ayther of theme one shepe, It[em] I give & bequethe to thom[a]s Webster son
of John Webster one shepe And also my mynd and will is that yf it shall happen At Any tyme here
After Any contencyon or varience to be betwene my said wife & Any of my childringe, or amonges
Any of my sayde childring That then they & ene[ry] of theme to be orderet by my sup[er]visours or
some of theme, whose names hereafter appereth, The Resydew of All my goodes & cattelles not
egasede nor bequested by dettes payed and funerall expences dischargede I give & bequethe vnto
Anne Salkelde my foresaid wife whom I ordayne & make my executryxe of this my Last will &
testiment, And she to vse and distribute the same goodes & cattelles as she shall think best for the
p[re]ferment of my childringe wyth thadvise and counsell of Richard salkelde esquyre george salkele
Richard Rigge John Rigge gentilmen & my said son os‹w›olde salkelde, whome I ordayne & make
the sup[er]visours of this my last will & testyment
[witnesses: Roger Webster, Richard (?) elesby yonger, Richard westgarthe, William Smythe, Richard
Salkeld of Morland (*his* brother, alive 1563, whereas Richard of *Thrymby* died 1557) & others.] One
illegible insertion, possibly Richard.

Inventory of John Salkeld
May 1563

iiij oxen	iiij^{li}
iiij kyne & ij calves	iiij^{li}
iiij yonge cattelle	xl^s
one nagge	vj^s viij^d
shepe	
x yooes & x lam[m]es	xxx^s
xj hogges	xxv^s viij^d
iiij wedders	x^s viij^d
Two swyne	ij^s
corne vpon ye grownde	
dyves viij estoppes by estimacion	xxxij^s
bygge iiij acrees	xx^s
wheat vpon the grownd one acree	vj^s viij^d
ij brasse pottes, iij pannes	)
one caldron, xij pewder dishes iij sawcers	)
one fryenge panne w[i]th other implements	) xxxij^s iiij^d
of howsald	)
Howsald stuff all together & beddynge w[i]th	)
sackes & windoclothes	) lv^s iiij^d
iij arkes one almery & iij chestes	xxj^s viij^d
Husbanry gere all together	xx^s
Alexander Hebson awe for wheat	ix^s

S[um]ma to[ta]lis xxiij^{li} ix^s whare of Dettes owyng to diu[er]se
p[er]sons as folowythe

To laurence Walker	v^s
To Rob[er]t Webstare	x^s
To William Smyth for wark	xij^d
To wylliam banke cowp[er] for warke	xviij^d
To george diuison for yran	ij^s vj^d
To Jhon Wynter wyffe	xx^d
To sanct oswald stocke	xv^s
To anthony broadlay	xvj^d

S[um]ma to[ta]lis xxxviij^s

Anne, will and inventory

<A>n inventory of all the <goods of An>ne salkeld wedowe Late wyff<e of> Jhon salkeld
pr[i]ced the xix day off aprille in an[n]o d[omi]nj 1567° By thes iiij sworne me[n] Roland
symson Ryc[hard] clesby, Ryc[hard] Wosgarthe and Jhon Webstare as followythe

Three Oxen, one kowe & one calfe	iiij^{li} xiij˙ iiij^d
Two meares & one foole	xxxiiij˙ iiij^d
Three yowes ij lam[m]es viij hogges at 6^d	xxix˙ iij^d
Twenty Bushells of ayles sawen	xx˙
Bygge iij b[ushels]	viij˙
Wheat one acre and Rye¹	vij˙
Otemele vj peckes	vj˙
malt iij b[ushels]	vj˙ viij^d
Three Brasse potts ij pan[n]es one caldron &	
viij pewder wessell	xxvj˙ viij^d
One almery iij chestes, ij arkes one masfat	
one gybyng tubbe & one slosthe fat	xviij˙
Beddynge one fedderbed, one mattres ij	
Bolstares ij cou[e]rletts ij blanketts Three	
pares of lynne shetes & ij pare of harden	xxv˙
husbandry gere one wayne and one pare of	
wheles w[i]th cowpe, plow, culter socke,	
temes, shackylls & Lynkes	xviij˙ x^d
vj sackes ij pookes & one wyndowchothe	v˙

S[um]ma to[ta]lis xiij^{li} xvij˙ xij^d

Whare of dettes owynge to diu[er]se p[er]sons as followythe

To george denison for terre & lyne	x˙
To Mr Rych[hard] cleburne for corne & lyne	x˙
To sam[ue]l oswald stocke	xv˙
To Esabell Salkeld my dowghter of	
Borawyd monay	xxxj˙
To else my dowghter of borowed monay	xiij˙
To Roger Salkeld my sone of borowed monay	xviij˙
In charges for suche thynges as was bowght	
in the tyme of hyr sekennes²	iiij˙
To Rog[e]r Symson for one pecke of bygge	³
To my ma[n]s[e]rwandes for hys wayges	xij˙

1 illegible
2 = her sickness
3 blank

Postscript – Thrimby

The period covered by the preceding pages can roughly be taken as starting at 1500
and ending about 1600, with some spill-over at each end; most but not all of those
mentioned were buried at Morland, only a few miles from Thrimby, and one of the
loveliest villages in Cumbria. Arthur Mee describes their resting place thus:

In a churchyard sweet with lavender and roses, watched over by a magnificent Spanish chestnut,
stands the venerable and dignified church of Norman and medieval times, two storeys of its sturdy

tower thought to have been here before the Conqueror came. Its top storey is 16th century – there are fragments of Norman work in the 13th-century nave arcades and in the sides of the 600-year-old chancel arch . . .

In the years that followed our period, the church register (which only from 1600 showed the necessary detail) records that from 1600 to 1742 some 200 folk from Thrimby were buried at Morland, but these included apparently only one Salkeld; there were 23 Websters, 17 Cleishes, 15 Simpsons, 14 Baxters, 10 Lancasters, nine Beathoms, seven Miles, and numerous Birds, Matthews, Smiths, Teasdales, Hobsons, Pearsons and others.

The Salkelds *of Thrimby* seem to have disappeared; perhaps they had become Quakers? or succumbed to the Plague? or just moved on?

Epilogue

In the first paragraph of this book I warned of the sideroads which must be avoided if eventually we are to reach our declared destination. With this epilogue we have reached it. So perhaps a peep down a few of the sideroads might now be permitted. But only a few; to attempt to treat each in the detail of this book would at least double its size and cost.

One of the most prominent of these sideroads carries off, from our mainstream road, at a point about A.D. 1500, all travellers for Northumberland and beyond. Once clear from the main road, the Northumberland signposts enable us to construct a complete picture of descendants right through Dorset (including the V.C. Philip Salkeld who was born in 1830), down to the present. But unfortunately although the John whose name is on this signpost is said to be 'of the Corby family' he cannot be identified – some future worker on Salkeld pedigrees may find the missing clue. But for this present study of the ancestors of Lilian Salkeld, none of these Northumberland nor Dorset Salkelds qualify for inclusion, as they were not her ancestors.

Another signpost, leaving the main road at the birth of Robert, son of Hugh I who married Christiana of Rosgill, takes us wandering through Goborro and several more generations, to Whitehall and the families of Lancelot Salkeld, who built themselves a great rambling mansion at this site, near Cockermouth. Perhaps the most distinguished of them was Lancelot who married Anne Strickland and was knighted in 1660, but a good case could be made for others, who lived in splendid style in Whitehall and who deserve a complete volume to themselves. But alas, they were *not* our ancestors and do not qualify therefore for inclusion in the present book. Perhaps these notes will stimulate some other Salkeld to examine the masses of information which exists on these Whitehall families, their successes and failures, starting perhaps at the wills they left.

This book has concentrated on tracing the fortunes of one family of Salkeld, against the varying background of their times. To do this it has been deemed necessary to keep a running commentary of those times and how and when changes have occurred. It has not, for example, been assumed that all readers know the difference between a joiner and a carpenter! Where such information seems to be part of that background, it has been added, with the risk of course of appearing to digress from the pure Salkeld history. Nor has too much genealogical 'purity' been insisted upon (for example, the exact date of a burial) if an estimate would suffice. If these and similar practices cause offence, my apologies are offered in advance.

References and Bibliography

Abbreviations

The following abbreviations are used:

C.W.A.A.S. *Transactions of the Cumberland and Westmorland Antiquarian and Archaeological Society*, New Series (unless Old Series specified).

C.P.R. *Calendar of Patent Rolls.*

N. & B. Joseph Nicholson and Richard Burn, *History and Antiquities of the Counties of Westmorland and Cumberland* (1777, reprinted 1976), 2 vols.

1. Pipe Roll of 10 John, 1208.
2. Pipe Roll of 10 Henry II, 1164.
3. F. W. Ragg, C.W.A.A.S., vol. 14, p. 1 *et seq.*
4. C. Roy Hudleston and R. S. Boumphrey, 'Cumberland Families and Heraldry', C.W.A.A.S., vol. 78, 1978.
5. C. Roy Hudleston, R. S. Boumphrey and J. Hughes, *An Armorial for Westmorland and Lonsdale* (Cumberland and Westmorland Antiquarian and Archaeological Society, 1975).
6. C.P.R., vol. 34, Ed. I.
7. G. H. de S. Plantagenet Harrison, *History of Yorkshire* (1885), p. 331.
8. T. H. B. Graham, C.W.A.A.S., vol. 21, p. 63.
9. William Flower, *Visitation of Yorkshire, 1563-4* (Harleian Society).
10. C.W.A.A.S., vol. 54, p. 302.
11. *Victoria County History, Cumberland*, vol. I, p. 311 *et seq.*
12. *see* note 11.
13. William Whellan, *History of Cumberland and Westmorland* (1860), p. 504.
14. C.P.R., vol. 11, Ed. II, p. 37.
15. C.W.A.A.S., vol. 25, facing p. 115.
16. J. E. Prescott, ed., *Register of Wetheral* (1897), p. 289.
17. C.W.A.A.S., vol. 56, p. 167.
18. N. Pevsner, *Buildings of England: Cumberland and Westmorland* (1973), p. 158.
19. C.W.A.A.S., vol. 6, p. 163.
20. C.P.R., vol. 9, Ed. I, p. 441.
21. C.P.R., vols. 8 & 14, Ed. III, p. 550.
22. N. & B.
23. R. S. Ferguson, ed., *Testamenta Karleolensia* (Cumberland and Westmorland Archaeological and Antiquarian Society Extra Series, vol. 9, 1893).
24. C.W.A.A.S., vol. 13, p. 169.
25. Dr. J. Mason, C.W.A.A.S., vol. 29, p. 98.
26. C.P.R., vol. 9, Ed. III, p. 171.
27. G. H. de S. Plantagenet Harrison, *History of Yorkshire* (1885), p. 333.
28. *Calendar of Inquisitions*, 21 Sept. 1316.

29. C.P.R., vol. 12, Ed. II, p. 235.

30. C.P.R., vol. 43, Ed. III, p. 243.

31. C.W.A.A.S., vol. 7, p. 236.

32. *Calendar of Esch.*, vol. 2, Rich. II, p. 13.

33. C.P.R., vol. 41, Ed. III, 2nd. No. 38.

34. *see* note 33.

35. C.P.R., 1348-50, p. 175.

36. F. W. Ragg, C.W.A.A.S., vol. 9, p. 275.

37. *Calendar of Close Rolls*, vol. 46, Ed. III, p. 363.

38. Marc Girouard, *Life in the English Country House* (Yale University Press, 1978).

39. F. W. Ragg, C.W.A.A.S., vol. 14, p. 23 *et seq.*

40. G. M. Trevelyan, *English Social History* (1945).

41. D. M. Stenton, *English Society in the Early Middle Ages, 1066-1307* (Penguin Books, 1952).

42. A. R. Myers, *England in the Late Middle Ages* (Penguin Books, 1969), pp. 42-3.

43. C.W.A.A.S., Old Series, vol. 4, p. 316.

44. C.W.A.A.S., vol. 71, pp. 75-89.

45. William Hutchinson, *History of the County of Cumberland* (1794), 2 vols.

46. ibid., p. 25, Sir Thomas Wharton's 'call out', 1543.

47. J. Bain, ed., *Calendar of the Border Papers*, vols. 1 & 2.

48. C.W.A.A.S., vol. 69, pp. 129-51.

49. C.W.A.A.S., vol. 63, p. 178.

50. C.W.A.A.S., vol. 5, p. 213.

51. C.W.A.A.S., vol. 10, pp. 411-94.

52. C.P.R., vol. 8, Ed. IV, 1469.

53. C.P.R., vol. 25, Ed. III, pp. 94 and 121.

54. 'Inglewood Forest', C.W.A.A.S., vols. 5, 6, 7, 9, 10, 11 and 20. Each volume has its own index.

55. *Calendar of Inquisitions Post Mortem*, 12 Rich. II, p. 109.

56. *Calendar of Inquisitions Post Mortem*, 25 Hen. VI, p. 234.

57. Graham, C.W.A.A.S., vol. 14, p. 244.

58. N. & B., vol. 2, p. 576.

59. C.W.A.A.S., vol. 11, p. 11.

60. Barrie and Jenkins, *The Steel Bonnets* (London, 1871), pp. 196, 329-31, 342.

61. William Camden, *Britannia* (London, 1789), vol. 3, p. 174 *et seq.*

62. C.W.A.A.S., vol. 16, pp. 246-69.

63. C.W.A.A.S., vol. 60, p. 89.

64. C.W.A.A.S., vol. 3, pp. 212-3.

65. C.W.A.A.S., Old Series, vol. 2, pp. 158-86.

66. *Gentleman's Magazine*, Dec. 1978, p. 279.

67. C. M. L. Bouch, *Prelates and People of the Lake Counties* (Kendal, 1948).

68. J. S. W. Gibson, *Wills and Where to Find Them* (Phillimore, 1974).

69. D. J. Steel, *General Sources of Births, Marriages and Deaths before 1837*, National Index of Parish Registers, vol. I (3rd. impression, Phillimore, 1976).

70. Sufferings of Friends, Friends House Library, Euston Road, London.

71. John F. Curwen, ed., *Records of the Barony of Kendale* (Kendal, 1926), p. 162 *et seq.*
72. Quaker Records, Book 1216, p. 336. Friends House Library, Euston Road, London.
73. Quaker Records, Book 1596, p. 152. Friends House Library, Euston Road, London.
74. Kendal Men's Monthly Meeting. Period 1670 to 1724. Cumbria Record Office, Kendal.
75. Marjorie Filbee, 'Dictionary of Country Furniture', *The Connoisseur*, (1977).
76. Elfrida Vipont Foulds, *Birthplace of Quakerism* (1973).
77. *Chambers Encyclopaedia*, vol.3, pp. 141-2, and D. Dymond and P. Northeast, *A History of Suffolk* (Phillimore, 1985).
78. Anthony Burgess, Paul Elek, *Coaching Days of England, 1784-1945* (1946).
79. Charles Dickens, *Sketches by Boz*, Chapter 15, March 1836.
80. C. A. and M. A. Weaver, *Woodbridge: a Short History and Guide* (published by the authors).
81. Records of the Woodbridge Meeting House, April 1707.
82. Public Record Office, Apprentice Records of the Inland Revenue, 1723.
83. White's *Suffolk*, (1844), p. 232.
84. F. A. Crisp, *Liber Admissionum, Seckford Grammar School, at Woodbridge, Suffolk* (Privately printed, 1900).
85. British Library, Additional MS 19148 Pedigrees S.-S. H. E. Davy's Suffolk Collection 72.
86. Forrest, ed., *Shrewsbury Burgess Roll* (1924).
87. Roll of the Drapers Company, Throgmorton Street, London.
88. Charles Nickson, *History of Runcorn* (Mackie & Co., 1887).
89. Briggs and Jordan, *Economic History of England* (1970), p. 210 *et seq.*
90. F. C. Mather, *After the Canal Duke* (Oxford, 1970).
91. William Bagshaw, *History, Gazetteer and Directory of Cheshire* (Sheffield, 1850).
92. 'The Silk Trade', *Chambers Encyclopaedia*, vol. 12, p. 552 *et seq.*
93. Wilfrid Palmer and Rainow Women's Institute, *The Story of Rainow* (1975), and George Ormerod, *The History of the County Palatine and City of Chester* (London, 1819), vol. III.
94. Graham Turner, *The North Country* (London, 1967).
95. Christopher Hibbert, *Agincourt* (1964).
96. Nicholas Harris, *Battle of Agincourt*.
97. 'The Salkeld Screen', C.W.A.A.S., vol. 56, pp. 119-27.
98. C. M. L. Bouch, C.W.A.A.S., vol. 57, p. 39 *et seq.*
99. N. & B., vol. 2, p. 303.
100. C.W.A.A.S., vol. 62, p. 355.
101. *Surtees Society*, vol. 172, p.158.
102. *Calendar of State Papers Domestic*, 1600-1603, p. 534 *et seq.*
103. *Calendar of State Papers Domestic*, 1653, p. 117.
104. Professor H. S. Reinmuth, C.W.A.A.S., vol. 66, p. 190, Kendal, April 1964.

Index

Compiled by Auriol Griffith-Jones

Women are indexed under their maiden names, where these are known. Salkeld men are indexed as far as possible using the system of Roman numerals, and thereafter by date and/or place of birth or residence.

List of Subscribers

Mr. & Mrs. Michael Cambridge
Mrs. Lorna R. Carleton
Alastair Salkeld Edwards
Ann Gilbert (*née* Salkeld)
Holesfoot Ancestral Research Centre,
    Cumbria
Mr. & Mrs. J. P. Howard
Mary Salkeld Larkin
Mr. & Mrs. Bruce M. Mackie,
    Adelaide, S. Australia
Robert Salkeld Matterson
Anna Pye
Alan Richard Salkeld
Albert Salkeld
Annie M. Salkeld
Anthony C. H. Salkeld
Brian Salkeld
Brian Frederick Salkeld
Brian Harold Entwisle Salkeld
C. Roy Salkeld
Cedric Frank Salkeld
David Robert Salkeld
Dorothy E. Salkeld
Duncan Salkeld, M. A.
Elizabeth Nkowles Salkeld
Esmée Wootton Salkeld
Frank Salkeld
Frederick Raymond Salkeld
Glenn Derrick Salkeld
G. M. Salkeld

George Salkeld
J. W. & C. F. Salkeld
Jack Salkeld
James Cheyne Salkeld
John Salkeld
John Salkeld, Cockermouth
Joseph Salkeld
Keith Salkeld
Norman Salkeld
Pat. & John Salkeld
Philip Frederick Salkeld
Raymond Salkeld
Richard Salkeld, Manchester
Richard Salkeld, Weymouth
Richard Andrew Salkeld
Robert Salkeld
Mr. Robert E. Salkeld, B.Sc.,
    M.I.H.T.
Sarah E. Salkeld
Thomas Salkeld
Thomas Robinson Salkeld
Trevor Salkeld
William H. Salkeld
Allen Macaulay Salkield
John Allen Salkield
Mrs. Leonard Unthank Salkield
Jessica Walmesley
C. W. & F. M. Weickhardt
Mrs. Joan Wilson